THE ECONOMY OF COMMUNIST CHINA

An Introduction

YUAN-LI WU

"A new bridge across the Yangtze River, a steel mill in Inner Mongolia, a railway extending westward toward Central Asia, these are all examples of tangible accomplishments which have bedazzled many an observer who is not aware of the cost of these undertakings and does not inquire into the alternatives that have been forgone."

Professor Wu's pioneering study of the economic goals and achievements of Communist China adds up the costs of the accomplishments and inquires into the alternatives. The author explores the broad structure and programs of the Chinese economy—a planned socialist system dedicated to rapid economic development and industrialization vigorous enough to make China a self-reliant nation. What distinguishes the Chinese from other planned economies, explains Professor Wu, is not its economic aims but rather its political *raison d'être* — economic development whose overriding national goal is the ever-greater power of the Communist Party.

It is within this framework that Professor Wu carefully examines the political and economic implications of the Chinese attempt to realize Party objectives. He traces the government's efforts to design an administrative machinery able to direct the economy both in its long-range plans

(Continued on back flap)

The
Economy
of
Communist
China

The Economy of Communist China

An Introduction

YUAN-LI WU

FREDERICK A. PRAEGER, *Publishers*

New York · Washington · London

FREDERICK A. PRAEGER, PUBLISHERS
111 Fourth Avenue, New York 3, N.Y., U.S.A.
77–79 Charlotte Street, London W.1, England

Published in the United States of America in 1965
by Frederick A. Praeger, Inc., Publishers

© 1965 by Frederick A. Praeger, Inc.
Library of Congress Catalog Card Number: 65–18082

Printed in the United States of America

This book is Number 166 in the series
Praeger Publications in Russian History and World Communism

To My Parents

IN MEMORIAM

Preface

The present book began as a series of lectures delivered at the University of San Francisco in connection with a seminar on comparative economic systems. In the course of the discussion on the economy of Communist China, the need for such an introductory text became apparent. It appears that up to the present time, economic studies on Communist China are either too narrow in their focus or too technical for the student who has had little more than a brief acquaintance with economics and/or with Chinese affairs. This volume is meant to fill the gap, and the subject matter is presented as a special case study of planned economies. While the setting is Chinese, the principles and problems are general.

The author is fortunate to have been able to draw upon the work of many other scholars who have written in this field in the last ten years. The names of many of these colleagues are mentioned in the text. However, since reference to publications cannot be complete, the acknowledgment of indebtedness is hereby extended to many more scholars who have published in Chinese economic studies. In particular, the author is grateful to Professor Ching-wen Kwang of the University of Buffalo and Dr. Dennis Doolin of the Hoover Institution for their comments and reading of the manuscript, to Professor K. N. Chang for his frequent advice, and to his co-workers, Mr. H. C. Ling and Miss Grace Hsiao, and his indefatigable secretary, Mrs. Joan Kleinman, for their assistance in many ways.

Special mention should be made of the Hoover Institution where the author has derived most of the information contained in this volume. Without the facilities made available to him by Dr. W. Glenn Campbell, Director of the Institution, and without the logistic support of the Hoover East Asian Collection under Eugene Wu, this book could never have been written. For their many courtesies, heartfelt thanks.

It is always a pleasure to mention the role played by the author's silent partners, his wife and daughter, without whose encouragement and whole-hearted support even such a slender volume would have been too onerous. So it is to them that all credit is due while all the errors and shortcomings in the book remain the author's own.

YUAN-LI WU

Menlo Park, California
1965

Contents

I. *National Goals and Their Selection*   3

II. *The Decision Makers and the Scope of the Economic Plan*   18

III. *Planning Resource Allocation: The Strategic Variables and the Criteria of Their Selection*   47

IV. *Planning Income Distribution: Accumulation, Socialization, Equity, and Incentive*   72

V. *The Over-all Economic Record, 1949–64: Allocation of the Gross Domestic Product by End Use*   87

VI. *Performance in the Industrial Sector*   107

VII. *Performance in the Agricultural Sector*   130

VIII. *Fluctuations and Growth*   157

IX. *Communist China in the World Economy*   170

X. *An Evaluation of the Communist Chinese Economy*   202

Appendixes   207

Index   217

The
Economy
of
Communist
China

CHAPTER I

National Goals and Their Selection

The Nature of Communist China's National Goals

At this time in history, the economy of Communist China may be described as a planned socialistic system dedicated to the rapid economic development of the country on a relatively self-sufficient basis for the principal purpose of enhancing national power under the Communist Party. Industrialization, which despite recent serious economic reverses continues to be identified with economic growth, the attainment of greater national power through industrialization, self-sufficiency, which is closely related to the aim of greater national power, and the establishment of a socialist and, eventually, communist society—these have been the unswerving national or collective goals of the Communist Party of China ever since the seizure of power, in 1949. The nature of these goals and the manner in which their fulfillment has been attempted carry certain implications that are very far-reaching indeed.

Before going any further, it should be noted that the goals of self-sufficiency and rapid industrialization, along with the establishment of socialism, coincide completely with the corresponding goals of the Soviet economy. This is one of the basic factors responsible for the many strong resemblances of the Chinese economy to its Soviet model and precursor.

The Element of Historical Continuity

An important question arises at this juncture: Would the Chinese population have chosen the same national goals if the Communist Party were not in power? The answer to this speculative

question should probably be in the affirmative. For industrialization, though not industrialization by forced draft, had also been
the professed objective of the pre-Communist Chinese governments ever since the early years of the 1911 Revolution, which
overthrew the Manchu regime, despite the vicissitudes of Chinese economic development. During the 1930's, the National Government under the Kuomintang attempted to introduce modern
industry, to attract foreign investment, and generally to encourage
economic development in modern terms in as wide a part of the
country as the influence of the central government could reach.
A new phase of economic advance, exhibiting in a number of
ways the symptoms of "take-off,"[1] could be detected after 1934,
when China forsook silver and adopted an exchange standard and
the end of the Depression and the temporary slowing down of
Japan's drive in North China offered the Chinese a breathing
space for economic expansion. This brief interval was marked by
considerable economic progress; it lasted until 1937, when renewed Japanese incursions brought on the Sino-Japanese War.
Economic progress continued during the war years, both in north-
ern China (under Japanese occupation) and in southwestern China
(under the beleaguered Nationalist Government) and development in Manchuria (then under the Japanese-sponsored Man-
chukuo) continued to accelerate, at least up to 1944. But the
war was also responsible for the monetary inflation, which
exerted an insidious influence on the continued growth of the
economy and contributed strongly to the downfall of the Nationalist regime and the rise of Communist China.[2] However, if one
were to take a long view, the 1940–49 decade may well be looked
upon as a prolonged interlude which postponed the "take-off" of
the Chinese economy but which also prepared for the "take-off"
and made its appearance when it finally came a more vigorous
one. Thus, Communist China's goal of economic development,
particularly industrialization, is by no means a new one. Its eleva-
tion by the Communists to the status of a national goal has
special significance only by virtue of their system of economic
planning and their mode of implementation.

Nor is the goal of self-sufficiency entirely a new phenomenon,

[1] W. W. Rostow, *The Stages of Economic Growth* (New York: Cambridge
University Press, 1960).
[2] See Yuan-li Wu, *An Economic Survey of Communist China* (New York:
Bookman Associates, 1956), chap. ii, and K. N. Chang, *The Inflationary
Spiral* (Cambridge, Mass.: The Technology Press, 1958).

for, as early as the 1930's, the Nationalist Government was already seriously concerned about industrial self-sufficiency. A special agency (the National Resources Commission) was established under the Supreme National Defense Council to supervise the establishment of a nucleus of heavy industry able to meet, at least partially, the country's needs for instruments of war as well as specific capital goods in the event of a national emergency. The fact that the NRC was a part of the broad defense establishment underlined its primary function. Thus, the desire for self-sufficiency in time of war also was not an innovation. Its significance as a national goal rests with the Communist regime's ideological conviction and political attitude in world affairs.

A Paramount Political Consideration

The distinguishing characteristic of the national goals enumerated above does not, therefore, lie in the purely economic aspects of the goals. It is not the hoped-for rapid pace of development through industrialization or the desire for self-sufficiency that sets the Chinese economy apart from its heritage and from that of many other less developed countries with a colonial past and therefore also given to extreme sensitivity and impatience in their desire for economic "independence." The distinguishing characteristic is the political goal: the establishment of a socialist, and eventually Communist, economy. This is a matter of a different order.[3]

Implied in the long-term goal of establishing Communism in China is the tacit and quite understandable conviction or assumption that this can be accomplished only through the Communist Party. Though obvious, this assumption is of far-reaching consequence. For establishment of Communism and, in the intermediate stage, attainment of the goals of a socialist economy, would, under this assumption, require the retention of political power in the hands of the Communist Party, perhaps even at any cost. It follows further that having a Communist government in power becomes in turn one of the implied goals of the economic effort and of Chinese society as a whole. This is an important rationalization. The Communist Party may therefore have to reconcile the goal of maintaining itself in power with that of rapid economic development and industrialization and/or with that of

[3] The difference between a socialist economy and a pluralistic, free economy rests, therefore, in the final analysis on a value difference.

achieving self-sufficiency if and when a conflict of goals arises. That this condition has important consequences in the selection of proximate or near-term objectives and in the choice of the economic plans will be demonstrated presently.

Comparison with the Goals of a Pluralistic Society

A second principal feature that distinguishes the Chinese planned economy from an economic system such as that of the United States lies in the manner in which national goals are regarded. It would be wrong to think that a free, pluralistic society has no national goals or, to put the matter more aptly, that there do not exist certain desiderata which an important segment of society would like to see stressed more strongly, as exemplified, for instance, in the report of the President's Commission of National Goals in November, 1960, which stated, *inter alia:* "The [U.S.] economy should grow at a maximum rate consistent with primary dependence upon free enterprise and the avoidance of marked inflation. Increased investment in the public sector is compatible with this goal. Such growth is essential to move toward our goal of full employment, to provide jobs for the approximately 13.5 million net new additions to the work force during the next ten years; to improve the standard of living; and to assure United States competitive strength."[4] Elsewhere in the Commission's report, it is stated: "In the present state of the world, rapid growth of the American economy may have an additional value."[5] Here the reference is to the challenge posed by the competition of Soviet growth and the possibility that the U.S. growth rate may have to be maintained at a level compatible with the anticipated growth of the Soviet economy. But growth is not without its cost, and the authors of the report's chapter on economic growth warn us that the cost may indeed exceed the worth of the effort. "The economic system must be compatible with the political system. The centers of economic power should be as diffused and as balanced as possible. Too great concentrations of economic power in corporations, unions, or other organizations can lead to abuse and loss of the productive results of fair competition. Individuals should have maximum freedom in their choice of jobs, goods, and

[4] *Program for Action in the 60's, Goal for Americans,* Report of the President's Commission on National Goals (Englewood Cliffs, N.J.: Prentice-Hall, 1960), p. 10.

[5] *Ibid.,* p. 175.

services."[6] The constraint under which growth may be maximized is clearly defined in the first sentence of the section on domestic goals: "The status of the individual must remain our primary concern. All our institutions—political, social, and economic—must further enhance the dignity of the citizen, promote the maximum development of his capabilities, stimulate their responsible exercise, and widen the range and effectiveness of opportunities for individual choice."[7]

If we examine the goals enunciated for the United States, two points stand out: (1) the resemblance to the goals of such Soviet-type economies as that of Communist China inherent in the demand for greater economic growth, and (2) the vital difference in the nature of the constraint under which economic growth is to be increased. In the case of the United States, economic growth is to be maximized provided that the individual's pursuit of his own private goals would not be unduly circumscribed while opportunities for their fulfillment would be enlarged. Even the demand for a greater growth rate is predicated upon the desire to find employment for new entrants to the labor force, because without employment they would not be able to avail themselves of the opportunities for the advancement of their own private goals. On the other hand, the Chinese desire for rapid economic development through industrialization is subject only to the constraint of the availability of material resources and the competing goal of maintaining the Communist Party in power. The last competing goal constitutes an ultimate test, because, by a twist of logic and an assertion of faith, the Communists seem to believe that their system is the only repository of truth and that their party is the only vehicle for fulfilling society's economic and other goals.

The Chinese–U.S. difference in the nature of the constraints under which the purely economic goals may be achieved implies that when obstacles to the realization of the selected goals are encountered, Communist China would not hesitate to move ruthlessly. One is reminded of the fact that in the Soviet Union the objectives of the Gosplan are prescribed in the form of laws which may not be violated without penalty. The same is true of Communist China.[8] But in the United States, the national goals defined

[6] *Ibid.*, p. 9.
[7] *Ibid.*, p. 3.
[8] See the article by Lin Li in *Hsüeh-hsi* (*Study*), Peking, April 15, 1953, cited in *Jen-min Shou-ts'e* (*People's Handbook*), 1953, pp. 72–73.

by the President's Commission in 1960 can serve only as recommendations with which the population at large may or may not agree. To some extent, of course, the government is in a position to exercise considerable influence on the country's economic development through its fiscal and monetary policies, and even through direct interventions. But these activities are very carefully circumscribed. In Communist China, however, the national goals set by the Communist Party are supreme, whereas personal activities for the fulfillment of private goals are always subordinated to the collective will of the Party. Herein lies the most important difference between the national goals of Communist China and those of a free society.

The Inevitable Conflict Between Private and National Goals

Of course, if the national goals selected by the Communist Party of China happened to coincide with what the population would collectively and voluntarily choose for itself, there would be little conflict. Yet the very nature of the Chinese economy precludes such a harmony of national and private goals. In the first place, Communist China, being a less-developed country, would have far too low a rate of voluntary saving to finance the rapid economic development of the country desired by the Party. This is evidenced by the low ratio of investment to the national product in prewar China, which, according to Ta-chung Liu, was only 1.8 per cent in 1933.[9] Because of the desire for self-sufficiency and the ideological position of the Communist Party, the low rate of domestic saving can hardly be compensated by a large inflow of foreign capital. Such a large inflow on terms acceptable to large potential creditors would be neither probable nor indeed tolerable to the Communist Party in power. A conflict between private and national goals is therefore inevitable in the allocation of resources in production between the present and the future.

Second, this conflict is further increased by the implied differences in the allocation of resources among different commodities and services to be produced. Since private demand for consump-

[9] See Liu Ta-chung and Yeh Kung-chia, *The Economy of the Chinese Mainland: National Income and Economic Development, 1933–1959*, RAND Memo. RM-3519-PR (Santa Monica, Calif., 1963), Table 8, p. 94, and Table 71, p. 355. (All references to this study are to the RAND edition.) See also the prewar Chinese national income study by Ou Pao-san, *Chung-kuo Kuomin So-te (The National Income of China)* (Shanghai, 1933).

tion deviates from the Communist Party's scale of priorities, it cannot be allowed to hold full sway, and therefore the types of goods and services to be produced must also be regulated. The degree of regulation is also more intensive than that characteristic of less-developed countries in general that are intent on rapid economic development.

Third, the differences that arise in the patterns of allocations are further augmented by differences in the distribution of income and wealth. Inasmuch as the establishment of Communism and, in the intermediate stage, socialism, is one of the Party's national goals, the nationalization of all means of production is implied. In the first instance, this process of nationalization is aimed at all nonlabor resources, although, by extension, it may also be interpreted to include manpower itself. The individual's choice in employment and his claim to property are therefore necessarily subordinated to the goals of the Party.

Finally, the national goal of the Party's consolidation of power and supremacy implies that all alternative rival centers of economic strength must be wiped out or subordinated. This requires the establishment of a "democratic dictatorship" by the peasants' and workers' alliance over all rival parties, as well as the elimination of relatively large employers and independent farm operators who may offer resistance to the Party's economic plans.

The Evolution of Near-term Objectives and Operational Plans

The long-term goals of course only deal with the ultimate objective, which must be approximated through a series of near-term objectives and operational plans. In this context, the Party's continual tactical shifts are rather impressive. Even its general approach to economic development does not lack flexibility. The thread of compulsive logic in these twists and turns emerges plainly in the following chronology of the Communist Party of China's CPC position.

1. The CP as an opposition party. During World War II, when the Chinese CP was still in armed opposition and bidding for domestic and foreign support, Mao Tse-tung wrote in *The New Democracy*[10] that the economic system he envisaged would have the following characteristics: (a) state control and operation of all monopolistic or large-scale enterprises so as to circumscribe the

[10] Mao Tse-tung, *Hsin Min-chu Chu-i (The New Democracy)*, Chieh-fang She Edition, 1940, p. 17.

influence of private capital in the country's economic life, (b) the partial nationalization of these private enterprises against compensation, (c) permission for other less important and less influential private enterprises to remain in operation, and (d) the adoption of necessary measures for the appropriation of land and its redistribution to poor peasants and the landless. In particular, the redistributed land was to remain under private ownership, hence there would not be any real socialization of land but only the abolition of the "feudalistic" relationship in farm production. This policy statement bore a strong resemblance to the political programs of social democratic parties elsewhere in the world in spite of the employment of some Communist terminology. Understandably, many Western observers not familiar with the Communist dynamics of political struggle thought the Communists were merely agrarian reformers.

A more militant attitude was struck by Mr. Mao in December, 1947, when the civil war again flared up following the efforts of the Marshall mission. In an address to the Central Committee of the Communist Party of China,[11] Mao called for (a) the confiscation of land owned by "exploiters" and its restitution to the peasantry, (b) the expropriation and reversion to state ownership of the "monopolistic" capital of four highly placed families[12] in the Nationalist Government, and (c) the protection of national industry and trade. This new policy statement delineated more clearly those segments of private capital holdings earmarked for expropriation. These potential victims were described as owners of "bureaucratic capital" (as opposed to another group labeled "national capitalists"), the criteria being their respective political positions in the Nationalist Government and their relationships to "foreign imperialist elements." The division of the owners of capital into two parts, a minority to be expropriated outright and a greater number to be left alone, was clearly a tactical move which reflected the political stratagem of Mao, whose dictum was to divide the enemy and to attack a minority while securing the neutrality of the majority.

[11] Mao Tse-tung on "The Current Situation and Our Task," Chieh-fang She Standard Edition of *Collective Official Documents,* 1949, p. 27. This was a report to the Central Committee of the Chinese Communist Party on December 25, 1947.

[12] The four families in question were those of Chiang Kai-shek, the Soong brothers (including T. V. Soong), H. H. Kung (a former Minister of Finance and Prime Minister), and the Chen brothers (Chen Li-fu and Chen Kuo-fu, who were high up in the hierarchy of the Kuomintang).

2. The Economic Policy of the Common Program,[13] 1949–53. The Communist Party of China came into power in October, 1949. But nominally, China still had a coalition government led by the CPC, and the platform adopted by the People's Consultative Conference was called "Common Program." The near-term goals of the Program therefore were designed to smooth the transition and to offer the Communist Party an opportunity to consolidate its power throughout the country. Having come to power as a revolutionary force, the CPC was expected to take certain drastic measures. But prudence demanded moderation in some areas. Hence the period of the Common Program may be best compared to that of the NEP[14] in the Soviet Union.

The revolutionary character of the new program was expressed in the call for land reform and, as a preliminary step, the elimination of "local despots" and the reduction of land rent and interest rates on loans.

Second, in terms of ownership and control, the economy was divided into five sectors. These were (a) a state sector of socialized enterprises, (b) a "semisocialist" sector of cooperative undertakings, (c) a sector of "state capitalism" composed of joint private and public enterprises or partially socialized businesses, (d) a sector of "national capitalists," and (e) a sector of small private enterprises, including farms, handicraft workshops, and other small businesses. This system of "mixed economy" was meant to be the landmark of Mao's "new democracy."

Third, the state sector was to act as the command post within the framework of a central economic plan; it was to supervise and regulate the provision of raw-material supplies and markets, the operation of business concerns, the working conditions governing labor, the promotion of technical facilities, and the enforcement of fiscal and monetary policies. In the related field of distribution, state trading companies were to be established to balance supply and demand, to stabilize prices, to curb speculation, and to promote the organization of cooperatives constituting the semisocialist sector. Furthermore, the participation of labor in

[13] The English text of the Common Program may be found in *Important Documents of the First Plenary Session of the Chinese People's Political Consultative Conference* (Peking: Foreign Languages Press, 1949).

[14] The New Economic Policy (NEP) period succeeded the so-called period of War Communism in 1921 as a result of the economic chaos and stagnation that had developed. A wide range of private economic activity was legalized under the NEP. See Alec Nove, *The Soviet Economy, An Introduction* (New York: Frederick A. Praeger, 1961).

the management of state enterprises and the introduction of collective bargaining in the private sectors were also stipulated.

Fourth, the goal of self-sufficiency was stressed in the statement that international trade was to be controlled under the principle of protection of domestic industry.

Fifth, in the approach to industrial development, first priority was accorded to the rehabilitation and expansion of such producer-goods industries as mining, ferrous metallurgy, electric power, the machine industry, chemicals, and the manufacture of electrical equipment. Secondary importance was assigned to textiles and other consumer-goods industries. Thus the strategy for economic development that Communist China was to follow at a later date was already broadly hinted at.

Last, the Common Program emphasized the need of strict control over all financial institutions and the establishment of a taxation policy and a balanced budget[15] that would assure supplies for the continued prosecution of the civil war and for the realization of the rehabilitation and investment program envisaged.

3. The Economic Program of the 1954 Constitution, 1954–57.[16] The next landmark in official pronouncements on economic goals was the promulgation of the 1954 Constitution. If the Common Program of 1949 had marked the beginning of a transition period toward socialism, the 1954 Constitution heralded the end of the transition.

First, in regard to the structure of the economy, the new Constitution proposed a policy of "voluntary cooperativization" (i.e., collectivization) in farming, together with the restriction and gradual elimination of "rich peasants"[17] as a class. Furthermore, the "national capitalists," who had been assured of protection because of their economic usefulness, were now to be subjected to a process of "utilization, restriction, and transformation (or reform)." Thus the socialization of all private business where the cooperative form did not or could not prevail became more or less imminent.

[15] The somewhat curious emphasis on the balanced budget by a Communist government reflected the Chinese people's bitter experience in the post-World War II hyperinflation and their conviction that it was a result of heavy government deficits. In the face of this public feeling, the Communist authors of the Common Program were apparently anxious to give the impression that they were in favor of orthodox public finance. For a discussion of this subject, see Yuan-li Wu, *op. cit.*, chap. iii, 1956.

[16] The text of the Constitution may be found in *Draft Constitution of the People's Republic of China* (Jen-min Ch'u-pan-she Edition, Peking, June, 1954, or in the English translation, Foreign Languages Press, Peking).

[17] The label "rich peasant" corresponds to the Russian *kulak*.

Second, in regard to the actual operation of the economy, the structure of the "command economy" was now given further consolidation and refinement through the adoption of the First Five-Year Plan (1953–57). Not only were the goals henceforth clearly defined as rapid industrialization under a socialist planned system, but the method of approach had been definitely worked out in considerable detail.

4. The Commune System and Subsequent Modifications, 1958 to the present. As matters developed, by the end of 1956, both the socialization of the nonagricultural sectors and the collectivization of agriculture had been virtually completed. This process will be discussed in more detail later on. At this point suffice it to mention that the CPC could, as a minimum, claim partial fulfillment of its initial goals. While still more radical changes in the economy were to follow in later years, there have been only two important modifications since 1954 as far as the major long-term goals are concerned.

First, in 1958, the agricultural cooperatives were replaced by the communes, which were both larger entities of farm operation, representing the consolidation of individual cooperatives, and a new form of labor mobilization and output distribution. In fact, in the heyday of the commune movement, the Party claimed that the commune represented a stage of institutional development closer to true Communism than any other form of social and economic organization evolved in any other socialist society. For a time, and in a number of places, distribution was carried out on the basis of need, although work was not always assigned according to ability. However, this state of affairs did not last long. Although the commune has been preserved in form, actual practice since 1961 has reverted to conditions predating the collective farm. In the second place, together with the institution of the commune, the original goal of rapid industrialization was greatly accelerated in 1958. But this, too, was sharply curtailed after the economic crisis of 1960–62, and the accelerated program was replaced by one of readjustments and moderate advance.

Contrasting Strategies of Economic Development

Even in 1964, the state of the Chinese economy was still so fluid that full recovery from the 1960–62 economic crisis and depression, to be followed by renewed, steady expansion, could not as yet be considered entirely assured. Consequently, the emphasis in 1962–64 on moderate economic growth and agriculture as against heavy industry should not definitely be regarded as a long-term policy; it may again be revised at short notice. However, changes in policy both in 1958 and in 1961–62 can at any rate be interpreted as important alterations of the long-term strategy.

Pertinent reference may be made to the experience of the Soviet Union. As Nicolas Spulber puts it, "Two main strategies were proposed in the 1920's. The first emphasized the development of agriculture or, alternatively, the simultaneous growth of various domestic industries. The proponents of this strategy stressed the importance of consumer demand—particularly of the peasant market—for sustained industrial growth, advocated reliance on comparative advantage in foreign trade, and favored a low rate of investment in the state-owned industries in order to avoid hampering the necessary growth of the other sectors. The second strategy stressed the priority for the development of heavy industry. Its proponents declared that the potential demand of state industry was unlimited, sought to gear the economy towards self-sufficiency, rejected comparative advantage, and finally, demanded a very high rate of capital accumulation in state hands."[18] It appears that the experience of Communist China has reflected rather faithfully at least one alternation between these two strategies. Between 1953 and 1957, Communist China adopted an approach to economic development similar to the second strategy described above. In 1962, something similar to the first strategy may have been adopted, that is, at least ostensibly, although one cannot yet say for how long. Before 1953, the main concern of the CPC was for economic rehabilitation and for the completion of preparations for the First Five-Year Plan.[19] The period between 1958 and 1960 represented, on the other hand, a modification of the strategy adopted during the First Five-Year Plan period. It was not, however, meant to be a replacement of the Plan's approach.

Determining Factors in the Modifications of Economic Policy and Near-term Goals

Even apparent changes in the long-term strategy of economic development would not be changes in long-term goals. They only

[18] *The Soviet Economy* (New York: W. W. Norton & Company, 1962), p. 210.

[19] The First Five-Year Plan was not, however, really completely formulated until 1954 or 1955.

reflect a different evaluation of what is feasible. The long-term national goals of the Chinese economy as envisaged by the Communist Party are fairly constant. They are determined by the ideology of Communism, the political ambition of the Chinese Communist Party and its leaders, and the status of China as an underdeveloped economy. The short-term goals, on the other hand, are always subject to change.

Even a cursory survey of the gradual modification of the series of official pronouncements on national goals enumerated earlier would be sufficient to bring to light the very great flexibility which the CPC has exhibited in this respect during its fifteen years in power. However, revisions of policy are by no means automatic; nor have Chinese planners always reacted rapidly to external changes and to the realized performance of their plans. On the basis of observations over a number of years, the principal determinants of plan readjustment appear to have been (a) the official evaluation of the state of the economy and its accomplishments, (b) the availability, scale, and content of external assistance, and (c) the objective conditions deemed necessary at the time for maintaining the Communist government in power.

Apparently the leadership of the Chinese Communist Party may react to unfavorable domestic economic developments, or new situations in external economic and political relations, quite differently, depending upon their evaluation of their own economic accomplishments in the recent past. Thus, if the official reports should indicate that economic accomplishments during the preceding period have been considerable, the leadership will probably revise the immediate economic goals upward. If some adverse condition should then develop, there may simply be a redoubling of the domestic effort instead of a reduction of the goals themselves. Such a decision may be made even in the absence of external assistance, or even if such assistance should be curtailed. Similarly, if domestic political opposition should develop, militating against the speed-up of the economic program, as long as economic performances in the immediate past have been judged satisfactory, the leadership may be induced to discount the political opposition and to increase the degree of repression as a countermeasure. The CP's confidence in its ability to meet opposition and to overcome objective difficulties increases with each success, so that even in case of an economic set-back after the first speed-up, the response of the leadership to such a set-back would again be a decision to redouble the effort in order to make up for lost time. In other words, political confidence and economic success tend to reinforce each other and to contribute to the momentum of an economic upswing, leading to successive upward revisions of the near-term goals.

On the other hand, an unfavorable economic record, especially over a period of time, would tend to produce caution. Under such conditions, the size and availability of foreign assistance would have a more decisive effect on the level of the economic goals set. A general retrenchment and downward adjustment of goals, while resisted and therefore delayed at first, would eventually take place in order to reduce the actual or potential opposition to the regime. In the face of strenuous opposition, tactical political retreats may even be thought advisable. Thus political uncertainty and economic decline may go hand in hand.

In reviewing the past, we find that the tentative goals set by the Communists as a wartime opposition party were replaced by the more positive statements of the Common Program, although the latter were still conciliatory and moderate statements designed to win over those who hoped for moderation. The next shift of position occurred with the outright proclamation of a socialist society in the 1954 Constitution. These successive steps clearly reflected the functional relationship between the degree of political success and consolidation, as perceived by the CP, on the one hand, and the tightening of control and the continual upward revision of the economic goals, on the other.

If we may anticipate some of our later discussion, the period that began in 1949, went through the phase of rehabilitation, and continued through the First Five-Year Plan was not free of reverses. These years saw alternate phases of tightening and liberalization, several large-scale drives against specific segments of the population, followed by the famous "Hundred Flower" campaign and, after that, anti-Rightist "rectification" campaigns. Then came the call for accelerated economic growth and a period of euphoria during the "Great Leap" period of 1958–59. This last phase, as we shall see, furnished us with a clear example of exaggerated optimism based on false information and distortion of the facts. The subsequent economic crisis was followed by a period of uncertainty, re-examination, and finally, adjustment. The downward revision of goals was accompanied by the relaxation of controls in the face of opposition. A breathing space then set in. Grain was imported from abroad; partial recovery of agricultural production followed some liberalization of controls and a general feeling of relief from the taxing demands of the Great Leap.

The principal point that emerges from the apparent alternations between relaxation and rigid control and between the continual upward revisions of the near-term economic goals and the intermittent reductions of the same goals is the fact that political stratagems play a dominant role in the selection of near-term economic goals and the methods used to achieve them.

Even in a free society, the individual's private economic plans are always affected by changing conditions over which he has no control. But in a pluralistic society and market economy, such changes are not always likely to be cataclysmic for a majority of the people. In a planned socialist economy, although the national goals may be constant, the intermediate and short-term plans and objectives are subject to continual revision, and each revision has the force of law to which all private plans of economic and other activities must conform. The uncertainty inherent in the frequent *volte-faces* is compounded by the harshness of the collective will as expressed by the Communist Party. The proposition may therefore be advanced, to wit, that the nature of the economy seems to reflect the nature of the political system, especially where the political system is imposed. This is a point that merits the attention of students of the Chinese economy.

CHAPTER II

The Decision Makers and the Scope of the Economic Plan

Relation of the National Goals to the Scope of the Economic Plan

Communist China is beset by the same type of economic problems as other countries. Every student of economics knows that these problems may be grouped under three headings, namely, (1) the allocation of resources, (2) the distribution of income, and (3) the movement of aggregate income, employment, and prices over time. In a pluralistic society, a vast number of decisions are continuously made by individual consumers and producers. These decisions, independently or together, determine what to produce, how and where production is to take place, who is to reap the benefits of the results of the productive effort, who is to own and exercise control over the resources, whether the entire economy will grow over time and at what rate, and what the path of change will be, i.e., whether it will be accompanied by fluctuations. The individual decisions are, however, modified in varying degrees by (1) the institutional framework inherited from the past, including the system of government and laws that determine the "rules of the game," (2) the deliberate current decisions of the government, especially in regard to the movement of economic aggregates such as total output and employment and the production of certain goods and services which, though needed by the society collectively, cannot be efficiently produced or supplied in adequate quantities on the basis of the individual's demand and effort alone, (3) governmental efforts to modify the distribution of income and wealth for noneconomic reasons, and

(4) the decisions of persons and governments in other countries. By and large, however, as long as the government of the country does not attempt to impose its will on the individual and does not seriously circumscribe his freedom of choice, a comprehensive national economic plan is not necessary.

Once certain national goals to which all individual goals must be subordinated in case of conflict are imposed from above, a national economic plan must be established so that both the long-term goals and the proximate objectives can be realized. Such a national plan must specify both the directions to be followed in allocating resources and distributing income and wealth and the manner in which these objectives are to be attained. Inevitably such a plan must go beyond the over-all regulation of output and employment through monetary and fiscal policies, the general supervision of business conduct and competitive behavior, and peripheral intervention in the allocation of resources which a government in a pluralistic society would be expected to undertake. The rigorously controlled direction and administration of the economy are needed because the long-term national goals as well as the intermediate objectives will almost inevitably be at variance with what the decisions would be if the individual were given a free choice.

In the case of Communist China, the first point of conflict arises out of the CPC's decision to develop as rapidly as the availability of resources permits. As pointed out earlier, this decision implies a higher rate of capital accumulation than voluntary saving alone would support. Accordingly, it is necessary to control the level of consumption out of the current output. Such consumption control can be accomplished through any one or a combination of the following measures: (a) control of gross income received by individuals through wage control, regulation of nonwage income, etc., (b) control of the level of disposable income through taxation, a savings program, sale of bonds, and capital levies, (c) control of expenditure through rationing and payment in kind, and (d) direct control over the availability of consumer goods. A further implication therefore is that the national economic plan must comprise such measures as trade control, wage control, control over the distribution of consumer goods and their production, budgetary control through a suitable taxation program, cost control in government-owned enterprises, etc.

In the second place, national and individual goals may come into conflict because of the specific types of goods demanded by the government. Inasmuch as the Communist Party follows a definite strategy of development based on self-sufficiency, an implication of the strategy is that some specific goods have to be produced in certain minimal quantities. This requirement may apply to a wide variety of goods, such as food grains, ingot steel, fuel, machines, etc. Such specific requirements given in terms of certain commodities will in turn necessitate the production of other goods which are used as inputs in the production of the former. In other words, the production goals set for some products will imply minimal goals in the production of other products. When carried to the extreme, as the number of goods with specified output goals increases, the economic plan must ultimately embrace all the sectors of the economy. In practice, of course, it may not be possible to have such a fully comprehensive economic plan inclusive of the entire input-output matrix. This is so especially if one or more segments of the economy are regarded as unessential or "noncritical" and can be left as a "residual sector" used to absorb the effects of plan failures and of all unexpected developments. Nevertheless, the specification of a certain number of output objectives would almost inevitably lead to conflicts between the planned goals and what the concrete results would be if the individual producers and consumers were left to their own devices. Accordingly, the national economic plan must also include detailed operational directives for the individual enterprises that produce commodities included directly or indirectly in the plan. These individual enterprises must then be placed in the operating sector of the economic plan and be administered by managers who take orders from the government administration. Implied in this arrangement is the provision of current production plans for various industries, plans for individual investment projects, and plans for the allocation of labor, scarce raw materials, machinery, etc.

In the third place, inasmuch as a high rate of economic growth is desired, the national economic plan must not only provide for a high rate of capital accumulation, it must also strive to maximize output from any given amount of resources employed. This means that the state of technological knowledge must not be treated as a constant. The national economic plan must therefore provide for the introduction from abroad of new knowledge, new methods of production, and new equipment, as well as for the encouragement of research and development at home. The planning authority will probably wish to allocate a different amount of resources to this use and in a different manner from what individuals would choose to do.

Finally, since a principal goal of the Communist Party is to alter the structure of the economy in terms of ownership and control over the means of production, those sectors of the economy which are not yet completely nationalized at any time must be regulated, and a point of "conflict" again arises. The "utilization, restriction, and transformation" of private enterprises proclaimed in the 1954 Constitution must be administered through certain government agencies, while the general goal of socialization must be promoted through other means as well. Included in these "other means" are political campaigns and drives, which, though commonly looked upon as an integral part of the political effort to establish Communism and Party domination, are not without their serious economic functions. As we shall see, a campaign directed primarily at the urban middle class in order to accelerate its subordination to the Communist state may simultaneously net the authorities a large supply of foreign exchange, and may therefore be regarded as an extraordinary form of capital levy. One may also consider the detention of "counterrevolutionaries" in forced labor battalions both a means of enforcing the political will of the Communist Party and a measure to marshal a large labor force whose incentive to work is stimulated by the instinctive desire to survive. Besides, such a labor force also has the advantage of being highly mobile.

The national economic plan thus derives a certain degree of support from the political and administrative machinery, and one must constantly look for the intertwined relationship between political intent and economic function. Except for this last aspect of economic planning in a totalitarian country like Communist China, the scope of the economic plan and its relation to national goals would make the Chinese economy (or for that matter the Soviet economy) in many ways comparable to the war economy of a pluralistic society. But the desire to change the nature of the economy and to subordinate the individual's role in decision-making indefinitely constitutes a major distinction between the World War II economies of countries like Britain or the United States and the present Soviet and Chinese systems.

The Scope and Structure of the National Economic Plan

The preceding section has outlined the scope of a national economic plan that attempts to provide a blueprint for the realization of the CPC's national goals. The national economic plan of Communist China, as described in Chinese literature,[1] corresponds entirely to our theoretical deductions.

The core of the national plan is a comprehensive plan of "balances" specifying interindustry and intersectoral relationships. It is supported by a set of sectoral and partial plans. The objectives and contents of these component plans may be outlined as follows:

1. A plan for industrial production. This is a two-part sectoral plan,—one for "heavy industry" and one for "light industry." The plan tells individual enterprises what products and how much they should produce during a given period of time. Furthermore, the plan also determines the respective growth rates of the producer-goods and consumer-goods sectors.

2. A production plan for agriculture. The corresponding plan for the agricultural sector fixes specific targets of agricultural output, including both the volume of consumption in the agricultural sector itself and the amount marketable in the nonagricultural sectors. The plan must include such items as targets in animal husbandry, plans of crop rotation, the acreages to be planted and the harvests expected, plans of agricultural technology, and other matters related to crop cultivation.

3. A transport plan. The objectives of the transport plan are the safeguarding of the adequate flow and distribution of industrial and farm products. The plan must specify the expected volume of traffic for freight and passengers by different carriers, including railways, waterway transport, highway transport, and civil aviation. Because of the dominance of rail transport in long-distance and bulk traffic, the core of the transportation plan is the railway plan.

4. A plan for capital construction[2] (or investment in fixed

[1] See Teng Hsiao-ying, "Kuo-min Ching-chi Chi-hua ti Ko-ko Pu-fen Pao-han-hsieh Sheng-mo Nei-jung" ("The Contents of the Component Sectors of the National Economic Plan"), *Jen-min Shou-ts'e (People's Handbook)*, 1953, pp. 70–72, and *Chung-hua Jen-min Kung-ho-kuo Fa-kuei Hui-pien (Compendium of Laws and Regulations of the People's Republic of China)*, Peking, July–December, 1955, pp. 131–275. For a description of Soviet plan formulations, see Spulber, *The Soviet Economy*, pp. 8–15.

[2] In Communist Chinese usage, "capital construction" is the major part of "accumulation," the remainder being work in progress and addition to in-

assets). The capital-construction plan specifies the volume of investment in fixed assets in individual economic sectors. It includes a list of the principal construction projects and an enumeration of the specific objectives of each project. The plan also specifies the schedule according to which existing and new enterprises are to be put into operation.

5. A labor plan. The principal purpose of this plan is to accomplish the desired continuous increase in labor productivity and to provide the economic apparatus with an adequate supply of skilled workers equal to the anticipated demand.

6. A technological plan. The purpose of the technological plan is to make sure that all sectors of the national economy would have the latest scientific and technological information at their command so that they can take advantage of all the "international advanced technological experiences." This plan covers the industrial, agricultural, and transportation sectors as well as the capital-construction projects.

7. A cost plan. The plan for production costs specifies the standard costs for each individual segment of the economy; it also fixes the targets of cost reduction and provides guidance to the correct relationship between increase in labor productivity and increase in wages. The ostensible purpose of the cost plan is the safeguarding of the rational operation of the individual production and capital-construction department, the supervision of the fulfillment of a continuing austerity program, and the facilitating of the accumulation of capital. Closely correlated with the cost plan is a plan of commodity prices.

8. A plan for the allocation and supply of materials. The purpose of this plan is the regulation of the supply of producer goods to the different sectors of the economy, the determination of the priority of supply, and the specification of the ratio of allocation

---

ventories and state stockpiles. "Accumulation," according to the same usage, is defined as that part of the domestic material product allocated to or used in making additions to fixed assets, net of depreciation, together with related ancillary expenditures, plus goods in process, projects under construction, inventories of commercial organizations and the stockpile of the state.

Reference may be made to the Soviet practice of defining "accumulation" as "capital formation, investment in process, addition to stocks, addition to state reserves in gold or foreign currency, and some outlays for defense." See Nicolas Spulber, op. cit., p. 28. Since the Chinese usage may also include some military construction in "capital construction" and, therefore, in "accumulation," the Soviet and Chinese definitions are virtually identical.

of producer goods between current production and capital construction.

9. A plan for the flow of commodities. The basic function of this plan is to make sure that the industrial and farm products demanded by the urban and rural workers will be available to them in planned quantities. The plan consists of two parts: one for wholesale trade, the other for retail trade. It is further subdivided by geographical areas, trading organizations, and, within each trading organization, by individual commodities.

10. A plan for the social and cultural welfare of the population. This plan is composed of three parts: a plan for public utilities and housing; a plan for the cultural, welfare, and educational activities of the population, including the training of Communist Party staff and activists, or "cadres"; and a public health plan.

Furthermore, the national economic plan also includes a foreign-trade plan, a set of financial plans, and a number of regional plans. The foreign-trade plan deals with export and import targets and foreign-exchange provisions. The financial plan deals with the national budget and the accumulation and allocation of capital funds and short-term credit. The regional plans have to do with regional specialization and the administration of enterprises under local control.

It should be fairly clear to the reader that the capital construction, cost, financial, and technological plans are concerned with the temporal allocation of resources and the maximization of the rate of growth. The industrial, agricultural, and transportation plans are concerned primarily with the allocation of resources among different sectors of production and "end use" and the maintenance of equilibrium in the input-output matrix, i.e., between intermediate and final demand and in interindustry relations. The plans of material allocation and labor are meant to guarantee the supply of factors for the attainment of the production targets. The cost plan also has the function of safeguarding the efficient employment of resources. The commodity flow or circulation plan, as well as parts of the financial plan, is concerned primarily with the distribution of consumer goods. The social, cultural, and educational plan is focused on collective consumption. The entire national economic plan (the structure of which is described above) therefore corresponds fully to the theoretical planning structure that we have outlined. The plan as a whole is an effort to resolve the problems of what to produce, how to produce, and for whom to produce. The only point that is not covered in the above set of plans but is a part of the broader theoretical structure for the fulfillment of the CPC's national goals is the system of provisions dealing with the modification of the economic structure and its conversion to a socialist economy. Nor does the problem of income distribution appear to be consciously tackled as a separate, component plan. This is probably due to the Communist position that conversion to a socialist and, eventually, communist economy is taken for granted, and that the national economic plan is predicated on the assumption that a socialist economy is already in existence.[3]

The Components of the State Apparatus in Economic Decision-Making

In lieu of the many individuals whose decisions determine the course of economic development in a pluralistic society, the Communist state apparatus in China has taken over the necessary functions of decision-making in this respect. Of course, within the realm not covered by the national economic plan, some degree of freedom of choice is still preserved. This is true in the area of the consumers' choice, outside of what the Communist Party has arrogated to itself as the realm of collective consumption. The consumers are still able to decide on what they prefer to consume, although their decisions must be made under two important and severe constraints. First, the kinds and quantities of consumer goods and services are determined primarily by the state and are very unresponsive to buyer preferences. Secondly, individual tastes and preferences are strongly influenced by the propaganda activities of the Communist Party. Outside this limited area of free choice, a vast apparatus of state administrative agencies has been set up to take care of the functions of the national economic plan and the structural change of the economy mentioned in the preceding paragraphs.

The government agencies that constitute the entire apparatus of economic decision-making may be classified either according to their functions or according to the procedural development of the national economic plan. When classified according to their functions, the various agencies may be grouped under the following categories: (1) those charged with the responsibility of re-

---

[3] The plan as described also betrays a strong preoccupation with production and supply rather than demand, which is characteristic of economically underdeveloped countries and of centrally planned systems.

source allocation, (2) those determining the distribution of money and real income, and (3) those responsible for the gradual transformation of the institutional framework of the economy. In the first group, several separate categories should be distinguished; namely, operational or production departments, agencies responsible for the supply and allocation of factors of production, and agencies exercising over-all supervision in plan execution.

On a procedural basis, we may distinguish the following categories of government agencies from one another: (1) agencies that gather information in order to provide the data for the formulation of operational economic plans and for the subsequent evaluation of plan fulfillment, (2) agencies that formulate the plans, and (3) agencies that implement the plans. These divisions are, of course, not mutually exclusive in the case of individual institutions. A ministry responsible for the implementation of the plan in a particular branch of the economy is also an essential link in plan formulation and a major source of statistical data. However, some specialization and division of labor are common among divisions within the same government department.

Regional vs. Central Planning Machinery

Superimposed upon the above functional and procedural classifications is the division of the entire apparatus into central and local government agencies. The latter include primarily the provincial, *hsien* (county), and commune agencies, or their equivalents in the municipalities and autonomous regions and districts. Prior to the abolition of the Greater Administrative Regions in 1954, another intermediate level existed between the central government and the provincial authority, although the entire administrative apparatus of planning and plan execution had not yet been fully developed. The larger and economically more developed provinces have planning as well as operational divisions similar to those of the central government.

However, prior to certain provisional changes in 1958 (to be implemented in the 1959 annual plan),[4] the provincial operational agencies, not to mention lower-level bodies, controlled only a limited number of small enterprises of local importance. The most important "plans of balances" with respect to major commodity

[4] Wang Kuei-wu, "Nien-tu Chi-hua Pien-chih Fang-fa ti Chung-ta Kai-ko" ("Principal Reforms in the Methods of Compiling the Annual Plan"), *Chi-hua Ching-chi* (*Planned Economy*), No. 9, Peking, 1958, pp. 13–15.

branches were also in the hands of the central government ministries in charge of the individual commodity branches. Provincial or regional plans were made an adjunct of the plans of the central government ministries. Following the provisional changes in the procedure of plan formulation, plans for the balancing of supply and end uses were placed on a regional basis, and even the plans of central government-controlled enterprises were to be integrated in the regional plans. This decentralization effort was clearly modeled after the Soviet reforms of 1957. However, with the failure of the Great Leap, little has been heard of the decentralization program, and there is some indication that the trend may have been reversed.

At any rate, both the central government ministries and the provincial planning agencies would have to have their plans integrated into the national plan at the central government planning level. Thus it is the central government planning agencies that reign supreme. Furthermore, since the larger enterprises and the more strategic sectors have always been kept as the central government's preserve, it is also the central government's operating units that are the more important ones.

Evolution of the Apparatus of Economic Decision-Making[5]

The apparatus of the central government's machinery for planning and plan execution did not come into being overnight. It has been subjected to continual modification and reshaping. The general nature of the more important agencies may be seen from the following:

1. The information-gathering agencies. In 1949, the highest statistical agency was the statistical department of the Planning Bureau in the Financial and Economic Commission of the Government or State Administrative Council, which corresponded to the cabinet. Subsequently, similar departments were established in each of the six Greater Administrative Regions. The effort to bring order to statistical reporting began in mid-1950, when a conference was held in Manchuria to discuss problems of standardization, training of personnel, and industrial census-taking.[6]

[5] For a more comprehensive survey of the governmental structure, see Appendices I and II.

[6] Yuan-li Wu, *An Economic Survey of Communist China,* pp. 254–55, and C. M. Li, *The Statistical System of Communist China* (Berkeley, Calif.: University of California Press, 1962), pp. 13–20.

Then in October, 1952, the State Statistical Bureau was established. Finally, a network of statistical offices was organized by the State Statistical Bureau at successive levels of local government, including the province (or its equivalent, the autonomous region), provincial municipalities, the special district, the *hsien*, and the communes. These local statistical offices were made an integral part of the local government structure but were operationally subject to a straight line command headed by the State Statistical Bureau itself. In the summer of 1956, a typical provincial statistical bureau reportedly consisted of a technical staff of eighty persons in five divisions, covering agriculture, industry, capital construction (investment), trade and communications, and health and culture. In the cities, the statistical staff was reported to be relatively small. Altogether, during 1953–56, a cumulative total of 160 offices and a quarter million statistical reporting units were established at the special district and the *hsien* levels, respectively.

In order to attain uniformity in statistical reporting, a system of "double-tracked reporting methods" was instituted in 1953 following a second statistical conference in December, 1952. Under this system, enterprises controlled by the central government ministries were required to report first to the specialized business bureaus and subsequently to the respective ministries, and finally, via the ministries, to the State Statistical Bureau. Secondly, they were also required to report to the provincial statistical bureaus and thence to the State Statistical Bureau in the central government. On the other hand, locally controlled enterprises would report (1) to their local business-affairs departments, then to the provincial statistical bureaus, and finally to the State Statistical Bureau at the center, and (2) to the statistical departments of the special districts or cities, which would in turn report to the provincial and central government statistical bureaus. Statistical data are compared and checked at the State Statistical Bureau in the case of reports from the central government-controlled enterprises or, in the case of the locally controlled enterprises, at the provincial bureau level. However, this checking procedure was applied only to statistical returns that presented a summary of the results of "national economic construction." In other words, the coverage was by no means complete. Nor were the methods of review and recording fully implemented to include all geographical areas and all the state and joint government-private enterprises. In March, 1954, the State Statistical

Bureau was further ordered to centralize the control and supply of basic national statistics; it was also made responsible for the accuracy of the data supplied. This directive was to lay the foundation for unified statistical reporting and for the centralization of the supply of statistical information to the planning authorities at various levels.

One is reminded of the resemblance between the Chinese statistical system developed through the First Five-Year Plan period and the Soviet system of statistical reporting. Constant efforts were apparently made to improve the system through unification and standardization of the returns and through the supply of uniform data to all the planners. However, at the sixth national statistical conference in Peking, held in September, 1957, a plan was drafted to decentralize control over the financing and operation of the industrial and commercial enterprises. This plan was to cover a large proportion, said to be 80 per cent, of the then centrally controlled enterprises; these were to be transferred to provincial jurisdiction. Essentially, this decentralization program, which was to take effect in 1958, but was apparently soon discontinued or never fully implemented, corresponded to the slightly earlier Soviet economic reorganization program and the establishment of the sovnarkhoz. According to Hsüeh Mu-ch'iao, then director of the State Statistical Bureau, this reorganization plan would have little effect on the statistical reporting system except that it might enhance the importance of the provincial bureaus as a source of data. In any event, there was a serious deterioration in statistical service during the 1958–60 period, although this might have been entirely due to the greatly increased load of statistical reporting, the consequent dilution of the technical staff, and the Party policy that "politics should take command" in statistics. Finally, in 1961, a new director of the statistical service, Wang Ssu-hua, who had previously been one of its assistant directors, was appointed, although the extent of reorganization carried out at the time was not clear.[7]

As mentioned earlier, in addition to the Bureau of Statistics, data gathering is, of course, undertaken by all government agencies. In particular, however, mention should be made of such agencies as the Ministry of Geology and the Central Meteorological Bureau, whose main function is gathering data on natural resources and the physical environment, and of the Scientific and

[7] *People's Daily*, Peking, July 24, 1961.

A CHRONOLOGICAL CHART OF GOVERNMENT DEPARTMENTS
RESPONSIBLE FOR ECONOMIC ACTIVITIES

CHART II-1. AGENCIES FOR THE COLLECTION AND EVALUATION OF PLAN DATA

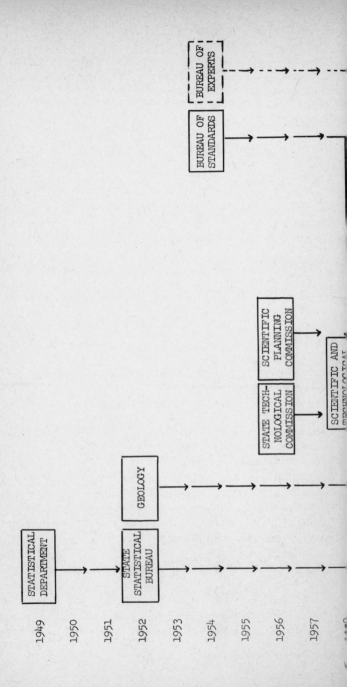

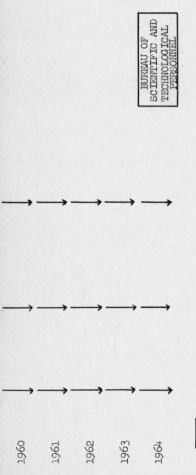

1960

1961

1962

1963

1964

BUREAU OF
SCIENTIFIC AND
TECHNOLOGICAL
PERSONNEL

DENOTES A GOVERNMENT AGENCY WITHIN THE SPECIFIC FUNCTIONAL CATEGORY ILLUSTRATED IN THE CHART.

DENOTES A GOVERNMENT AGENCY WHICH IS ORGANIZATIONALLY RELATED TO ONE OR MORE AGENCIES IN THE CHART, BUT WHICH IS FUNCTIONALLY OUTSIDE OF THE SPECIFIC CATEGORY ILLUSTRATED IN THE CHART.

CONTINUED EXISTENCE IN TIME.

NOTE: THE TERM "MINISTRY" IS OMITTED IN THE CHARTS. THUS "GEOLOGY" MEANS "MINISTRY OF GEOLOGY."

SOURCES:
1. CHUNG-HUA JEN-MIN KUNG-HO-KUO FA-KUEI HUI-PIEN(COMPENDIUM OF LAWS AND REGULATIONS OF THE PEOPLE'S REPUBLIC OF CHINA), PEKING, VOLS. I-IX, 1954-1959.

2. CHUNG-KUNG SHIH-NIEN(A DECADE OF COMMUNIST CHINA), HONG KONG: UNION RESEARCH INSTITUTE, 1960, pp.42-48.

3. SHIH CHŪGOKU NENKAN(NEW CHINA YEARBOOK),TOKYO, 1963.

4. CHŪKA JINMIN KYŌWAKOKU SOSHIKIBETSU JIMMEI HYŌ(THE DIRECTORY OF PERSONNEL AND ORGANIZA-TIONS OF THE PEOPLE'S REPUBLIC OF CHINA), CABINET RESEARCH OFFICE, JAPAN, JANUARY, 1964.

5. WEN-T'I YÜ YEN-CHIU(ISSUES AND RESEARCH), VOL. III, NO. 10, JULY, 1964, TAIPEI, pp.66-69.

Technological Commission, which is in charge of the collection of technical information from abroad and the dissemination of new knowledge.

2. The planning organs. The responsibility of plan formulation for the long-run economic development of the country is lodged in the State Planning Commission established in November, 1952. This agency is responsible for the drafting of the national economic plan, including the integration, revision, and appraisal of all the partial plans of the individual central government ministries and of local, provincial, and municipal governments. Individual sections within the commission are responsible for the allocation of essential producer goods, stockpiling and storage, financial planning, the credit plans of the state bank, and all other segments of the national economic plan described earlier. In addition, the agency is responsible for the evaluation of the results of plan implementation by the individual ministries, in individual geographical areas, and with respect to the national plan as a whole.[8] It also formulates the planning procedure and standards used in planning.

Until May, 1956, the State Planning Commission was responsible both for the long-term economic plans and for the annual plans. In May, 1956, a new State Economic Commission was set up to formulate the annual plans within the framework of the Five-Year and longer-term plans prepared by the State Planning Commission. Implementation and appraisal of the annual plan were also made a part of the Economic Commission's responsibility. The Commission was also charged with the responsibility for coordinating the work of individual government departments and enterprises in order to maintain balance in the allocation of materials among central and local government-controlled enterprises.[9]

The division between long-term and short-term planning offers another parallel between the Soviet and Chinese systems. The State Planning Commission and the State Economic Commission thus correspond unmistakably to the Soviet Gosplan and the Gosekonom kommissia.

3. The executive departments. The largest group of government agencies is concerned with the implementation of the na-

[8] Chung-hua Jen-min Kung-ho-kuo Fa-kuei Hui-pien (Compendium of Laws and Regulations of the People's Republic of China), Peking, July–December, 1955, pp. 72–76.
[9] Ibid., January–June, 1956, p. 82.

CHART II-2. THE PLANNING ORGANS

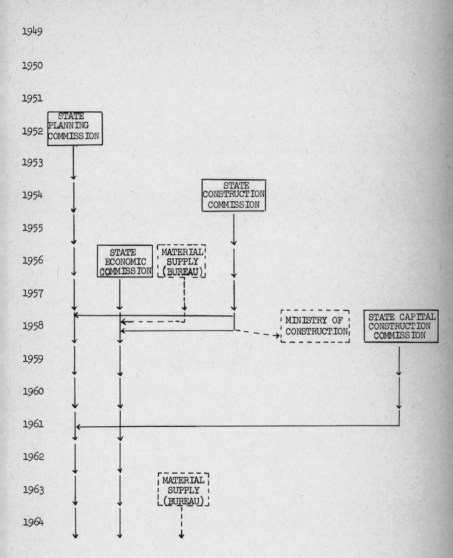

tional economic plan. Within this category, by far the greatest number of agencies are responsible for the general allocation of resources within the plan. In the first place, there are those whose responsibility lies in the supervision of the financial transactions which correspond to the physical production plans; thus they act as the controllers of the state enterprises. These are the People's Bank of China, together with its various subordinate specialized agencies such as the People's Construction Bank and the Agricultural Bank, and the Ministry of Finance. The banks do not allocate funds independently as a rule, thus influencing resource allocation, as they do in a market economy. The banking system is responsible for the provision of money to finance the transactions of the enterprises according to their individual plans, which are determined independently, whereas the Ministry of Finance is in charge of budgetary appropriation and the devising of taxation and other sources of state revenue. The banks also act as auditors of plan implementation by making sure that disbursements correspond to plan provisions.

Next, there are a number of agencies which are responsible for the supply of the necessary factors of production to the productive enterprises. The Ministry of Labor, the Ministry of Health, and the Ministry of Education are responsible for the supply and training of the labor force. The Ministry of Public Security is responsible for the supervision and direction of the forced-labor battalions. The Ministry of Foreign Trade, which splintered off the Ministry of Trade in 1952, is responsible for the supply of imported equipment and raw materials. The Bureau of Material Supply—first an agency under the direct jurisdiction of the State Council in 1956, then absorbed by the State Economic Commission in 1958, and again an independent agency in 1963—is responsible for the allocation of producer goods to all the individual enterprises, both for current production and for investment.

Finally, a great many government agencies are found in the operating sector and are directly responsible either for the current production of goods and services or for the implementation of the capital-construction projects. The number of ministries in charge of individual commodity groups has fluctuated almost constantly. Mergers, regroupings, and divisions have continued to take place through the years. At present, there are individual departments or ministries responsible respectively for enterprises producing such consumer goods as textiles, food, aquatic products, and other "light-industrial products," together with producer-goods indus-

CHART II-3. AGENCIES FOR FINANCIAL AND MONETARY PLANNING AND SUPERVISION

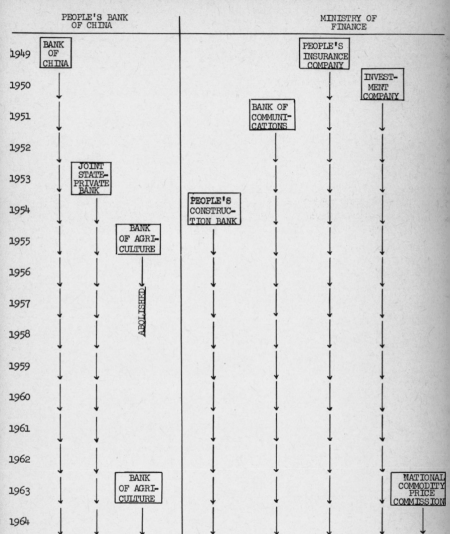

tries such as petroleum, coal, chemicals, construction, agricultural products, railway transportation, waterway and highway transportation, water conservation and electric power, postal and telecommunications service, forest products, machine production, and state-farm production (together with land reclamation). In particular, the number of ministries responsible for the production of machines has undergone very complicated changes. As of the end of 1964, there were eight ministries in charge of the manufacture of different types of machinery, including the former Ministry of Agricultural Machinery. Apart from these ministries, which are responsible for the individual enterprises, a separate commission of capital construction existed during 1958–61, and was apparently in charge of the supervision of plant construction and equipment installation in individual capital-construction projects.

Of special interest is the continual administrative shifts of the ministries in charge of commodity production. These shifts appear to have been the result both of administrative streamlining and of the proliferation of new commodity groups. In this respect, the Chinese system of individual ministries responsible for different types of commodity production closely resembles the Soviet system prior to the organization of the sovnarkhoz and the decentralization program of 1957. Even following the provisional changes in planning procedure in 1959, the central government ministries have never lost control over the principal enterprises. The "ministerial system," therefore, has been preserved relatively intact in Communist China.

The erstwhile Capital Construction Commission may also be regarded as a part of the group of government agencies playing a critical role in the future expansion of the economy. The other part of this group of executive departments is represented by the State Technological Commission and the Scientific Planning Commission, both established in 1956. These two agencies were merged into the Scientific and Technological Commission in 1958, which, together with the Bureau of Standards and the Academy of Sciences and other related institutions,[10] forms the backbone of

[10] The Scientific and Technological Commission is headed by Nieh Jung-chen, a marshal of the Communist Chinese Army; the Academy of Sciences, by Kuo Mo-jo; the Bureau of Standards, by Li Cheng-kan. Research institutes in atomic energy and nuclear physics were established in 1957–58, under the active direction of Western-trained physicists. See Sidney H. Gould, *Sciences in Communist China* (Washington, D.C.: American Association for the Advancement of Science, 1961), and Liu Chi-chuen, "A Study of the Chinese Communist Nuclear Program," *Issues and Studies* (Taipei), I, No. 2 (November, 1964).

CHART II-4. AGENCIES FOR THE CONTROL OF FACTORS OF PRODUCTION

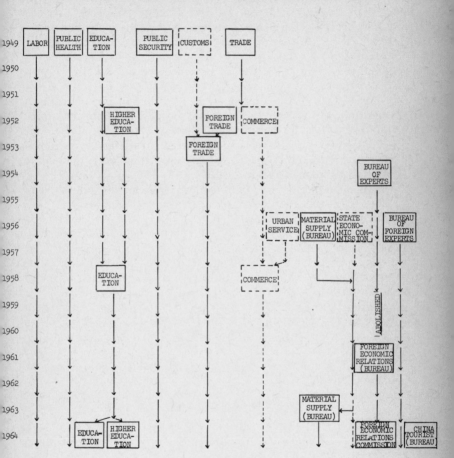

the entire research and development sector of Communist China.

A sales and purchase section is part of every producing department of the producer-goods enterprises. These sections are concerned primarily with the transfer of producer goods between enterprises. The Ministry of (domestic) Commerce, which splintered off the Ministry of (domestic and foreign) Trade in 1952, on the other hand, is responsible for the distribution of consumer goods other than food. The Ministry of Food, in turn, is responsible for the distribution of food staples.

These agencies in charge of the distribution of commodities constitute the executive departments which in effect determine the distribution of consumption in real terms. At the same time, the Ministry of Labor and the agencies governing the socialization of private enterprises are instrumental in determining the distribution of income and wealth.

Finally, there is the Administrative Bureau of Industry and Commerce, which handles the conversion of private enterprises into state-owned and -operated enterprises and the subsequent disposition of their affairs. A separate bureau for the administration of the handicraft industry, also established in 1954, was, until 1965, in charge of the organization of the handicraft workshops into cooperatives. It was reorganized as the Second Ministry of Light Industry in February, 1965.

Often the appearance or disappearance of new government agencies may be taken as an indication of important changes in economic policy inasmuch as, from an administrative point of view, the establishment of a specialized agency may reflect an increase in activity of a particular nature. For instance, the merger of the Ministries of Electric Power and Water Conservancy in 1958 and the formation of the Ministry of Electric Power and Water Conservancy coincided with a policy decision to emphasize the development of hydroelectric power in large multipurpose water-control projects. Similarly, the formation of a Foreign Economic Relations Bureau in 1961 may be regarded as an effort to develop a new administrative organ to handle the increased external trade activities with the Afro-Asian and other less-developed countries, as well as some Communist countries. The continual subdivision of Ministries of Machine Building offers a distinct example of expansion in specialized fields, including military equipment such as missiles.

CHART II-5. THE PRODUCTION AGENCIES

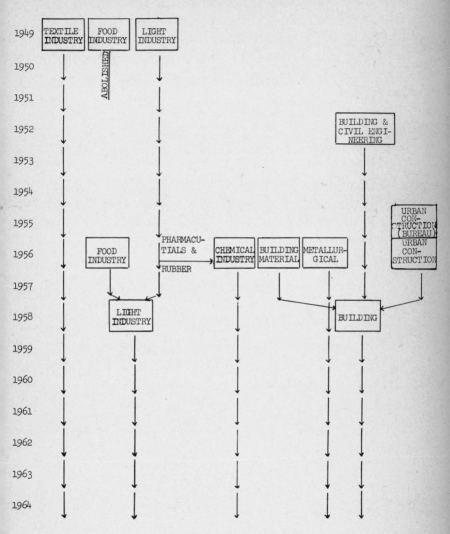

NOTE: A NEW SECOND MINISTRY OF LIGHT INDUSTRY WAS ESTABLISHED IN FEBRUARY, 1965.
THE ORIGINAL MINISTRY OF LIGHT INDUSTRY WAS CHANGED TO THE FIRST MINISTRY OF
LIGHT INDUSTRY.

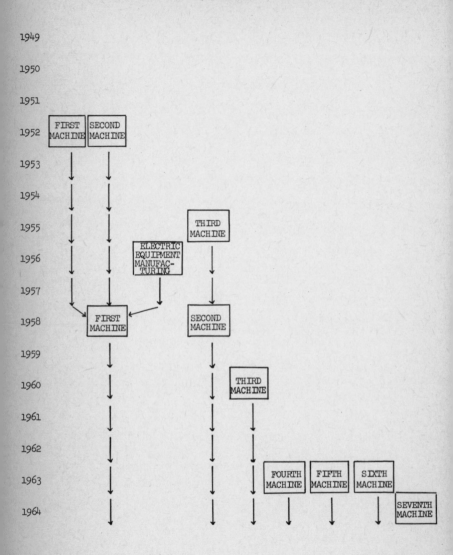

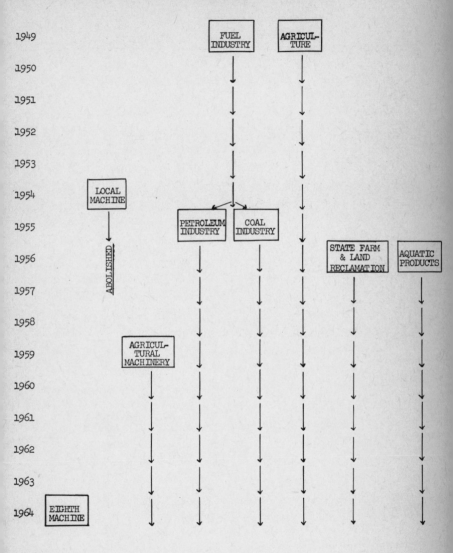

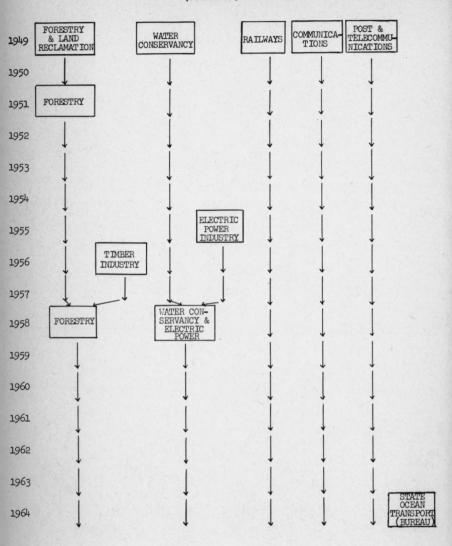

CHART II-6. THE DISTRIBUTION ORGANS

(6a)   SPECIALIZED TRADING
        CORPORATIONS

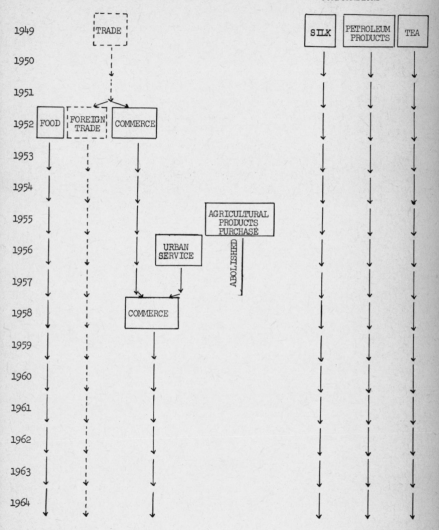

NOTE: IN FEBRUARY, 1958, THE MINISTRY OF COMMERCE WAS CHANGED TO THE FIRST MINISTRY
       OF COMMERCE, AND THE MINISTRY OF URBAN SERVICE TO THE SECOND MINISTRY OF
       COMMERCE. IN SEPTEMBER OF THE SAME YEAR, THE FIRST AND SECOND MINISTRIES OF
       COMMERCE WERE AGAIN COMBINED INTO THE MINISTRY OF COMMERCE.

(6) THE DISTRIBUTION ORGANS

(6a) SPECIALIZED TRADING CORPORATIONS
(CONTINUED)

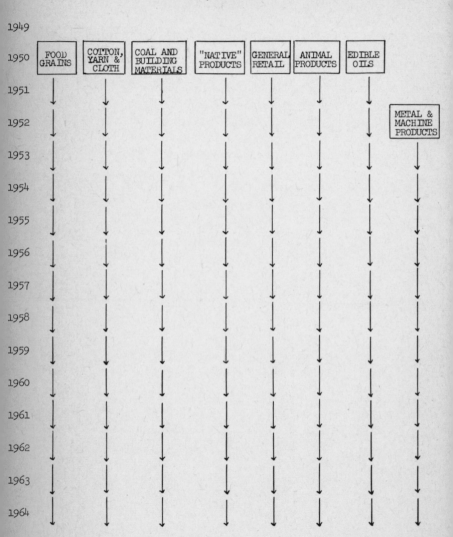

(6a) SPECIALIZED TRADING CORPORATIONS
(CONTINUED)

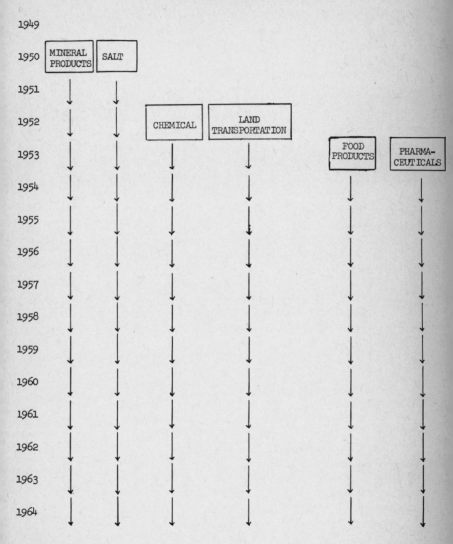

(6) THE DISTRIBUTION ORGANS

(6a) SPECIALIZED TRADING CORPORATIONS
(CONTINUED)

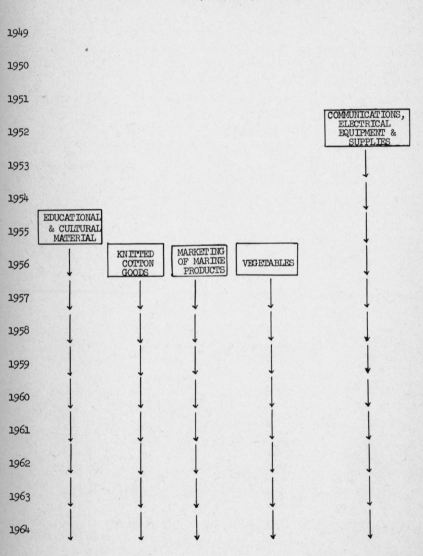

CHAPTER III

Planning Resource Allocation: The Strategic Variables and the Criteria of Their Selection

Formulation of the Plan

Schematically speaking, the formulation of the national economic plan is quite simple. In the case of the annual plan, the State Economic Commission must first decide upon a number of target figures to be employed in drafting the plan on the basis of statistical data supplied by the State Statistical Bureau and the political directives of the CPC.[1] These "control figures" consist of output targets in physical and value terms, input and cost coefficients to be observed in operation, and some general and aggregative indicators governing various phases of economic activity that are covered in the component plans described in the last chapter. The relevant "control figures" are then transmitted to the central-government ministries, as well as to the provincial governments. The planning agencies in these respective organs must in turn transmit the relevant "control figures" to the individual enterprises under their jurisdiction. Some adjustments of these initial "control figures" are permitted at this level. Finally, the individual enterprises must draft their production plans on the basis of the output targets and operational requirements stipulated. When completed, these plans are submitted to the higher-level agencies for integration and approval.

[1] The number of targets the central planning agency had to set was reduced in the 1959 decentralization program. But the changes were only in their scope, not really in kind.

As pointed out in Chapter I, prior to the adoption of the provisional regulations governing the annual plan of 1959, integration of the plans of the individual enterprises was carried out by the central-government ministries in charge of the individual industrial branches. Beginning with the 1959 annual plan, and in addition to the commodity-branch plans which the central ministries had to prepare, integration of the plans of both the central government and the local government enterprises was also to be undertaken at the provincial or regional (for the "autonomous" regions) government level. Finally, both the commodity-branch and the territorial plans are submitted to the central planning agency, which then proceeds to integrate and revise the partial plans. In theory, the resultant national plan should possess internal consistency in the sense that the expected supplies of goods and services must be equated to the expected demand, both in terms of single items and in terms of aggregate supply and demand. The revised control figures are then transmitted to the central government ministries and lower government levels for further transmission to the operating agencies and enterprises. They have now become targets which the operating units must strive to attain. The degree of plan fulfillment must then be reported regularly by the operating enterprises and the results appraised by the State Economic Commission.

While the above procedure has been described with reference to the annual plan, a priori, the long-term plan must follow essentially the same procedure, except that it would now be subject to revision on the basis of the fulfillment of the short-term plan. Furthermore, at any time, the long-term "control figures" would serve as a reference for the initial control figures adopted in the annual plan.

The Two Basic Sets of Decisions

The relative simplicity of the preceding schematic description has, however, concealed some very important issues. These concern the selection of the "control figures" and the manner in which internal consistency of the many partial plans is arrived at.

Although the national economic plan comprises not only the allocation of resources, but also the distribution of the products and the transformation of the economic system into socialism, in a narrower sense it is the allocation of resources that preoccupies the planners. In this regard, two basic sets of decisions are involved before any instruction can be handed down by the planning authority to the executive departments and operators in the economic system.

In the first place, a pattern of allocation by end use must be decided upon. That is to say, some decision has to be made concerning the allocation of resources between present consumption and addition to the capacity to increase future output, which, of course, may or may not mean greater future consumption. This is the problem of determining the ratio between investment and consumption, including both personal and collective consumption; collective consumption should also be construed to include the military use of resources. Alternatively, the problem may be formulated as one of determining the investment-income or saving-income ratio. In the second place, resources must be allocated by commodities and by productive sectors from which the national output originates. That is to say, the planners must decide upon the kinds and quantities of goods and services to be produced, technically known as the "commodity mix."

The first set of decisions will enable the planning authority to determine the size of the wage fund, which corresponds to the bulk of the population's income, and the consumption and commodity sales plans. The supply of goods may then be matched with the corresponding effective demand. Simultaneously, the same decision on the rate of investment will be the basis of plans for the financing of investment expenditures. Such expenditures must come out of available sources of revenue, whether through or outside of the budget.

There is little doubt that China's economists and planning officials are aware of the important relationship between investment (or accumulation)[2] and consumption. They recognize that the level of the saving-income ratio is reflected in the ratios between "Department I" and "Department II" in industrial output (that is, in the production of producer versus consumer goods), between agricultural and industrial output, and between the production of "heavy" industry and that of "light" industry, etc.[3] However, the over-all consumption and investment figures must be disaggre-

[2] For the definition of "accumulation" see Chapter II, fn. 2, pp. 22–23.

[3] Tung Fu-jeng, "Chüeh-ting Chi-lei ho Hsiao-fei Pi-li ti Jo-kan Fang-fa-lun Wen-t'i ti T'an-t'ao" (Inquiry into the Problems Concerning the Theories in the Determination of the Accumulation-Consumption Ratio), *Ching-chi Yen-chiu* (*Economic Research*), No. 11, 1959, pp. 38–46.

gated into commodities and investment projects. Investment projects must in turn be disaggregated into (1) fixed capital investments or capital-construction expenditures, and (2) investment in working capital. These subcategories must themselves be disaggregated into commodities. Since any given set of over-all consumption and investment targets can presumably be matched with varying sets of commodity targets, the second set of decisions regarding what commodities to produce at home or to procure from abroad does not follow automatically from the first set of decisions. Each set of decisions, therefore, has to be made separately, although in relation to one another.

Two Principles for General Guidance

What criteria should the planners employ in making the decisions? What criteria do they actually employ? Before we can answer these questions in any detail with reference to the case of Communist China, it may be worth-while to mention the two "objective laws" that, it is said, govern socialist economic planning in general. These "laws" are mentioned time and again in the literature of Soviet as well as Chinese economic planning.[4] The first "law" speaks of the development of a socialist economy that would continuously increase the material and cultural requirements of the society. The second "law" speaks of the planned proportional development of the economy or the process of "balanced growth."

If the above generalizations are to be given a little more meaningful content, one interpretation of these "objective laws" would be as follows: (1) that collective and personal consumption should be allowed to rise as the economy develops, and (2) that plans should be laid to make available goods needed for the production of these consumer goods and for the distribution and use of all goods produced. This interpretation, however, still leaves unanswered why certain final goods are to be produced at all and how rapidly consumption should be allowed to rise, assuming, of course, that the alternative of leaving the rate of increase in consumption entirely to private individual decisions is precluded. Apparently the really meaningful answers cannot be found in general statements; they must be sought in the individual national plans themselves.

[4] See, for instance, Nicolas Spulber, *The Soviet Economy*, p. 9.

Choosing the Investment-Income Ratio in Communist China

Speaking to the first session of the Eighth Central Committee of the Communist Party of China on September 18, 1956, Po I-po, Chairman of the State Economic Commission, stated that it would be "relatively prudent" to set the proportion of accumulation in national income for some years to come at "not less, or a little higher, than 20 per cent."[5] Furthermore, "for the sake of the country's industrialization," that is to say, "in our people's long-run collective interest, not only should the rate of increase in the people's consumption level be less than that of the social output, especially that of the increase in labor productivity, it should also be lower than the rate of increase in accumulation."[6] Po went even further by pointing out that the envisaged normal proportion of accumulation in national income should be accompanied by appropriate ratios of the national budget to the national income and of capital construction to budget expenditure. The normal budget receipts to national income ratio was set at about 30 per cent, while the ratio of capital construction to total budget expenditure was set at approximately 40 per cent.

According to Po, the above accumulation-income ratio was chosen on the basis of actual experience in 1953–56. During this period, the ratio was said to have fluctuated from 15.7 per cent in 1952 to 18.3 per cent in 1953, 21.6 per cent in 1954, 20.5 per cent in 1955, and 22.8 per cent in 1956. Po felt that because of the increase in national income, industrial output, and agricultural output during 1953–56—despite the greater rates of increase registered (1) by heavy industry than light industry, (2) by industry than agriculture, and (3) by investment than consumption—consumption nevertheless managed to increase. This convinced Po that the higher rates of accumulation in the latter part of the four-year period were quite reasonable.

However, he was also aware of the shortages in supply that were felt during those years when accumulation and capital construction were high. Thus, stated Po, "Whenever we wanted to add to industrial or other construction projects, and to expand the national budget and investment in capital construction accordingly, we always noticed that greater speed was not the same

[5] Po I-po, "Cheng-ch'üeh Ch'u-li Chi-lei ho Hsiao-fei ti Kuan-hsi" (On the Correct Handling of the Relationship Between Accumulation and Consumption), *People's Handbook*, 1957, p. 73.
[6] *Ibid.*

as greater accomplishment."[7] Elsewhere in the same speech, Po pointed out that if the consumption level of the population could not be increased during the industrialization process, then the development of the entire economy would be handicapped and the further consolidation of the "workers' and peasants' alliance" would be adversely affected. This would in turn reduce the speed of industrialization and lower the level of accumulation. Alternatively, a number of undesirable political and economic effects would be felt.

The above considerations relate to the level of investment financed by domestic saving. Implied in Po's statement was the undependability of foreign-capital inflow. Communist China has to rely solely on domestic accumulation, according to Po, "because of the inherent characteristic of our social system."[8] This was an admission that foreign capital had to be ruled out because of the socialist system that China was trying to establish. As a further implication, foreign capital from other socialist countries, including the Soviet Union, was apparently not expected at any substantial level.

In the years following Po's 1956 statement, a great deal of discussion took place on the upper limit of the investment-income ratio. Some Chinese economists believed that 20 per cent would be a maximum ratio. Others, however, disputed this. Chang Chu-chung, for instance, believed that there was no natural limit to the ratio of investment to income. On the contrary, he claimed that the economic limit to increasing investment was merely the need to safeguard the normal increase in the level of consumption of the people, which was by no means inflexible. According to Chang, the accumulation-income ratio during 1952 was 19.7 per cent,[9] and it rose to 23.7 in 1957. Consequently, an increase to 25 per cent would be entirely feasible. The 20 per cent figure employed by Po was, therefore, a rather conservative estimate, and in Chang's opinion its choice was partly influenced by the Soviet record, which was said to be around 25 per cent "in recent years."[10] However, because of the higher relative prices of means

[7] Ibid.

[8] Ibid., p. 72.

[9] Chang Chu-chung, "P'ing Chi-lei Pi-chung Ku-ting Lun" (On the Variability of the Accumulation Ratio), Chi-hua Ching-chi (The Planned Economy), No. 8, 1958, pp. 23–25. It should be noted that the accumulation-income ratio in 1952 quoted by Chang (19.7 per cent) differed from Po I-po's official estimate of 15.7 per cent.

[10] See also Spulber, op. cit., p. 137 et seq.

of production in China compared with corresponding Soviet prices, a 25 per cent investment-income ratio would be equivalent to only 20 per cent in the Soviet Union. Thus, even in the light of the Soviet model, an increase to 25 per cent or more would be well within reason.

Chang went on to describe how one might estimate the possible range of the appropriate investment-income ratio. This was, on the one hand, defined by the minimum investment required for equipping the expected increase in the labor force at a ratio of invested capital per worker equal to that of the base period. This minimum investment requirement would include investment both in fixed capital and in working capital; it would also include both productive and "unproductive" investments (such as housing, hospitals, etc.), inclusive of capital needed to produce additional consumer goods required for the growing population. On the other hand, the investment-income ratio would be defined by a ceiling determined by the availability of resources, and specifically by the size of the producer- and consumer-goods industries. As income increased, the flexible range of sustainable investment would widen.[11]

Throughout the first fifteen years of Communist rule (1949–64 inclusive), the Chinese population was urged incessantly to "practice economy" so that both national income and accumulation could be raised. In the words of Mao Tse-tung, "Practice of economy on a sustained and universal basis is a way to resolve the 'contradiction' between poverty and the desired large-scale construction."[12]

The problem of practicing economy and increasing accumulation so as to hold the ratio of investment to income at a given level is complicated by the existence of collective ownership along with state ownership. Where collective ownership exists, as in the case of cooperative farms, the distribution of output is not entirely in the hands of the government. Thus the volume of consumption in relation to saving cannot be determined with any degree of certainty. On the other hand, in the case of state-owned enterprises, pricing of the product and absorption of a major part of

[11] According to Chang, the increase in income in 1958 over that of 1957 was 34 per cent, while the corresponding increase in accumulation was 97 per cent, and the increase in per-capita consumption 7.8 per cent.

[12] Mao Tse-tung, "Kuan-yü Cheng-ch'üeh Ch'u-li Jen-min Nei-pu Mao-tun" (On the Correct Handling of Inner Contradictions among the People), *Jen-min Ch'u-pan She*, p. 35.

the output through profit, which accrues to the state, are directly under the control of the government. This is recognized by the Chinese planners, and explains *in part* why the investment-income ratio showed an upward trend during 1952–57 as the process of socialization advanced, and why it was stepped up further during the Great Leap following the establishment of the communes.

Selecting the Commodity-Output Targets

A major portion of the "control figures" used initially in plan formulation, and subsequently as instructions to the operating agencies, consists of commodity-output targets. After 1953, the lists giving commodity specifications in both industry and agriculture have grown longer, indicating the gradual expansion of the scope of the control figures. Some of the commodities involved are final products while others are intermediate goods. But how are the particular goods and output targets selected?

One would think that the planning literature of China, which has increased during more than a decade of Communist rule, would provide some explicit answers to this particular question. Yet no clear answer has ever been offered. A probable explanation for this conspicuous lack is the nonexistence of a complete set of principles governing the determination of these targets and the fluidity of such principles that may exist at any time.

Nevertheless, certain important considerations can be inferred on an a priori basis, while others are deducible from observation of actual practice: (1) In the case of some intermediate goods (e.g., pig iron), the physical output targets can be deduced from the corresponding targets for end products (e.g., finished steel) under the assumption of fairly stable technical input coefficients. (2) In the case of some final products—essential consumer goods that would be invariably included in any bill of goods representing a rather basic level of consumption—minimum requirements can be estimated on the basis of the physical needs of the population. The minimum domestic requirements, modified possibly by such considerations as supply to the export market, can then be used as output targets. Food grains, cotton cloth, and other simple staples are good examples in this category. (3) In the case of a number of final and intermediate goods in chronic short supply, such as petroleum, chemical fertilizers, and certain machine tools, the current production targets can probably be set at the level of full capacity production by the existing plants. (4) The domestic production of goods used in construction projects may be determined by the selection of specific investment projects, which may in turn be influenced by "exogenous" factors such as foreign-aid negotiations. For instance, a particular industrial plant may be scheduled for construction under Soviet-aid arrangements, or with the aid of other external credit, and the plant may in turn determine which goods and what quantities should be supplied domestically. (5) Where imports constitute an irreplaceable component among the inputs used in production, their availability may set the maximum limit to certain domestic-production targets. This may be regarded as a corollary to the preceding case. (6) "Arbitrary" political decisions may be made on items of collective consumption, such as hospitals, schools, welfare institutions, supplies, and military procurements; a number of specific capital-construction projects in existing industries; and pilot plants for certain new products. These decisions may be made on completely noneconomic grounds. (7) Given the volume of output deemed necessary because of one or more of the preceding reasons, a somewhat larger figure may then be set as the total output target in order to allow for other uses. (8) As time passes, adjustments of the pattern of consumption and production in the preceding plan period may be made so as to modify the conditions of shortage or oversupply.

Necessary Conditions for the Optimal Allocation of Resources

The preceding description of plan formulation and the earlier discussion on the decision-making apparatus have shown that the economic planning system of Communist China is highly centralized. This appears to be the case in spite of decentralization efforts in 1959, when the Second Five-Year Plan period began. Since the First Five-Year Plan was not announced until 1955, and since the planning apparatus had not been fully developed until then, it is also clear that the economic plan remained rather rudimentary during the greater part of 1953–57. Yet the plan at all times has had the structure of a system of material balances, which are expressed in large part in physical units. A pertinent question, therefore, is whether such a system is capable of allocating resources in an optimal manner.

To facilitate analysis, let us consider this question in three steps: (1) Can the optimum be defined? (2) Will the decision makers in economic planning be able and willing to make any necessary readjustments to reach a well-defined optimum? (3) Are the operators in the productive enterprises willing and able to follow certain clear rules of behavior in making these readjustments? If plan modifications are possible and can be implemented, and if an optimum can be unambiguously defined, then an initial plan containing many arbitrary elements need not by itself preclude an eventual optimal solution.

But how can an optimal pattern of resource allocation be defined? What are the conditions necessary for such a clear definition? In plain language, an optimal allocation of resources may be said to have been reached when it is not worthwhile to produce one commodity rather than another, or to produce more of any commodity than the given amount, or to adopt a different method of production, including different proportions of factors of production employed, or to allocate long-term investment in a different manner. In order to ascertain such an optimum, it is necessary to be able to compare costs with benefits. Furthermore, such a comparison should be made in terms of small variations "at the margin" whenever divisible units can be applied in measuring input and output.

There are certain conditions under which such a comparison would be possible. In the first place, since the comparison must be made between physically distinct goods and services, a common denominator must be employed. Hence one must employ money as a measuring rod, and a price system under which the relative values of different goods and services can be assessed must be presupposed. In the second place, a valid comparison can be made only if both costs and benefits can be accurately measured and related to each other; furthermore, costs must be inclusive of all scarce resources consumed. Third, a basis of comparison must be found for values (both benefits and costs) which accrue at different dates over a period of time. Finally, the price system employed must reflect the subjective scale of priorities of the decision makers both in demanding end products and in supplying prime factors of production so that the comparison of costs and benefits can be made meaningful. Only then would it be possible to determine whether any economic activity is worthwhile.

In the case of Communist China, money prices are used, so that the first condition for an optimal allocation of resources exists. In the second place, benefits that may be ascribed to specific economic activities are frequently qualified by the CPC's political assessment of their advantages and disadvantages. Thus prices are not employed as a full reflection of benefits and costs. But even more important than this defect is the fact that according to Communist Chinese practice, costs are not fully inclusive of all the scarce factors used in production. In the third place, comparison of values over time is made difficult because of the absence of proper accounting for interest charges. The evaluation of long-term investments and of the relative merits of different types of durable equipment to be produced or used is virtually impossible for the same reason. This phenomenon stems from the same failure to include interest charges in the cost of production other than interest on bank loans for working capital. Finally, even if all the above-mentioned problems did not exist, the optimal allocation of resources in Communist China could be defined only with reference to the subjective priority and preference scale of the planners. This raises the question whether the price system used would not necessarily deviate widely from those prices that would reflect individual preferences if the latter were allowed to play their full role.

Degree of Inclusiveness of the Cost Concept and the Profit Rate

In accordance with Marxian economic concepts, the Chinese Communists regard the costs of production as composed of $c+v$, that is, "constant capital" plus "variable capital." Constant capital represents the amount of past labor embodied in materials used up in the production process. It is, therefore, the sum of depreciation plus material cost. Variable capital, on the other hand, is the amount of current labor and is represented by the wage bill. This concept of production cost does not include either interest or land rent, with one exception: interest charges on borrowed working capital are considered a part of cost. Where land is an important element in the production process, as in agricultural production, failure to account for land rent would imply that all land, regardless of its fertility, usefulness, and location, is treated uniformly. There would be no basis of comparison between returns from different uses of land of varying fertility, location, etc., and therefore no basis to evaluate the efficiency in the use of land and other cooperating factors of production. Even more important, of course, is the absence of interest charges and its adverse effect on the economic use of capital.

There are economists in Communist China who are well aware of the importance of accounting for interest and for the efficient use of capital. For instance, in an article published in *Economic*

Research in 1962, three economists[13] undertook to point out the relative unimportance of depreciation in production cost. "With the exception of a few industrial branches, such as electric power and mining, in which depreciation constitutes a fairly high proportion of production cost," the authors maintain, "the relative importance of depreciation in cost is universally less than 10 per cent in most Chinese industries. That is to say, even if the amount of fixed assets employed in these industries were increased or reduced by one half, the effect on production cost would be less than 5 per cent. Furthermore, depreciation is charged only on productive equipment actually employed. It is not allowed for in the case of equipment held in reserve or not used in the enterprises. The possession of such equipment does not therefore have any effect on cost."[14]

Earlier, in a 1958 article in *Planned Economy*,[15] Fan Jo-i pointed out the vast discrepancies in different branches of production between rates of profit over cost and the corresponding rates of return over capital investment. Specifically, the following figures were quoted:

	Rate of Profit over Cost	Rate of Profit on Investment
	Per Cent	
Commercial Activities	11.0	82.3
Agricultural Cooperatives	56.1	32.1
Light Industry	32.0	47.1
Heavy Industry	43.0	23.1

Thus, in goods production, the rate of profit on investment was lowest in heavy industry and higher in light industry and agriculture. Furthermore, according to Fan, during 1953–55, the large-scale central-government-operated enterprises employed about ten times more invested capital than the smaller local-government enterprises. In addition, the value output per yuan of investment decreased steadily from year to year in the large enterprises, whereas in the small enterprises output per yuan of investment during the same period was 1,200 per cent higher than in the

[13] Ho Chien-chang, *et al*, "Kuan-yü She-hui-chu-i ch'i-yeh Ching-chi-he-suan ti Nei-jung Wen-t'i" (On the Meaning of Enterprise Economic Accounting Under Socialism), *Ching-chi Yen-chiu*, No. 4, April, 1962, pp. 1–10.

[14] *Ibid.*, p. 6.

[15] Fan Jo-i, "Lüeh-lun Ts'u-ching Li-jun-lü yü Tuo-k'uai-hao-sheng ti Chien-she Fang-cheng" (On the Rate of Profit on Capital Construction and Development Policy), *Chi-hua Ching-chi*, No. 8, August, 1958, pp. 21–23.

larger ones. Fan also spoke of the much greater investment cost
in the development of new areas because of the overhead investments required. The latter, including investments in municipal
constructions, transportation, etc., it was said, may be as high as
investment in the new factories themselves.

Considerable discussion on the subject of the profit rate took
place during 1961–63. While some favored computing the rate of
profit over production cost, excluding interest, others preferred to
use the rate of profit over investment. Actual practice in Communist China has been mostly the former. Although there has
been some shift of emphasis to the latter, there is little evidence
that the more rational practice has been uniformly adopted, even
if only as a matter of ostensible policy.

It can be shown that the two rates would be identical only if
the rate of turnover of fixed capital were the same as that of
working capital. This, of course, would imply the absence of any
durable equipment which would last beyond one period of turnover of the working capital.[16]

[16] Let t_v be the number of times the working capital of an enterprise turns
over during a unit accounting period, and t_f the number of times fixed capital turns over in the same period (t_f is usually less than 1).

Let K_f be the amount of fixed capital in the enterprise, and K_v the amount
of working capital.

Within the accounting period, let S denote the profit or "surplus value"; d,
the amount of depreciation; r, the material cost; v, the wage bill.

The rate of profit over cost $= \dfrac{S}{C+V} = \dfrac{S}{d+(r+v)}$

The rate of profit over investment $= \dfrac{S}{K_f + K_v} = \dfrac{S}{\dfrac{d}{t_f} + \dfrac{r+v}{t_v}}$

If the two rates are equal, $\dfrac{S}{d+(r+v)} = \dfrac{S}{\dfrac{d}{t_f} + \dfrac{r+v}{t_v}}$

Then $d+(r+v) = \dfrac{d}{t_f} + \dfrac{r+v}{t_v}$

Let us choose an accounting period such that $t_v = 1$

Then, $d+(r+v) = \dfrac{d}{t_f} + (r+v)$, and $d = \dfrac{d}{t_f}$, which can be true only if
$t_f = 1$.

This is tantamount to saying that there is no fixed capital of a longer durability than the period of turnover of the working capital, that is, no fixed
capital at all.

Possibility of Adjustment Toward Optimal Resource Allocation

In the competitive model of a private-enterprise economy, mal-allocation of resources would result in oversupply or overdemand, which would in turn lead to price changes. The price changes would bring about an alteration of the relative profitability of different economic activities. The entrepreneurs, in trying to maximize profit, would then undertake to make the adjustments needed to bring about optimal allocation.

Playing a different role, the Chinese commodity price, F.O.B. factory, is composed of three parts: cost (including raw materials, depreciation, and labor), profit, and tax. Cost is in turn based on the average costs of different enterprises in the same industrial branch, weighted by the planned outputs of the enterprises. The profit and tax margins, compared with cost, are a matter of major concern and are often used in evaluating the adequacy of pricing. This implies that commodity prices in Communist China are really constructed on a cost-plus basis.

According to Fan Jo-i,[17] an outspoken and severe critic of Chinese planning, the practice of setting "transfer prices" for heavy-industry products in inter-enterprise transactions began in 1953. These are prices employed in the purchase and sale of commodities between government enterprises. At the same time, separate market prices existed for transactions by enterprises not yet socialized, which as a rule were higher than the transfer prices. A double-price system was therefore brought into existence.

Furthermore, in 1953, when transfer prices were introduced, individual prices were generally increased above their 1952 level. Between 1954 and 1957, the transfer prices on the whole remained relatively unchanged, although there were some individual price reductions. The question of further reducing the transfer prices of certain heavy-industry products was again a subject of considerable discussion during 1957. It was in this connection that the rigidity of prices and their disuse as a regulator of demand and supply were forcefully pointed out by Fan.

If prices were fixed at too low a level [stated Fan], then many enterprises would go out of business and supply would fall short of demand. If prices were set too high, then the inefficient enterprises would be given protection. If the profits and losses of individual enterprises were used to offset one another, then the many differ-

[17] Fan Jo-i, *op. cit.*, pp. 21–23.

ences that exist among the central and local government enterprises, as well as between the more developed and the less efficient ones, would be disregarded. If such were the case, production would fail to increase and the number of administrative personnel would instead have to rise. Consequently, prices should be used to render assistance to planning, and, according to the actual relationship between supply and demand, they should be employed to regulate production and to resolve the "contradiction" between production and demand. That is to say, prices should be lowered when the output of the larger enterprises is sufficient to meet the consumption demand of the country. Under these conditions the disappearance of the smaller and less efficient enterprises would not present any problem.

During 1954–55, both prices and profits in the government-operated heavy-industry enterprises were high. The capital-construction departments were anxious to purchase imports, especially Soviet imports. Within the country, they would rather purchase their supplies from private enterprises at lower prices or produce them themselves: They were not willing to receive the same supplies under central allocation. On the other hand, whenever supplies fell short of demand, the same capital-construction departments would immediately apply for central allocation while trying simultaneously to increase their purchases from the market.

Fan's comment on this situation was that if the government was able to set prices, there would be little reason for it to continue the irrational pricing that would increase the "contradiction" between supply and demand. Under such conditions why should the government employ solely administrative means to balance demand and supply instead of using the price level? Fan's criticism was centered on (1) the disregard of demand and supply, and (2) pricing on the basis of cost. The employment of the cost-plus pricing system led to higher prices with higher cost. An example given by Fan was the higher price of beet sugar compared with cane sugar because of the higher beet sugar production cost. To take the position that an equal profit-cost ratio should be maintained for all enterprises would thus lead to erroneous instructions being issued by the planners to the operating enterprises.

Among the measures recommended by Fan that might improve the economic accounting system, the following were of special interest: (1) Necessary price adjustments should be made, and improvements in the fiscal and planning systems should be carried out; (2) differences in profits due to the different material endowments of the industrial or mining enterprises or varying locational advantages should be offset by taxes in the same way as differential land rents; (3) because of differences in the amount of working capital employed in the individual enterprises and in the organic structure of their fixed assets, profits should be computed on the basis of investment; such profit may then be returned to the state; (4) the larger part of cost savings should be retained by the enterprises and distributed to the workers according to their individual efforts. None of these recommendations was, however, enforced in 1957, at the end of the First Five-Year Plan. Nor was the situation markedly altered during 1961–63, in spite of the renewed interest and discussion on the country's need to allocate its resources rationally following the economic debacle in 1960–62.

To recapitulate, the emergence of an excess supply or demand in Communist China would not necessarily lead to price changes. They definitely would not result in continued price changes initiated by the managers of individual enterprises, inasmuch as the transfer prices of goods sold by one state-owned factory to another, as well as the wholesale and retail market prices of commodities, are all determined by the planning agency, and the plans are fairly rigid in the short run. Furthermore, even if price changes were to take place, they would not necessarily affect profitability. This is a necessary result if the performance of individual enterprises is gauged according to planned profits valued at planned prices rather than real profit that must be earned on the market. In other words, an enterprise may have been instructed to produce a certain output which at given planned prices and standard costs would yield a certain planned profit. Following the inception of the planning period, however, the price of the product may be changed even though such changes are infrequent. Although this has taken place, the planner may nevertheless wish to judge the performance of the enterprise on the basis of the planned price and profit, in which case the price change would not automatically affect the planned profit of the enterprise. The manager of the enterprise would be reluctant to deviate from the criteria officially employed in judging performance.

Of course, the noninclusiveness of production costs would make "profit" an unreliable criterion in resource allocation in any case, as we have already pointed out. The doctrinaire reluctance to employ profit as such a criterion stems from the Marxian position that profit is surplus value and that it is a concept characteristic of the capitalist economy. Therefore, with the establishment of

Among the indicators used in economic accounting and embodied in the control figures issued to the individual enterprises as instructions are specifications about the value output, the physical output, quality requirements, unit cost (mostly excluding the cost of capital), profit over cost, and the productivity of labor. Furthermore, the cost category includes such items as specific input coefficients and coefficients of equipment utilization. As stated by Ts'ui Ch'i in an article in the *Planned Economy*,[22] the purpose of the cost plan of an enterprise is to discover how raw-material-consumption coefficients may be reduced, the expenditure of labor economized, and the potential of equipment capacity fully exploited. Alternatively, the main content of the cost plan which every enterprise has to follow may be said to aim at the gradual increase in labor productivity and the continued reduction of cost, excluding, however, interest charges.

The usefulness of the cost and profit indices are, of course, vitiated by the noninclusiveness of cost. The labor-productivity index also disregards the role of other inputs. Moreover, the output indices may be misleading when they are not sufficiently specific with respect to the quality of the products and their technical characteristics. Another major difficulty arises from the possibility that the individual indicators employed in economic accounting may not yield consistent results. For instance, an enterprise may be able to fulfill the planned output target but not the profit or cost requirement. Whenever such conflicts occur, there is the question as to which of the control figures and indicators should be given preference. During the discussion of 1963, there were those who believed that the physical- and value-output figures were the most important, inasmuch as they were the principal indicators in the plan. Some, on the other hand, thought that the cost and profit indicators should constitute the focus of attention. No agreement of opinion or practice exists to date.

Financial and Direct Controls

Although the system of planning described above may not permit the optimum allocation of resources and the efficient management of the individual enterprise, the Chinese planners nevertheless have certain means at their disposal for the implementation

[22] Ts'ui Ch'i, "Pien-chih Sheng-ch'an Tzu-liao Ch'an-p'in Ch'u-ch'ang Chia-ko Chi-hua-chung ti Ho-suan Fen-hsi Kung-tso (Accounting and Analysis in Compiling the Plan of Producer-Goods Prices [ex factory]), *Chi-hua Ching-chi*, No. 3, 1957, pp. 18–21.

of their plans. In other words, even if the plan targets do not correspond to the optimum allocation of resources, and even if, under the given system of planning, it may be difficult to discover what the optimum is, attainment of the targets as such is nevertheless possible in theory.

There are two principal categories of control. On the one hand, direct control can be exercised through the assignment of labor to jobs and control over transfers of labor from one enterprise or geographical area to another. This control is reinforced by direct allocation of important raw materials, so that in the..ry no unauthorized production could take place. On the other hand, strict indirect control can also be exercised through monetary control. Inasmuch as most transactions are in terms of money through bank transfers, the flow of goods is necessarily accompanied by a counterflow of funds. By requiring that all purchases and sales of goods be matched against authorized payments and receipts, it is possible to use financial control over the budget of an enterprise as a regulator of its production. This procedure, of course, parallels the internal financial control practiced in all large corporations in a market economy.

Shortly after the Communist seizure of power, the commercial banks at all major economic centers in mainland China became targets of rigorous state control. At first the purpose of such control was twofold. One immediate purpose was the suppression of the postwar hyperinflation through the concentration of bank deposits in government banks, reduction of the liquidity of the commercial banks, and direct restrictions in the extension of bank credit. At the same time, it was recognized that the commercial banks occupied a unique position in the Chinese economy as large-scale suppliers of funds for long-term as well as short-term investment. Thus any design to control the direction and volume of investment would be furthered by control over the banks. Many commercial banks were required first to increase their capitalization and then gradually to consolidate their operations. The amalgamation process led ultimately to the formation of a single joint government private bank, which took over the business of all the commercial banks. With increasing control over the banks, which were put under the supervision of the People's Bank of China, a system of monetary control began to take shape.[23]

[23] Yuan-li Wu, *An Economic Survey of Communist China*, pp. 411–12 and 414–17, on the process of controlling the hyperinflation and the nationalization of the banks.

The system of monetary and currency control established in 1950 required all government enterprises, cooperatives, and certain joint enterprises to conduct their business with other similar units through the People's Bank. All transactions were to be cleared through the bank and only minor operations could be financed by currency. All enterprise units within the system were required to prepare monthly and quarterly plans of receipts and expenditures both for currency and for bank transfers. These expenditures and receipts had to be in balance with the exception of those cases where planned credit was provided for. No overdraft or unplanned credit was permitted. The bank in its turn prepared similar plans for transactions involving private business and persons. These were consolidated with the plans of the government and related enterprises, and together they became the basis of the national plan of monetary expenditures and receipts. The bank would credit or debit an account against a special transfer check or non-negotiable clearing certificate. Copies of all contracts involving any unit within the system had to be deposited with the bank, so that it could act as the government's watchdog for making payments and play a role corresponding to the controller in a giant corporation. The bank was also empowered to hold up transactions that appeared to be unauthorized under an existent contract. Enterprises could borrow from the bank only according to plan and for short-term financing only. Special care was to be exercised in controlling the unauthorized use of funds for long-term investment as against its employment as short-term working capital. This system of monetary control has remained relatively unchanged since 1950. In addition, separate agencies have been developed to finance long-term capital construction and investments in particular sectors in order to facilitate control.

Assurance that the State Economic Commission's production and allocation plan would be adhered to is further derived from the government's control over the distribution of goods. The gradual nationalization of the distributive channels and the formation of government-sponsored marketing and producers' cooperatives in order to replace the many individual small retail outlets were begun very early under the Communist regime, and the process became virtually complete by the end of 1956. The authorities had gradually extended their control over these trading channels by offering to supply them with goods produced by state enterprises and by employing them as outlets for the consignment of goods produced in the government sector. However, with the extension of full government control over these retail channels, it was obvious that no other goods could be sold except the output of government-controlled or -sanctioned enterprises. By closing off the outlet for the sale of unauthorized goods, it would theoretically be possible to make sure that only production within the plan could be carried out. An exception to this institutional framework is the free market, which has been reinstituted since the collapse of the commune movement. A number of products—mostly goods produced by the peasants on their private plots or in their homes—can be bought and sold on the free market, but there is a definite restriction on the types of goods that can pass through these uncontrolled channels.[24]

Divergence Between Theory and Practice

Even though the Communist authorities possess the tools to implement their production plans, actual practice may prevent the realization of the plans for various reasons. In the first place, the data on which the plans are based may be incomplete or

[24] Between 1953 and 1956, a system of market control was developed for agricultural products and scrap metals, the controlled commodities being divided at the time into two groups. Grain, cotton, edible oils, and oil seeds constituted the first group and were placed under the system of compulsory government purchase. After tax payment in kind, peasants producing these commodities were required to sell their entire output to the government at fixed prices, except what they were permitted to keep for their own use. The same regulation is still in force today (1965), except that up to August, 1957, peasants were allowed to sell the stock retained for their own use; they have not been allowed to do so since. The second group consisted of such products as cured tobacco, hemp, jute and ramie, sugar cane and sugar, silk cocoons, tea, live hogs, wool, cow hide, paper produced by handicraft, wood oil, scrap copper, lead and tin, major types of timber, medicinal herbs, apples, oranges and marine products. For this category the government was to determine, and still determines, the proportion of the commodities it desired to purchase while the producers were permitted to sell the amount over and above the purchase quotas. Prior to August, 1957, all sales were to be made on officially supervised markets; since then, sales have been permitted only to purchasing agents designated by the government. In the summer of 1956, a third list of commodities, known as "minor native products," was promulgated. These commodities were to be sold freely, presumably at uncontrolled prices. Goods produced on private farm plots since the modification of the communes probably should be bracketed with this group. There have doubtless been reclassifications from time to time, especially between the second and third categories.

To these three categories of goods a fourth group in the distribution process might be added: those industrial products produced by government enterprises which are subject to direct allocation.

management to follow practices that would convince outsiders that everything was well. Such "window-dressing" practices are fairly common in business and other activity. The "red executive" is not immune to such practices; nor are they his sole prerogative.

At a still different level, the problems of rational resource allocation are complicated by the planners' regional or departmental outlook. Prior to the 1959 decentralization attempts, inasmuch as the supply and demand of individual commodities were balanced at the departmental level, the central government ministries often paid no regard to the demands placed on the transport system while attempting to balance the material requirements of their own enterprises. Following the 1959 decentralization program, however, regionalism began to rear its head, and there has since been a reversion to greater centralization of control.

Nor is the allocation of resources always according to plan. In fact, among the "crimes" the Communist authorities have tried to stamp out are the matter of unauthorized invoices and purchase orders, purchase and sale of raw materials on the black market, and production in "underground factories."[27] These "deviations" became especially prominent in the spring of 1963 and required the institution of official drives to eliminate them along with the "rectification" of various "individualistic trends" contrary to the spirit of planning. The 1963 drives were reminiscent of similar campaigns in 1952.

The Soviet *tolkachi* (pushers) most definitely have their Chinese counterparts. Thus, while optimal resource allocation may be precluded in Chinese planning, further deviations may occur between the plan and actual practice.

[27] Wang Hsiao-t'ang, "Kung-fei ti Hsin-wu-fan Yün-tung" ("The New Five-Anti Campaign of Communist China"), *Fei-ch'ing Yen-chiu* (*Studies on Mainland China*), VII, No. 1 (Taiwan, January, 1964), 52–58.

CHAPTER IV

Planning Income Distribution: Accumulation, Socialization, Equity, and Incentive

Principles in Income Distribution

There are few expressly formulated principles of income distribution in Communist China. However, it can perhaps be said that payment of labor according to work and the abolition of private property as a source of income constitute the major theoretical propositions. All other propositions are based on practical considerations of economic policy and the need to adjust practice to the stage of economic development and the prevailing political environment. Among such practical considerations are the maintenance of a high rate of investment and, by necessity, a low level of consumption, increase in labor productivity, observation of strict labor discipline, avoidance of gross popular discontent, and maintenance of some degree of equity in income distribution.

In the first place, the Communist regime's answer to the question "for whom to produce" is of course affected by the "national goals" the CPC has chosen for the economy. In particular we may single out the following:

First, since rapid and accelerated accumulation is desired, and since the total output of the economy is low, a high rate of saving can best be assured by pre-empting a large part of the national product for the purpose of investment before it can reach the individual consumer. Since the Communist society wishes to regulate the rate of collective consumption as well, and, even more, to channel it into very specific directions, it would be expedient to add to the share pre-empted for investment an amount set aside for collective consumption. The latter corresponds to expenditures for "defense," "government administration," and "social and cultural activities," all of which are standard expenditure categories in the state budget.

The following description of the distribution process by an economist in Communist China is worth quoting:

> In the case of those peasants who have joined agricultural cooperatives, in the first phase of distribution of the national product created every year, a part of the product becomes the personal income of the peasants . . . another part constitutes the collective income of the cooperative farm. In the second stage of redistribution, a part of the collective income received by the collective farm during the first stage has to be forwarded to the treasury via the agricultural tax; the remainder will be used within the cooperative for investment in further production . . . and for expenditure on collective-welfare items for the benefit of the cooperative's members. . . . Furthermore, out of the national income annually produced by government industrial enterprises, during the first stage of distribution, a part consists of the workers' wages while the remainder constitutes the gross income of the enterprise. In the second stage of redistribution, with the exception of a part of the gross income retained as the "reward fund" of the enterprise, or profit reserved to it, which may be disposed of by the enterprise itself, the greater part is transmitted to the treasury either as tax or as profit. The wage income received by the employees in the first stage of the distribution may also be transferred to the government treasury or to the credit institution through purchase of bonds or savings deposits.[1]

The previous observation that a sizable portion of the national product has to be pre-empted for collective consumption or government investment means that the second stage of redistribution must produce large transfers of funds to the government.

In order to safeguard the share pre-empted for purposes of investment and collective consumption, it would be expedient if the amount of income distributed to the individuals could be closely regulated by the government. Within the framework of Marxian concepts, this proposition means that the amount of personal income distributed to the farmers or to the wage earners in the first stage of distribution preferably should be limited. Such a situa-

[1] Yang P'o, "Shih-lun Wo-kuo Kuo-min-shou-ju ti Fen-p'ei Wen-t'i" (On the Distribution of China's National Income), *Ching-chi Yen-chiu*, No. 6, 1957, pp. 1–11.

tion can be promoted by enlarging the relative share of wages in the national income, by correspondingly reducing both the share and the absolute amount of property income, and by careful government regulation of the form and structure of wage payments.

Since transition to socialism is a "national goal" of the CPC, nationalization of private property becomes an important means of reducing the relative and absolute amount of property income. Thus the pattern of income distribution to be established is invariably associated with the continual redistribution of wealth, which is in turn an integral part of the political and social revolution. In practice, since tactical considerations preclude the completion of the revolutionary process in one stroke, the redistribution of wealth and income must also proceed by stages. So long as property income is not completely eliminated, it will be necessary to regulate the size of the income, as well as its disposition, in order to safeguard the planned accumulation of resources and collective consumption.

Finally, since equity is a major consideration in a socialist economy both for ideological and for practical political reasons, and since increase in labor productivity is a principal goal of a developing economy, the final pattern of income distribution has necessarily to be resolved in a tug of war between two forces—the provision of adequate incentive on the one hand and the desire for equity and limitation of individual consumption on the other. It is in this light that one has to evaluate the attempt of Chinese planners to predicate wage increments on increases in productivity, to institute appropriate wage differentials, and to create a workable and efficient system of nonmonetary rewards and punishments. How all these measures are implemented and what problems are encountered may be seen in the following sections. One may note in passing that most of the measures and problems are common to Soviet-type economies.

Reduction of Property Income

The reduction of the share and absolute amount of property income goes hand in hand with the nationalization of private enterprise. The entire process may be conveniently explained with respect to the urban and rural areas separately.

The process of nationalization of nonagricultural enterprises in the urban areas proceeded by several stages during 1949–56. At the beginning of their rule, the Communist authorities took over the state enterprises of the Nationalist regime and confiscated property owned by the so-called "counterrevolutionaries." The confiscation of banking and manufacturing interests of owners identified with the Nationalist government had the effect of giving the Communists a nucleus of important financial and manufacturing enterprises, in addition to the many former state-owned enterprises. Obviously, because of the political power wielded by the Communist Party, an enterprise would behave as if it were completely nationalized as soon as the Communist government had established a minority interest.

In the second stage, which happened during the first half of 1952, the nationalization process took place as a part of the "five-anti" campaign. The latter was an attempt to bring a larger number of private business enterprises under Communist control, ostensibly as a countermeasure to the efforts of the capitalists to undermine the new order as a class. The five economic "crimes" against which the campaign was directed were bribery of public officials, evasion of taxes, theft of government-owned assets, fraud in filling government contracts, and betrayal and misuse of the state's economic secrets. Prosecution of "offenders" served to cloak the government's real intention—i.e., an unprecedentedly large capital levy and the expansion of the sphere of joint and public enterprises. The large number of business firms investigated under this campaign probably included most of the larger firms. Infringement of government regulations was classified into several categories, and punishment ranging from fines to confiscation was meted out to the offenders by special tribunals.[2] The officially reported sharp decline of the proportion of capitalist enterprises in the gross value of industrial output (excluding handicrafts) from 28.7 per cent in 1951, to 17.1 per cent in 1952, and 14.0 per cent in 1953,[3] serves as an indication of the scale of socialization during the five-anti campaign and immediately afterward.

The third stage of socialization was reached in 1955–56, when businesses were brought under the aegis of whole or partial state ownership on a wholesale basis. At this time, joint enterprises were formed by entire trade groups. The same official statistics cited above show that the proportion of the capitalist enterprises in the gross value of output of industry had declined to .1 per cent by 1956.

[2] See Yuan-li Wu, *An Economic Survey of Communist China*, pp. 228–31.
[3] *Wei-ta ti Shih-nien (Great Ten Years)*, Peking, 1959, p. 32.

With the virtual elimination of private enterprise in the nonagricultural sectors in 1956, the former owners of these enterprises were given a nominal "dividend" payment under a resolution passed by the State Council on February 8, 1956. A nominal "fixed interest" or "dividend" of 1–6 per cent a year, payable quarterly, regardless of the profit or loss of the enterprises in question, was promised to private stockholders for a period of six years. The amount was subsequently revised to a uniform 5 per cent per annum. Inasmuch as the payments were to be terminated at the end of six years, this arrangement was tantamount to confiscation with partial compensation at the rate of 30 per cent of the estimated value of the private owners' investment, payable over a six-year period. The value of the investment itself was, of course, subject to the arbitrary influence and decision of the authorities. Prior to the 1956 regulation, it was customary to allot at least one quarter of the net profit of all joint enterprises to private stockholders. Thus, with the 1956 regulation, the source of property income in the urban sector was effectively eliminated.[4] Although the practice of paying 5 per cent a year to the original stockholders was extended in 1962 for another three years, compensation would still be limited to 45 per cent of the property value assigned to it by the authorities.

In the agricultural sector, socialization and the redistribution of wealth were also carried out in several stages. The first stage consisted of land reform, which began in 1950 under a new Land Reform Law. It was completed toward the end of 1952 and in 1953. Under the redistribution program, those farmers who leased land to others or had tenants, and some of the "rich peasants," were deprived of their land and other means of production. The latter were distributed to the poorer farmers and farm workers. The same reform also eliminated rental and interest payments as sources of income. However, nominally at any rate, the land received in distribution was to remain as the private property of the owner-cultivator. Thus property income was not entirely eliminated at this point.

The second stage of socialization, however, followed immedi-

---

[4] *Fa-kuei Hui-pien,* January–June, 1956, pp. 282–83.
Discussions on the theme of "fixed interest" may be found in various articles in *Ching-chi Yen-chiu,* No. 1, 1957. The further extension of the "dividend" payment measure for 1963–65 was reported at the end of the third session of the second National People's Congress, March 27–April 16, 1962. *People's Daily,* Peking, April 17, 1962.

ately after land reform. This phase was heralded by the establishment of "mutual-aid teams," which in turn led to the formation of agricultural cooperatives of the first degree. The mutual-aid teams were precisely what their name implied. They were formed by groups of farmers who helped one another with equipment or labor for specific purposes or at certain times of the year. In many ways they were a traditional form of mutual assistance among individual farmers. The important transition was from a temporary mutual-aid team to a permanent one, and then to the cooperative farm of the first degree. While the mutual-aid team served an average of 20 households each in 1952, the cooperative farm of the first degree comprised an average of 48 households in 1957, and the advanced cooperative farm, an average of 158 households.[5]

The mutual-aid teams were a form of organization of production only. Even the cooperative farms organized at that time still retained a category of property income, namely, a part of the output of the farm which was distributed to the members on the basis of the land and other means of production they had contributed to the cooperative. However, such property income was not to exceed the amount distributed on the basis of labor performed.

The third stage of socialization was the formation of the advanced type collective farms. Distribution on the basis of property contribution was eliminated completely at this point. This stage of socialization in the agricultural sector corresponded roughly to the same time period as the completion of socialization in the nonagricultural sectors.

Then, in 1958, the communes were established,[6] and for a time income distribution was made up almost entirely of commodity supplies, so that some enthusiastic CPC members were able to claim that Communist China had already reached the ultimate phase of distribution according to need. The amount of money

[5] See *Ching-chi Chou-pao* (*Economic Weekly*), No. 38, 1952, p. 747, and Yuan-li Wu, "Some Economic Effects of Land 'Reform,' Agricultural Collectivization and the Commune System in Communist China," *Land Tenure, Industrialization and Social Stability: Experience and Prospects in Asia* (Milwaukee: The Marquette University Press, 1961), pp. 21–22.

[6] The state farm may be regarded as the epitome of nationalization in agriculture, and differs from the communes of 1958 in ownership and management. It is an instance of state rather than collective ownership and is probably more centrally managed. It is also more mechanized. However, there were only 2,490 state farms at the end of 1960, accounting for 4.6 per cent of the total cultivated land.

income was reduced to a minimum, and distribution was carried out largely without reference to the amount of work performed. Under the commune, which averaged 4,600 households in September, 1958,[7] the peasant members were organized into production brigades and teams. During the period when the commune was in full swing (April, 1958–April, 1959), the production brigade was solely a unit for production, corresponding roughly in size to the advanced cooperative farm, while the production team was a smaller unit under the brigade. After April, 1959, but only for a very short period, the production brigade was given the function of income distribution and made into an independent accounting unit.

Finally, beginning in the middle of 1961, and again in 1962, the method of distribution within the commune was once more readjusted to the same pattern that had existed prior to the formation of the more advanced cooperative. The category of property income was restored through the granting of private plots to the farmers, who were permitted to retain their own output either for personal consumption or for sale on the free market.

Pre-emption of National Income for Accumulation

In the early years, when the Communist authorities were not yet in a position to control fully the allocation of resources and the flow of income, political means were employed to curtail consumption. Prior to the establishment of the First Five-Year Plan, police and parapolice methods were often employed to discourage persons from consuming more than what was considered politically acceptable. People were afraid of being accused of the "crime" of conspicuous consumption; heavy taxation (including levies of "back-taxes"), compulsory bond purchases, and forced savings were also relied upon. Subsequently, as the scope of nationalization widened and greater control of the income flow was established, profit from the state enterprises and the depreciation fund became a major source of the investment fund. Reinforced by rationing and centralized distribution of various commodities, including food, clothing, and other basic consumer goods, the level of consumption was kept at an "acceptable" volume. At the same time, the level of investment was augmented by employing hitherto unemployed or semi-employed labor, including peasants, prisoner labor, and the Communist Chinese Army. These workers

[7] T'ung-chi Kung-tso (Statistical Work), Peking, No. 20, 1958, p. 23.

were employed in mass labor projects for water conservation, road and railway building, and other similar labor-intensive work; they numbered 23 million in 1953, according to one estimate.[8]

The Principle of Low Wages

In the course of the program to establish control over resources for accumulation, a principle of low wages and low farm income was evolved. The system of low wages, according to Communist Chinese authors, is one under which all workers would have enough to eat while improvements in the standard of living would be gradual and would be granted only on the basis of further development in production. It is said to be the only principle which, under Communist China's present condition of low output, would permit the practice of rewarding labor according to the amount of work performed. To quote Hsü Kang, "Payment according to labor performed means that the compensation of the worker must be appropriate in the light of the productivity of all social labor. Furthermore, compensation to each individual worker must be in accordance with the amount and quality of the labor performed, subject to the condition that all workers must, as far as possible, be given enough food to eat."[9] The underlying idea that there should be sufficient wage differentials to reflect differences in productivity along with a total wage bill that would permit adequate accumulation is also brought out in the statement:

If we assume the lowest level of consumption that would accrue to a worker on the basis of the quantity and quality of his work or the lowest standard of living to be 3, even if the labor differentials should be 3:6:9:12, the distribution of the consumption fund to the individuals need not maintain the differences of 3:6:9:12 but may be at the ratios of 3:4:5:6. This would reflect the principle of letting everybody have enough to eat and of distributing the rest on the basis of differences in the quality and quantity of labor. Such an

[8] Estimate by Li T'ien-min, quoted in Yuan-li Wu, *op. cit.*, 1956, pp. 322–23. A later *China Post* (Taipei, March 11, 1965) report puts the number of forced labor camps at over 350, and the cumulative total of inmates in fourteen years at 90 million. Seventeen labor reform farms are said to have a population of 2 million.

[9] Hsü Kang, "Lao-tung Kung-tzu Kung-tso Pi-hsü Tseng-hsü T'ung-ch'ou Chien-ku Ch'in-chien Chien-kuo ti Fang-tsun" (Pursuit of Labor and Wage Policy in the Light of the Over-all Policy of National Construction under Austerity), *Ching-chi Yen-chiu*, No. 2, 1958, pp. 21–30.

arrangement would still satisfy the requirements of the law of distribution according to labor, but would at the same time allow for the low productivity of the economy. Therefore, a rational low wage system does not contravene the law of distribution according to labor . . . it is not equalitarianism.[10]

In the agricultural sector, even on a cooperative farm of the advanced type or in a commune, there exists some remnant of collective ownership instead of outright state ownership. An attempt must therefore be made to minimize the distribution of output as personal income and to provide appropriate differentials for the sake of safeguarding incentive. This dual purpose is realized in several ways, namely (1) by determining the real value of the wage unit after the total number of wage units is known and the amount available for distribution as personal income has been determined; (2) by requiring the collective farm or the commune and its subdivisions to pre-empt a certain amount of the gross output for collective consumption and investment purposes; (3) by requiring the same distribution units to set aside supplies allocated to the tax fund and for compulsory sales to the government, (4) in the case of the commune during 1958–60, by paying personal income mostly in kind, and (5) by specifying in advance the work unit for each person and for each job. As practiced by the cooperative farm and the commune prior to the latter's modification in 1961–62, this method of controlling personal consumption on the farm was probably no less effective in maintaining a high level of accumulation than the low wage policy practiced in the nonagricultural sectors.

Labor Productivity and the Wage Rate

In practice, according to official statistics, the low-wage principle resulted in an annual increase of 14 per cent in the money-wage rate during 1952–56. The corresponding increase in the real-wage rate was 13 per cent. These rates may be compared with a 22 per cent annual increase of labor productivity in the material-production department. The official sources of these statistics also show that the annual increment was not at all even and that the ratio between the rates of increase in wages and in labor productivity at times varied violently. The most notorious example occurred in 1955 and 1956. During 1955, a 15 per cent

[10] T'ang Kuo-chün, "Wo-kuo Kuan-yü 'An-lao Fen-p'ei' ti T'ao-lun" (National Discussion on the Principle of Payment According to Work), *ibid.*, No. 7, 1958, pp. 72–76.

increase in labor productivity over the corresponding level in 1954 was accompanied by a 1 per cent increase in real wages and a 3 per cent increase in money wages over the preceding year. On the other hand, in 1956, the rates of increase were 30 per cent in labor productivity (1955 = 100), 25 per cent in real wages, and 28 per cent in the money wage rate. In the case of individual industries, workers sometimes fared much worse than the average indicated.

However, while the increase in the wage rate may lag far behind that reported for labor productivity, the average lag being about 50 per cent or less, it is nevertheless possible for the wage-rate increase to exceed that of the supply of consumer goods on which wages are spent. This point is noted by Hsü Heng-mo,[11] according to whom retail prices rose precisely because of such a discrepancy. Employing what he alleges to be hypothetical figures, Hsü showed that if the increase in the total wage bill was 48 per cent in 1955–56 while the supply of consumer goods increased by only 32 per cent, an increase in retail prices might be expected. It is conceivable to have some price inflation even though the phemonenon can be largely suppressed by direct controls. The low wage policy does not always work out as well as it should in principle.

The Wage System and Labor Incentive

Throughout the decade and a half of their rule, the problem of providing enough incentive for labor has incessantly plagued the Chinese Communists. The authorities oscillated between stressing material incentives and stressing nonmaterial incentives. The frequent back-and-forth swings between these two approaches mirror the state of the economy and its subjective interpretation by the Communist Party leaders. In the early years and through the First Five-Year Plan, primary emphasis was placed on the employment of material incentives, and considerable efforts were exerted in order gradually to evolve a wage system based primarily on piece rates and adequate wage differentials. Such a system, it was thought, would be calculated to encourage workers to put forth their best effort. Toward the last two years of the First Five-Year Plan and during the Great Leap, the pendulum swung toward the nonmaterial incentives. Piece rates gave way

[11] Hsü Heng-mo, "Ju-ho Fen-hsi Yen-chiu Chih-kung Kung-tzu Wen-t'i" (Method of Analysis of the Problem of Wages of Workers and Employees), *Tung-chi Kung-tso* (*Statistical Work*), No. 7, 1957, pp. 8–10.

to time rates, at least in principle, and to the time-worn "supply" or ration system, which provided for relatively equal distribution regardless of the amount of work completed or output produced. These measures were reintroduced in the commune, and, to a lesser extent, in the nonagricultural sectors. With the collapse of the Great Leap, the pendulum swung back to the material incentives, as may be noted in the restoration of piece rates and the permission granted the peasants to cultivate their private plots and to keep the produce for themselves. The most significant concessions were the reversion to output distribution by the production team on the basis of work units and setting a value on the work unit in advance.[12]

The regular material incentives in the nonagricultural sectors consist of the basic wage plus supplementary payments for overtime, night or holiday work, hazardous working conditions, regional allowances, and bonuses and other special emoluments. Subsidized housing and other welfare benefits provided under a labor insurance scheme are also part of the total compensation. According to official statistics, the number of workers under the labor-insurance system increased from 3.3 million in 1952 to 13.8 million in 1958;[13] the coverage includes maternity, injury, illness, and death benefits, although the level of benefits is necessarily very low. In addition, during the First Five-Year Plan, a system was evolved establishing awards for rationalization proposals, innovations, and inventions. These were generally based on the amount of cost savings to the enterprises.

The most notable advance in the development of the wage system, however, was made in June, 1956. The wage reform of that year consisted mainly of (1) the abolition of the former wage point system, which was introduced during a period of hyperinflation and under which the actual amount depended upon the monetary value of the wage point which varied with certain commodity prices, (2) the establishment of an eight-grade wage scale in money for most industries and enterprises, (3) the widening of wage differentials to correspond more closely to differences in skill and training, and (4) the establishment of common standards in differentiating the various grades in each industry. Wage rates of the highest grades in Manchurian industries[14] were

12 *People's Daily*, Peking, March 30, 1963.
13 *Wei-ta ti Shih-nien* (*Great Ten Years*) (Peking, 1959), pp. 192–94.
14 Charles Hoffmann, "Work Incentives in Communist China," Social Science Research Council, Berkeley, Calif., 1964.

about 2.5 to 3.2 times those of the lowest grades, while in general an average ratio of 1 to 3 prevailed. In particular, greater wage increases were granted to workers employed in those industries that were deemed important in the priority scale of the economic plan—that is, workers in "heavy" rather than "light" industry; production workers rather than administrative workers; engineering, technical, and highly skilled managerial personnel rather than the ordinary administrative workers; professors, scientific researchers, and other intellectuals rather than the common run of workers.[15]

There were several reasons for the brief return to egalitarianism during the Great Leap. One of these was the ideological attitude that the communes represented a stage of development approaching real Communism and that compensation of labor according to work would be incongruent in these circumstances. Secondly, the industrial and agricultural output, partly due to faulty accounting and inaccurate records, was advancing at such a rate at the time that any attempt to maintain the same piece rates would have resulted in a very sharp increase in personal wage income and consumption. Hence, emphasis was shifted to ideological rewards and the psychic compensation that one should find in being a good Communist and an exemplary worker; the materialistic incentives, on the other hand, were denounced as unduly "bourgeois."

Where the nonmaterial incentives are employed, often they take the form of special honors given to "model workers," "labor heroes," and "advanced workers," who frequently are the winners of emulation campaigns and competitive drives conducted among different groups of workers either within the same industry or between industries. These emulation campaigns are comparable to the Stakhanovist drives of the Soviet Union. One disadvantage of such emulation campaigns and competitions, often not understood by planners and officials, is that such measures are disruptive of production based on predetermined plans. For, if such output drives are not to be stalled because of lack of raw material or spare parts, the participating enterprises and workers should have at their disposal a larger supply of raw materials and other inputs than what the plans call for. This would imply an increase in working-capital requirements. Since quality may also suffer in

[15] Ma Wen-jui, "Report to the Third Session of the First National People's Congress," *Current Background*, No. 405. See also the article by Charles Hoffmann, "Work Incentive Policy in Communist China," *The China Quarterly*, No. 17, January–March, 1964, pp. 92–110.

consequence of the output drive, the effort to increase labor productivity may actually end up in creating an increase in goods of dubious quality, aggravated by new bottlenecks.

Attention should also be called to the role of negative incentives. Strict labor discipline which cuts down absenteeism and forbids slowdowns and strikes is based both on the collective discipline exercised by the labor union and the ever-present threat that an unsatisfactory worker may be treated as a counter-revolutionary by the authorities. The penalties are both monetary and nonmonetary. The role of the trade union in Communist China, similar to that of other Communist countries, is no longer that of the guardian of the workers' interest, vis-à-vis the employer. In state-owned and -controlled industries, the workers, in their capacity as citizens, are said to be the real owners of the enterprises. Consequently, they would not want to strike against themselves. They must also be protected against such base feelings should they be so misguided as to regard themselves and management as opponents. The trade union, of course, performs certain welfare functions as agents of the state, dealing with such matters as labor insurance, safety, living conditions, mutual savings, female workers, health and hygiene, etc.[16]

Finally, although little is usually said of the forced-labor camps, such labor contingents under the direct control of the Ministry of Public Security exist in Communist China.[17] The possibility of direct allocation of forced labor to specific locations, enterprises, and industries, and the possibility of sending industrial workers to farms or to labor camps are very potent weapons of enforcement of labor discipline. These negative incentives are and can be used to supplement what an otherwise undesirable pattern and method of income distribution may fail to achieve, at least in the short run.

Income Differentials Between Farmers and Industrial Workers

One of the principal "contradictions" that exist in the Communist Chinese society is the disparity between the incomes of

[16] The multifarious welfare and related functions of the union under the direction of the national and territorial federations of labor unions and the national industrial union are illustrated in Yuan-li Wu, op. cit., pp. 426 ff.

[17] For a discussion on the "Regulations Governing Labor Service for Reform" proclaimed in 1954, see Yuan-li Wu, op. cit., pp. 320–23.

industrial and farm workers. The phenomenon is well recognized by Mao Tse-tung and economists and officials.[18] In 1952, the per-capita annual "consumption" of wage earners' families averaged 167.7 yuan, while the corresponding average consumption of farmers' families, including possibly some production costs, was only 72.8 yuan. In 1956, the corresponding values were 199.8 yuan per head for workers' families, while the per-capita value of farmers' families was 84.2 yuan. A ratio of 2.3:1 was maintained during the First Five-Year Plan. The preceding data are based on official figures that include collective consumption. The 1955 figures net of collective consumption, but inclusive of consumption of self-produced goods valued at retail prices, were 148 yuan per capita of personal income for workers' families and 138 yuan of per-capita expenditure, while the corresponding figures for farmers' families were 98 yuan of income (probably gross) and 93 yuan of expenditure. These figures exclude such items as rent, utilities, and transportation expenditures. If the latter were included, workers' families would have a per-capita income of 183 yuan and a per-capita expenditure of 173 yuan, while the corresponding figures for peasant families would be 102 yuan of income and 97 yuan of expenditure.[19] In any case, there was a large discrepancy of income and expenditure between farmers and nonfarmers. On the basis of the first set of figures, the discrepancy varied from 50 per cent of the farmers' income to 80 per cent of expenditure.[20] The discrepancy in income may also be seen in the larger relative expenditure of the farmers on staple foods and vegetables in comparison with a much larger expenditure on meat, cooking oil, and sugar by the urban workers.

During the first phase of the commune in 1958, when the peasants were paid mostly in kind, the per capita annual personal income of the commune members was estimated at 77 yuan in one study.[21] Of this amount, 51 yuan consisted of food rations;

[18] See fn. 12, Chapter III.

[19] At 1952 prices and in terms of the 1952 "product mix," 1 yuan would be equivalent to 33 cents in U.S. currency for industrial consumer goods, and 95 cents for agricultural products. See Yuan-li Wu, *et al., op. cit.,* p. 353.

[20] See "Wo-kuo Kuo-min Shou-ju Sheng-ch'an ho Fen-p'ei ti Ts'u-pu Yen-chiu" (A Preliminary Study on the Distribution and Production of China's National Income), *T'ung-chi Yen-chiu,* No. 1, 1958, pp. 11–15, and "Kuan-yü Kung-nung Sheng-ho Shui-p'ing Wen-t'i" (On the Standards of Living of Workers and Peasants), *ibid.,* No. 13, 1957, pp. 4–5 and 24.

[21] Yuan-li Wu, "Some Economic Effects of Land 'Reform,' Agricultural Collectivization and the Commune System in Communist China," in *Land*

the remainder represented the sum total of monetary receipts, including both regular and bonus wages. The discrepancy between agricultural income and industrial wages was probably largest during this period.

Particularly annoying to the peasants was the higher income of the unskilled industrial workers. The inequity was recognized by the Communist authorities and partly corrected through a reduction of the basic wage of the lowest three grades of unskilled industrial workers. The wage and income differentials between farm and other workers have, however, persisted, and attempts are made by the authorities to explain them away. First, it is said that considerable differences in productivity exist between these two groups of workers. Secondly, it is pointed out that the income differences are to some extent offset by opposite price differences, so that the differences in real income are much less. Thirdly, farm workers allegedly do not have certain expenditures incurred by workers living in urban areas. The fact that the farmers may prefer to enjoy some of the urban amenities is not mentioned. The real issue, of course, is that there are too many farm workers, and any increase in their wages would lead to a sharp increase in potential consumption. Although it is conceivable to increase the farmers' pay and then to try to tax away the excess income, this is a far less reliable method. The same consideration has probably caused the Communists to rely more on the turnover tax and the state's share of the profit margin rather than the direct income tax as a major source of government revenue, even though the price structure is unnecessarily distorted as a result and the indirect taxes are highly regressive. Since the lower income of the farmer is a reflection of China's excess farm population, the solution lies in the absorption of more farm labor by other sectors of employment. It was partly to resolve this problem, as we shall see in Chapter 7, that the communes and the small-local-industry movement were initiated in 1958.

Tenure, Industrialization and Social Stability (Milwaukee: The Marquette University Press, 1961), pp. 17–37.

CHAPTER V

The Over-All Economic Record, 1949–64: Allocation of the Gross Domestic Product by End Use

Performance as Measured by the Growth of the Total Output

Having discussed the manner in which Communist China's planning is carried out in order to realize the CPC's "national goals" and the inherent problems confronting the planners in allocating resources and distributing income, we now turn to the actual performance of the economy. A convenient and often-used aggregative index in such an evaluation is the gross national product or one of its related concepts. An alternative index, *inter alia,* would be the level of aggregate consumption or investment.

As far as the national-product index is concerned, a number of widely divergent official Communist and Western estimates are available. First, according to official statistics,[1] the "net material

---

[1] *Wei-ta ti Shih-nien (Great Ten Years)*, Peking, 1959, p. 18; and *The Peking Review*, III, No. 4, 1960.

The following "national-income" concepts are employed in various sources: The "Gross National Product" is defined as the total value of final products, including depreciation, at market prices.

The "Gross Domestic Product" is equal to the gross national product minus net factor income received from abroad. If depreciation is excluded, the result would be the "Net Domestic Product."

The "Net Material Product" is equal to the net value produced by agriculture, industry, construction, freight transportation, the part of communications serving other productive sectors, and trade. It is therefore the net value of production of the material sectors only. It excludes such nonmaterial sectors as government administration; military and police forces; cultural, educational, and social organizations; and personal services.

product" increased by 53 per cent in 1952–57 (1952 = 100). Two years later, in 1959, it was nearly 150 per cent higher than in 1952. Second, according to T. C. Liu and K. C. Yeh, the increase in the "net domestic product" between 1952 and 1957 was only 34 per cent, while the increase to 1959 (1952 = 100) was 75 per cent.[2] An earlier estimate by William Hollister shows, on the other hand, an increment of 51 per cent in the gross national product from 1952 to 1957, which is much closer to the official estimate than Liu's. On the other hand, Hollister's preliminary estimate of the increase in 1952–59 was only 112 per cent[3] instead of the official 150 per cent. Finally, one Western estimate of the gross domestic product, based on certain revisions and extensions of Liu's data, shows an increase of about 33 per cent between 1952 and 1957, which was followed by another increase of 20 per cent between 1957 and 1960, and a decline of 31 per cent in 1960–61.[4] These diverse estimates differ both with respect to the rates of growth for a given period and with respect to the period covered. If we take the 1952–57 period, the official estimate gives us an annual increment of 8.9 per cent, as against Liu's estimate of 6 per cent, Hollister's 8.6 per cent, and the author's own (and fourth) estimate of 5.2 per cent. If one goes beyond the period of the Great Leap, the years 1960–61 would indicate a sharp decline of production, thus making it all the more difficult to assess *the* rate of growth of aggregate production.

Furthermore, the several official and Western estimates of Communist China's national or domestic or material product also manifest considerable variation in their respective annual growth rates from year to year. For instance, the mean deviation in per-

[2] T. C. Liu and K. C. Yeh, *National Income and Economic Development of the Chinese Mainland, 1933 and 1952–1959* (Santa Monica, Calif.: The RAND Corporation, 1963), chap. ii. The same study has also appeared as a Princeton University Press study, entitled *The Economy of the Chinese Mainland*, in 1965.

[3] William W. Hollister, *China's Gross National Product and Social Accounts, 1950–57* (Chicago: The Free Press of Glencoe, 1958), pp. 132–33; also the same author's paper in *The Realities of Communist China*, edited by Yuan-li Wu (Milwaukee: The Marquette University Press, 1960). For another estimate of the Chinese GNP in 1952, see Alexander Eckstein, *The National Income of Communist China* (Chicago: The Free Press of Glencoe, 1961).

[4] Yuan-li Wu, *et al.*, *The Economic Potential of Communist China* (Menlo Park, Calif.: Stanford Research Institute, 1963), tables 51 and 80, pp. 241 and 340.

centage points of the annual rate of growth in 1952–57 was 4.1 in the official estimate, which compares with an average annual rate of 8.9 per cent. In the estimate by Liu, the mean deviation comes to 2.4 as compared with an annual growth rate of 6 per cent for the same period. The annual fluctuation, as well as the different results obtained by taking different time periods, suggests that perhaps the path of economic expansion is not really very assured and that the pattern of development, especially the allocation of investment and the choice of its growth rate, may themselves have played a significant role in the instability of the growth rate. We shall return to this point in Chapter VIII.

The Ratio of Investment

Given the consistent emphasis on "accumulation" until after the 1960–62 crisis, a high rate of realized investment should be expected. Available statistics demonstrate without exception that this was the case. Official data on "accumulation" show the ratio of accumulation to the material product to have increased substantially in 1952–56, reaching, according to Hsü Ti-hsin, 26 per cent in 1956.[5] Much higher estimates, on the other hand, are given for the period of the Great Leap. According to Liu, net domestic investments varied from nearly 16 per cent of the "net domestic product" in 1952, to 22 per cent in 1956. Alternatively, Liu's ratio of "gross domestic investment" to "gross domestic product" was more than 19 per cent in 1952, and 26 per cent in 1956. (Somewhat lower estimates are given by Hollister.) Later estimates by this author show comparable levels for the First Five-Year Plan as well as for the later years, while a high of 34 per cent was registered in 1959. With the exception of Hollister's estimate, which showed a slight decline in 1955, perhaps the most significant fact is the uninterrupted increase in the absolute value of investment from 1952 to 1957 and its even sharper increase in 1958–60. The higher investment-income ratio during the

[5] *Ibid.*, p. 252. It should be noted that the different ratios available for any given year are due to differences in the price base and/or in the dates and coverage of the estimates. In 1952, both Hsü Ti-hsin and the State Statistical Bureau give 18.2 per cent as the accumulation-income ratio. Both are at 1952 prices. In contrast, an estimate by Niu Chung-huang, also at 1952 prices, gives a ratio of 16.1 per cent. As noted in Chapter III, Po I-po's official but preliminary estimate is 15.7 per cent, while the figure quoted by Chang Chu-chung is 19.7 per cent.

Great Leap was a result of the organization of the communes, and perhaps one of its principal causes.[6]

The Level of Consumption

Given the steady rise of investment and the increasing proportion of investment in the total output of the economy for most of the years up to the general economic crisis in the latter part of 1960, the level of consumption had to become more and more stringent. As a matter of fact, a much slower rate of increase was shown by data on consumption up to 1958. A sharp decline then ensued in 1958–61. If we take the gross-domestic-product estimates and subtract the estimated values of investment and government consumption, and if the residual, which may be regarded as personal consumption, is then divided by the corresponding midyear population estimates, the resultant per-capita figures would show both (1) a very low rate of increase and (2) an absolute level which in most years approximated what has been described in one study as the minimum subsistence level that must be upheld in the long run in order to maintain political viability.[7]

Such a minimum subsistence level has been estimated at 168 yuan per capita for the urban population and 79.6 yuan for the rural population, or a mean of 92.6 yuan for the population as a whole. The per-capita consumption estimates derived as a residual were slightly below this mean subsistence level in 1953–55, and substantially below it in 1960–62. One may compare these figures further with the official estimates of consumption for 1955 in T'ung-chi Kung-tso.[8] According to these, personal-consumption expenditure was then at the level of 173 yuan per urban worker and employee, while the corresponding rural figure was 97 yuan. These estimates are inclusive of imputed expenditures in the non-market sector. If only the wage earners at the lower end of the

[6] People's Daily, September 19, 1958, and T'ung-chi Yen-chiu, No. 8, 1958. Some reports put the ratio of accumulation to income in some communes as high as 70 per cent, in contrast to the 70 per cent of output (probably before taxes) distributed as personal income on the collective farm in 1956. See Cheng Chu-yuan, Communist China's Economy, 1949–62, Seton-Hall, 1963, p. 42. Cf. also Chapter VII below.

[7] Yuan-li Wu, et al., op. cit., II, Table D–5, 74.

[8] Kuan-yü Kung-nung Sheng-huo Shui-p'ing Wen-t'i (On the Relative Standards of Living of Workers and Peasants), T'ung-chi Kung-tso, No. 13, 1957, p. 4.

pay scale were considered, the estimate per head in 1955 would be only 159 yuan, which would be below the minimum subsistence level cited above.

According to the same source, 58 per cent of the farmers' expenditures in 1955 were devoted to food, 15 per cent to clothing, 22 per cent to other consumer goods, and 5 per cent to services. In the case of urban workers, 55 per cent were devoted to food,

TABLE V-1. ESTIMATES OF GROSS DOMESTIC PRODUCT, INVESTMENT AND CONSUMPTION, 1952–62

	Gross Domestic Product	Gross Domestic Investment	Government Consumption	Residual	Midyear Population (In millions)	Per Capita Personal Consumption (In yuan)
	(In billions of 1952 yuan)					
1952	75.6	14.5	7.3	53.8	568.9	94.6
1953	78.9	19.0	9.1	50.8	582.6	87.2
1954	82.2	20.6	8.0	53.6	594.8	90.1
1955	86.1	22.1	8.4	55.6	608.2	91.4
1956	96.6	25.3	8.5	62.8	621.2	101.1
1957	100.0	25.8	10.3	63.9	637.2	100.3
1958	110.7	29.9	10.6	70.2	654.0	107.3
1959	119.1	40.3	11.0	67.8	668.0	101.5
1960	120.7	52.8	13.1	54.8	682.0	80.4
1961	82.1	17.6	11.2	53.3	693.0	76.9
1962[a]	109.0	35.8	11.4	61.8	705.0	87.7

SOURCE: Yuan-li Wu, et al., op. cit., pp. 16, 28, 241, 340. The 1953 population is a census figure; the remaining population data are interpolated.

[a] Revised estimate

12 per cent to clothing, 13 per cent to other consumer goods, and 20 per cent to services, rent, utilities, transportation, and remittances to family members still living in rural areas. These budgets are typical of the expenditure patterns of low-income families in poor communities anywhere in the world.

Population Growth and Consumption

Given the official desire to maintain a maximum rate of capital investment, the need to curtail personal consumption has been further accentuated by population growth. The 1953 official census put the Chinese population on the mainland at 588 million at year end. By 1963, the year-end population was estimated at 715 million.[9] The average growth rate between 1949 and 1958 was in the neighborhood of 2.2 per cent. This reflects a crude birth rate of approximately 33 per thousand and a crude death rate of 11 per thousand. Since the death rate had allegedly experienced a considerable decline from 17 per thousand in 1953,[10] any further large decrease would be most improbable in the short run. It already compares well, for instance, with the crude death rates of the United States (9.5 per thousand in 1957–58) and the United Kingdom (11.7 per thousand). As a result of overwork, food shortage, and nutritional deficiencies, the post-1958 economic crisis had the effect of temporarily raising mortality and curbing live births. However, if there was indeed a "bottoming out" of the crisis in 1962, the decline in the rate of population growth may also have ceased.

While the Communist Chinese authorities had emphasized birth-control measures in their usual mass-propaganda fashion prior to the Great Leap Forward, the active campaign was temporarily curtailed, if not entirely suspended, during the Great Leap. The present drive to reduce population growth relies largely upon raising the marriage age and condoning abortion. However, even with these measures, the population continues to grow at about 2 per cent a year.

Thus an increase in personal consumption at approximately the same population growth rate would seem to be unavoidable. Furthermore, in the long run, some improvement in the level of per-capita consumption is necessary in order to provide the population with sufficient incentive for sustained hard work over extended periods. Population growth and the need to permit some increase in per-capita consumption therefore constitute one of the basic constraints to the increase in investment. Together they define the upper limit of the ratio of capital investment in relation to the national product. A continuously rising proportion is possible in the circumstances only if the growth rate of the national product exceeds the population growth rate plus the improvement factor. Whether this is possible would in turn depend upon the productivity of new investments.

[9] Yuan-li Wu *et al.*, *op. cit.*, Table 3, p. 28.
[10] S. Chandrasekhar, *China's Population: Census and Vital Statistics* (2d ed.; Hong Kong, 1960), p. 53.

Financing Investments

How was the steady increase in investment, both absolute and in relation to the national product, brought about? In what manner was the national product pre-empted for investment purposes?

The first point that should be mentioned in this connection is the relatively negligible proportion of foreign-capital inflow. There are various estimates of the volume of Soviet aid to Communist China, the major source of foreign capital prior to the Sino-Soviet dispute. One estimate puts the total between 1950 and 1957 at 5.2 billion yuan.[11] According to Feng-hua Mah,[12] during the First Five-Year Plan, only 727 million yuan out of approximately 3 billion yuan in Soviet loans to Communist China consisted of economic loans, the rest being military loans and transfers of assets already in China. The economic loans, not all of which represented import components in investment, were a little more than 0.5 per cent of total budget revenue during the period, and about 1.5 per cent of Mah's estimated state capital investment during the First Five-Year Plan. Thus, the major source of capital investment was domestic capital formation.

The bulk of capital investment consisted of additions to fixed assets. The importance of capital-construction spending in total budget expenditure can therefore be treated as a good index of the magnitude of investment financing. Official estimates indicate the ratio of capital construction to total investment expenditure to have risen from a low of 26 per cent in 1952, the last preplan year, to 48 per cent in 1956 and 1957.[13] How capital investment was financed may in part be seen in the distribution of government revenue by sources.

In this connection, of 17 billion yuan of budgetary revenue in 1952, tax revenue totaled 9.8 billion yuan, while nontax revenue accounted for the smaller portion, or a little more than 7 billion yuan.[14] In particular, industrial and commercial taxes accounted for more than 6 billion yuan, while agricultural taxes were responsible for 2.7 billion. Customs receipts, the salt tax, and other miscellaneous taxes that were important in pre-Communist days now play a minor role. At the same time, the most important

[11] Yuan-li Wu et al., op. cit., p. 302.
[12] F. H. Mah, "The Financing of Public Investment in Communist China," The Journal of Asian Studies, XXI, No. 1, 1961.
[13] Wei-ta ti Shih-nien (Great Ten Years), pp. 21 and 46.
[14] Yuan-li Wu et al., op. cit., p. 264.

source in the category of nontax revenue was profits from state enterprises, which were responsible for 4.6 billion yuan in 1952. This was followed by 1.08 billion yuan of depreciation allowance and other income from state enterprises, followed by 1.3 billion yuan of receipts from foreign loans (not all of which were for investment purposes or even economic loans), and smaller amounts from miscellaneous budgetary receipts. In 1957, however, less than 16 billion of the 31 billion yuan of total budgetary revenue were derived from taxes. Nontax revenue had increased in importance. Of the tax revenue, industrial and commercial taxes still accounted for the bulk, or 11.4 billion yuan, while agricultural taxes remained at a fairly stable level of under 3 billion yuan. In the category of nontax revenue, profits from state enterprises had risen to 11.4 billion yuan as a result of the wholesale nationalization of private business in 1955–56, while the depreciation reserve and other incomes of state enterprises had almost tripled, reaching a level of 3.1 billion yuan. The increasing importance of profit from state enterprises should not, however, be construed as evidence of a diminishing burden on the farmers. The low prices paid to the farmers when agricultural products are purchased from them and the higher prices at which the same products, as well as industrial goods, are sold by the government to the farmers are responsible for a portion of the profit earned by the state trading organs being derived from the farmers. This phenomenon is often described in Chinese and Soviet literature as the effect of the "scissors."

By 1957, receipts from foreign loans had fallen to .02 billion yuan and were less important than receipts from domestic loans, government insurance operations, and other miscellaneous budgetary receipts. Furthermore, increase in savings deposits and note circulation also remained relatively small.

Thus the most significant point in financing investment was the large relative and absolute increase in profits from the state enterprises and in depreciation reserves as sources of government revenue and indirectly of financing for investment expenditure. Deficit financing through increase in note circulation, borrowing from the domestic population, and forced saving was also much in evidence. Yet it is an indisputable fact that the high rate of capital investment was financed primarily by pre-empting the national product for investment purposes and only secondarily by resorting to taxing the income of persons and enterprises after it has been earned by them. As the degree of nationalization advanced, the importance of pre-emption of the national product for investment purposes also increased.

Financing of Investment and Price Stability

Prices increased rapidly during the first two or three years of Communist rule. If March, 1950, is used as the base period, the wholesale price index in Shanghai at the end of September, 1949, would be 13.6, while at the end of February, 1950, it was 110.6.[15] While considerable variations were found in different regions of the country partly due to the breakdown of transport, in general prices increased very rapidly between the initial establishment of the Communist regime and March, 1950, and again during a part of 1951. Outward price stability was not achieved, therefore, until sometime in 1952.

There are several official price indices available. Taking 1952 as 100, the national wholesale-price index showed a remarkable stability during the First Five-Year Plan, declining first to 98.7 in 1953, then rising steadily but slowly to 100.1 in 1957.[16] The retail-price index, on the other hand, showed a somewhat greater increase, reaching 108.6 in 1957.[17] The retail-price index for industrial products marketed in the rural areas followed approximately the same trend as the national wholesale-price index, declining first to 98.5 in 1953, then rising to 101.6 in 1957. Another retail-price index of eight large cities showed first a decline to 94.6 in 1951, then a steady increase to 102.2 in 1957, with March, 1950, as 100.[18]

The relative stability of the official price indices may of course be taken as a measure of success in financing investment without evoking open inflationary symptoms. However, the existence of repressed inflation testifying to the presence of an excess in effective demand may be seen in the gradual extension of the rationing system, which began with the government's initiation in 1953

[15] Yuan-li Wu, An Economic Survey of Communist China, pp. 87–96.
[16] Wei-ta ti Shih-nien, 1959, p. 152.
[17] Ibid., p. 153.
[18] Ibid., p. 154. The March, 1950, price level rested on a plateau reached at the time when the price-stabilization program was first introduced. The latter consisted of a sharp contraction of bank credit, increase in tax payments, liquidation of government-held commodity stocks, and the liberal employment of police methods. For a description of the financial stabilization measures in 1950, see Wu, An Economic Survey of Communist China, chapter iii, pp. 64–108.

of centralized control over the purchase and sale of food grain and, later, of cotton cloth. The government-controlled distribution system has since been extended to many commodity markets, some of which are put entirely under government purchase and allocation or rationing, while others are subject to less stringent controls. In the latter case, the state trading organs are interested only in acquiring specific quantities of the commodities in question, leaving the remainder for disposal on the market.[19]

Following the re-establishment of the free market for certain commodities—essentially consumer goods produced by the peasants on their private plots—after the admitted failure of the Great Leap, considerable discrepancies emerged between the official, controlled prices and the free-market prices. These discrepancies were very marked for certain commodities during 1960–62 for which partial reports are available.[20] However, it is difficult to generalize as to the extent of overt price inflation and the degree of difficulties encountered in financing a high rate of investment.

Allocation of Investment by Sectors

How effective was the high rate of investment in increasing output and in fulfilling the goals set by the planners? The productivity of the total investment is of course determined by its allocation among the various sectors of the economy and by the relative productivity of investments in the individual sectors.

During 1952, 39 per cent of total investment in capital construction went to industry; 17.4 per cent went to transportation and communications; and only 13.8 per cent went to agriculture, forestry, water conservation, and meteorological installations. By 1957, industry's share had increased to 53.2 per cent, followed by 15 per cent in transportation and communications, and 8.6 per cent in agriculture, forestry, water conservation and meteorological installations. After the initiation of the Great Leap Forward,

[19] See fn. 24, Chapter III.

[20] For some time in 1961, the official, posted retail price of rice in Nanking was 0.13 yuan per *shih* catty (1.1 lb.), while the free-market price was 3 yuan. The official, posted price of cooking oil in Shanghai was 0.61 yuan per catty, while the free-market price was 30 yuan. The free-market prices of various consumer products at a Han-ning free market in Hupeh were from 8 to nearly 200 per cent higher than the official prices. These sporadic reports are indicative of the divergence between the two sets of prices. See *People's Daily*, March 14, 1961.

investment in capital construction in industry rose to nearly 66 per cent in 1959, in comparison with 20.5 per cent in transportation and communications, and only 7.1 per cent in agriculture, forestry, etc. Within the industrial sector, the share of investment in "heavy industry" varied from 75.7 per cent in 1952 to 84.8 per cent in 1957. In contrast, investment in "light industry" was only 24.3 per cent of total investment in industry in 1952 and declined to 15.2 per cent in 1957.

Thus the investment pattern reflected faithfully the priority scale of the planners described earlier. However, as Fan Jo-i pointed out in his 1958 article in *Planned Economy*, at 82.3 per cent, the rate of profit over investment was highest in trading enterprises; it was followed by 32.1 per cent in agriculture, 47.1 per cent in light industry, and 23.1 per cent in heavy industry.[21] Thus the investment pattern adopted also points to a strong emphasis on those sectors which showed smaller rates of return to investment.[22]

Furthermore, one might note in this connection that, according to one Western estimate, the gross value-added in modern industry rose from 9.4 billion yuan at 1952 prices to 37.7 billion yuan in 1959, while the corresponding gross value-added in agriculture increased only from 35.9 billion yuan in 1952 to 37.0 billion yuan in 1959, after having passed a peak of 39.3 billion yuan in 1958.[23] The small rate of increase in agriculture as opposed to the much greater rate of increase in modern industry doubtlessly was, to a considerable extent, even though not exclusively, a result of the priorities pattern in investment.

Change in Investment Policy After the First Five-Year Plan

Two major and dramatic changes in investment policy took place after the completion of the First Five-Year Plan. The first, an important part of the Great Leap program, was characterized by large-scale investment in small enterprises, many of which

[21] Fan Jo-i, "Lüeh-lun Tzu-chin Li-jun-lü yü To-k'uai-hao-sheng ti Chien-she Fang-chen" ("On the Profit Rate over Capital and the Policy of Massive, Rapid, Superior, and Economical Development"), *Chi-hua Ching-chi*, No. 8, 1958, pp. 21–23.

[22] The above data on investments are based on original official statistics given in the *Great Ten Years*, pp. 59–62. See also Yuan-li Wu *et al., op. cit.*, tables 56 and 62, pp. 261 and 275.

[23] Yuan-li Wu *et al., op. cit.*, p. 241.

employed traditional methods of production and were located in the communes. The second dramatic shift in investment policy took place after the failure of the Great Leap and consisted of a sharp retrenchment of investment. Both developments merit closer attention.

Pros and Cons of the Small-Industry Drive

In theory, a small-industry drive has a number of points in its favor.

First, a fundamental advantage of the small plant as exemplified by the backyard furnace for iron-making is the low incremental capital to output ratio. Supplemented by the short construction period required for establishing such small plants, this low capital requirement should theoretically make possible a larger and faster increase in output after an initial investment. Since the initial investment consists primarily of labor input (very little capital goods being needed in plant construction), much of the increase in output could be brought about by an initial expenditure of labor drawn from the large pool of hitherto unemployed workers mobilized through the commune organization. Furthermore, since such investments can be carried out with crude tools and labor, it would be possible to spread the small industrial establishments throughout a very large area, thus reaping at once both the benefit of decentralized planning and that of geographical industrial dispersion.

Since, according to some planners, the rate of investment should probably have been increased as the First Five-Year Plan drew to a close, because of population growth and a rising capital-output ratio—a consequence of the completion of the recovery phase and the attainment of full utilization of existing plants and equipment—the prospect of shortening the construction period and reducing the capital intensity of production came as a real boon. Lastly, the many obstacles and the high capital-output ratio encountered in the development of new industrial centers in the inland and less developed regions of Mainland China would be reduced if the effect of industrial dispersion and decentralization that would accompany the small-industry movement could be brought to bear.

Of particular interest to students of economic development are the principle and practice of "dualistic economic development" represented by the small plants that were built upon the basis of "traditional or native methods of production." That these small plants, which employed rather primitive methods of production and incurred higher production costs than the modern plants theoretically producing similar products could nevertheless co-exist with the latter is an example of the so-called dual economy. It is of course known that during the initial phase of economic development in underdeveloped countries with a private market economy, handicraft workshops and cottage industry often fall victim to the competition of new industries using machines. Problems of technological unemployment and of small-business failures caused by the effective competition of machine industry thus often arise. Why the Communist Chinese were able to boast of the development of traditional methods of production simultaneously with that of modern industry poses an interesting question.

The explanation, however, is simply that the existence of an adequate effective demand for the more costly products was never in question. On the one hand, the development of the modern enterprises was limited only by the amount of capital investment allotted. On the other hand, new plants in the traditional sector did not have to concern themselves with the competition of the modern enterprises since the government sponsored the purchase of the goods thus produced. Industries in which the amount of investment allocated in the central plan was small were to undergo only a low level of modernization, thus leaving considerable scope for the complementary development of a traditional sector. And industries which were faced with a high demand in spite of large allotments of planned investment were also supposed to accommodate a growing sector of small plants.

During the Great Leap Forward, the traditional sector had the function of supplementing the modern sector while preparing for its own conversion to modern enterprises at a later date. To the extent that the products of the traditional sector were adequate enough to replace some of the output that the modern sector would otherwise have had to supply—especially in the steel industry and machine production—to that extent the modern enterprises were assumed to be able to undertake experimentation and upgrade and diversify their products without unduly curtailing the total output of both sectors. By making possible the establishment of many small plants in both urban and rural areas, the small-industry drive was also meant to help popularize industrial technology. Thus it was hoped that the sense of participation of the common man in the industrial development of the country would be enhanced. It was partly for this reason that steel was selected as the focus of the small-industry drive. In fact, steel and food grain, which spearheaded the Great Leap, were symbolic of industrial power and economic self-sufficiency, the primary national economic goals of Communist China.

Unfortunately for Communist China, the above-mentioned advantages of the small-industry drive are based upon several implicit assumptions which were unfounded in reality. First, although it was recognized that the traditional methods of production, especially in the iron-smelting and steel-making industries, would be less efficient than the modern methods, it was assumed that the end products, allowing for their lower quality, would at least be worth more than the raw materials used in their production. This, however, was not true in the case of the pig iron and steel produced in the native furnaces in 1958. On the contrary, it has been estimated that the value-added in this native sector was actually negative; that is, the product was of lesser value than the materials used in its manufacture.[24]

Secondly, it was assumed that the cost of erecting and running the small industrial plants would be minimal because of the low capital-goods input in construction, while the labor force employed in building and operating the plants would be drawn from the large pool of unemployed or semi-employed who had previously produced nothing to speak of. Again, this assumption proved to be unrealistic in practice. The Communist planners, especially the local Party functionaries, failed to appreciate fully the concept of opportunity cost. For when otherwise unemployed workers were drafted to build and operate a small plant, the opportunity cost was indeed nil. But if, having been thus employed, they were abruptly shifted to the construction of another plant or to some other activity before the first project was completed, the unfinished project would now become the opportunity cost of the new project. Apparently, the simultaneous initiation of many such projects in many areas, such as backyard-furnace construction, ore collection, intensive farm work, digging of irrigation ditches, etc., took place during the Great Leap. The fact that the farm labor surplus in some areas was seasonal only contributed further to the miscalculation of cost. Since some of the unfinished projects, such as irrigation ponds without proper outlets or haphazard

[24] See Wu, *The Steel Industry in Communist China*, chap. iv.

mine diggings without adequate pit props and designs, might actually turn out to harm the future exploitation of available resources, the productivity of existing industrial plants might in fact be lowered in subsequent periods.

One reason for the failure to recognize the true opportunity costs was the commune system and the absence of monetary wage payments under it during the Great Leap. Since the workers at this time were paid principally in rations, the accounting units represented by the enterprises where the workers were employed often failed to realize that a real opportunity cost was actually incurred even in the absence of monetary payments. The commune was also responsible for the high mobility of labor without which constant switchings of workers from one job to another and from one locality to another could not have occurred. In the final analysis, however, the true culprit was the desire and the political slogan to increase output, which prompted the frenzied production drive regardless of cost. The drive for record-breaking output resulted in lowering the standard of statistics gathering, exaggerating the actual output, and underestimating the failures in quality maintenance. The exaggerated output figures were in turn used to spur the production units to even greater and faster advances, thus compounding a false sense of accomplishment on the part of both enterprises and planners.

Moreover, there was an obvious failure to appreciate the need for balanced economic development or the difficulties that would ensue should gross sectoral imbalance develop. Inasmuch as local transportation had always been handicapped by serious shortages, it was clear that the tremendous output that the many small new plants were supposedly producing could, if actually produced, never have been shipped to their destinations. At the same time, the transport industry was itself engaged in the game of piling up output. Since output in the transport sector was measured by the volume of freight shipments, unnecessary shipment to increase the recorded freight traffic became a practice.[25]

A further drawback of the small-industry drive was the low durability of the equipment installed and its high maintenance cost. Many of the small, native pig-iron furnaces could not be used more than a few days without breaking down. The high

[25] For instance, examples of heavy traffic due to cross-hauls of coal in 1958 are given in the April issue of *Chi-hua Ching-chi,* pp. 25–26. Similar examples are available regarding ores, construction materials, etc., in the literature, especially during the period of the Great Leap.

labor input required therefore added to the construction cost, although such cost was not always properly accounted for.

Finally, an implicit assumption of the advantage of the unproductive labor-intensive methods of production employing hitherto unemployed labor is the maintenance of aggregate consumption at the old level or an increase in the consumption level smaller than the output of the newly employed labor. In practice, notwithstanding the doubtful output of labor thus employed, in the initial phase of the 1958 Great Leap, there was probably an actual increase in total consumption because of the organization of the commune system and the prevalent feeling that as much as possible could be consumed because nobody owned any of the things that were consumed.[26] To some extent, the short-term increase in consumption was a reaction of the peasantry to the "communization" of the cooperatives, the abolition of private property, and the subjection of the population to harsh military discipline in everyday life. Later on, as control of consumption became more stringent, the unintended increase in consumption was halted. However, this was accompanied by a sharp drop in output. The consequent decline of consumption exerted a further adverse effect on health, incentive, and productivity.

Retrenchment of Investment During the Economic Crisis

Following the collapse of the Great Leap and the belated recognition by the Communist Chinese authorities, a set of new directives was promulgated in 1961. These directives constitute a new investment policy, which has been closely followed up to this writing (spring, 1964). In the first place, all industrial enterprises which suffered losses under the economic-accounting system were to cease operation.[27] Secondly, all capital-construction work with the exception of specified projects was to be halted, including projects that had planned on expansion or new con-

[26] According to a report of Theodore Shabad in *The New York Times* of April 16, 1964, Khrushchev, in commenting on the Chinese commune system, said that one of his aides who visited China found neither chickens nor eggs, because commune members had eaten them themselves, in their mess halls. The Soviet Union would not follow China's example and set up Chinese-type communes because, as Khrushchev remarked, "We ate all our chickens once before."

[27] In determining whether losses were incurred, it is not clear whether interest charges were included. The presumption is that they were not, inasmuch as the inclusiveness of the cost concept was far from being settled.

struction. There was not to be any planless investment. Thirdly, the management of productive enterprises was instructed not to transfer workers at will and to notify the shop foremen whenever skilled workers had to be transferred. Industrial units were instructed not to recruit workers from the villages for three years. Local governments also were ordered not to transfer workers at will for a three-year period and to make transfers only with the knowledge of the county or province authorities. Strict product standards were to be inaugurated and inspectors were to be held responsible for the quality of the products they had checked. These rules were accompanied by other stipulations governing the wage system, a census of equipment and machinery available at the various enterprises, inventory-taking at the same enterprises, the focusing of production policy to meet market demand, the restoration of producers' cooperatives that had previously been amalgamated into state-owned factories, and a number of other readjustments aimed at a more orderly, and consequently a slower, course of industrial development. According to preliminary estimates, the drop of the investment rate was 67 per cent in 1960–61, followed by a recovery in 1961–62.[28]

The Transformation versus the Saving Bottleneck

It is possible that the curtailment of investment during 1961 and, even more so, the reduction of current industrial production at the time overcompensated for the previous, ill-conceived advances. However, one of the causes of the industrial cutback and the curtailment of investment activity was the reduction of shipments of machinery from the Soviet Union following the recall of Soviet technicians and the slowdown of deliveries. The agricultural crisis, which by 1960 had brought about a reversal in food import policy from self-sufficiency to import, had also seriously reduced the ability of the Chinese economy to import industrial goods. Lack of industrial equipment needed for investment there-

[28] The 1962 gross investment (35.8 billion yuan) may be twice as much as the sharply reduced 1961 figure (17.6 billion yuan) (see Table V–1). A comparison may be made with the decline of gross domestic investment in the United States during the Great Depression, which was at the rate of 33 per cent in 1929–30, 33 per cent in 1930–31, 73 per cent in 1931–32, and 33 per cent in 1932–33. The decline from 1929–33 was even greater than the Chinese "Great Slide," but was less precipitate (except in 1930–31). See Wu *et al.*, *op. cit.*, I, 371.

fore became an important factor in slowing down the rate of development in the modern sector.

At the same time, although the failures in the traditional sector were to a large measure a result of mismanagement, they were no less an object lesson in the imperfect substitutability of labor for capital, especially in the production of certain capital goods used in modern industry. The labor-intensive methods employing mass conscript labor, which had proved useful in building certain large water-conservation works, particularly on the Huai River and its tributaries, in the early phase of Communist rule,[29] proved to be ill adapted to modern manufacturing and fabrication. The "dualistic" approach in economic development was somewhat limited in its usefulness. Consequently, further industrialization would have to rely upon the expansion of the modern sector, which is in turn rather rigorously limited by the availability of imported capital goods. Thus the rate of economic growth is not only subjected to the limitation of available savings, it is also constrained by the availability of imported machinery. The effective constraint therefore lies in the capability of the Chinese economy to convert resources not used up in consumption into the desired kinds of capital goods. Inasmuch as domestic industry is still inadequate, it is therefore essentially a constraint of the balance of international payments.

In a recent study by the present author on the possible rate of economic growth in the future, an attempt has been made to relate the amount of industrial investment to the volume of imports. According to this thesis, the rate of industrial investment may for some time to come be limited by the availability of imported equipment, while equipment import will be governed by three factors: the availability of long-term credit, export capacity, and the existence of any priority import for nonindustrial purposes. The last factor depends upon the extent of agricultural recovery and the need for imported food and other agricultural products. As long as industrial development lags, export capacity will also depend upon the extent of agricultural recovery, which is essential for an expanded supply of agricultural exports and for the production of raw materials for consumer goods and other light industry whose products might be exportable. The availability of credit will depend upon (1) the extent of Soviet and other bloc assistance, which would have to be predicated upon the satisfactory resolution of the Sino-Soviet dispute, and (2) the

[29] See Wu, *An Economic Survey of Communist China*, chap. ix.

willingness of Western countries to step into the breach. Both
conditions are governed by political factors.

Productivity of Investment in the Modern Sector

Whether the emphasis on industrial investment and, within the
industrial sector, on investment in "heavy" industry during the
First Five-Year Plan and again in the abortive Great Leap was
wise should of course be measured in terms of the productivity
of the investment. We have already pointed to the apparent un-
profitability of such investment in the traditional sector, as exemplified in the small-industry drive. Can a reasonable appraisal
be made for the modern sector?

As Fan Jo-i stated, the large enterprises were less profitable in
terms of investment than the smaller modern enterprises, while
the heavy-industry sector was also less profitable than the less
capital-intensive sector.[30] Furthermore, if Western estimates of
values-added in the agricultural and modern industrial sectors
are compared with the capital-construction estimates in their
respective sectors, the result would show a very slightly higher
output-investment ratio in the modern industrial sector than in
agriculture. However, the latter result is not clear-cut because of
the crudity of the statistics and the added complications owing
to the different periods of construction needed for investments
in the two sectors.

An even more serious problem stems from the pricing system.
Inasmuch as industrial producer goods have been priced at relatively high levels in comparison with consumer goods and agricultural products, there is a built-in bias in favor of industrial
output, which is heavily weighted with producer goods, thus
tending to increase the relative output-capital ratio for industry.
Since these prices do not reflect either consumer preferences or
the relative scarcities of resources, there is some ambiguity about
the meaningfulness of the price system and, consequently, of the
comparative advantage of investments in the different sectors.
Lack of proper investment criteria thus precludes an adequate
evaluation of the appropriateness of the allocation of investment.

One may, however, appeal to certain more obvious errors in
resource allocation such as the emergence of gross shortages or
surpluses in different industries. Intrasectoral imbalance in the
steel industry and in the generation of hydro- versus thermal-

[30] Fan Jo-i, *op. cit.*, pp. 21–23.

electric power offer two examples of the improper allocation of investment. The possibly premature emphasis on the development of the inland provinces in a period of capital shortage presents another example of malallocation of resources in locational planning. Insofar as the economic crisis of 1960–62 was a result of insufficient development of the agricultural sector and in the production of consumer goods, the sharp setback in production as a result of the crisis and the reduction of the growth rate of the GNP over a longer period can also be regarded as further evidence of errors in resource allocation. Further reference to this topic will be made in Chapter VIII.

CHAPTER VI

Performance in the Industrial Sector

Introduction

Since Communist China's policy during the period of economic rehabilitation and for approximately the entire decade covered by the First and Second Five-Year Plans was marked by a single-minded purpose—to industrialize the country rapidly—one good measure of the appropriateness of such a policy and of the efficiency of its implementation would be the development of the industrial sector, specifically that of modern industry. In this connection, the industrial record may be appraised from several points of view. In the first place, a quantitative assessment of the growth rate of this sector in comparison with other sectors and other periods would be informative. The growth of output may also be viewed in relation to the large share of industrial investment in total investment, although available statistics are somewhat inconclusive as to the relative profitability of industrial versus nonindustrial investments in terms of economic growth. In the second place, a qualitative assessment of the industrial record may be undertaken from two different, albeit related, points of view. On the one hand, it would be interesting to see whether developments during the Communist period have sharply altered the character of the industrial sector of the earlier years. On the other hand, it would be useful to learn whether developments during the recent period, and largely engineered by the present regime, have on balance succeeded in removing some of the more serious impediments to further industrialization and economic growth. A priori, any radical change from the pre-Communist state of affairs in the industrial sector may be either beneficial or detrimental to further development. The same may be said of conditions that have remained relatively stationary between the pre-Communist and the Communist periods.

In anticipation of later discussion, we may note that there is a certain unity and mutual dependence between the quantitative and qualitative approaches in evaluating China's industrial performance. Not only is the qualitative transformation of the industrial sector vitally affected by its rate of expansion, and vice versa, but the quantitative assessment itself must be predicated upon certain qualitative interpretations of the statistical measurements. This somewhat puzzling statement will be clarified as we proceed, but it is inserted here as a warning against any oversimplified view of economic performance.

The Quantitative Record—Coverage and Measurement

According to the Communist Minister of Railways, T'eng Tai-yüan, the greater part of "capital construction" expenditure on transportation and industry in 1950–51 was devoted to the rehabilitation of the transportation system.[1] However, once the railway network was restored, by far the largest proportion of investment in 1952–60 went to the industrial sector. This investment pattern was plainly indicated in the preceding chapter. Such a heavy and general emphasis on industrial production should therefore lead us to anticipate a sharp increase in industrial output, even though some of the investment projects did not begin operation until the latter part of the period covered, while others may not have been completed even at this writing.

Following the Soviet pattern, Communist China's output statistics, apart from physical production data, are represented in the main by the series of "gross value output of industry and agriculture."[2] Of this, the industrial component is in turn made

---

[1] See Yuan-li Wu, *An Economic Survey of Communist China,* p. 347.
[2] According to Communist Chinese usage, the gross-value output of agriculture is defined to include the value output of the following categories:
    1. Plant products
        a. Food crops: paddy rice, wheat, miscellaneous cereals, potatoes (sweet and Irish)
        b. Soybeans

up of three parts: modern industry, factory handicraft, and cottage handicraft. Up to 1957, it was possible to segregate modern-industry output from that of the handicraft industry and, within the handicraft industry, to distinguish the output of the factory-type workshops from that of non-workshop handicraft industry. From 1958 to 1960, however, the published industrial output statistics no longer differentiated between the modern subsector and the handicraft subsector. One possible explanation was the fiction maintained during the Great Leap that modern industrial production was no longer limited to the modern factory but was being carried on in numerous small industrial establishments employing traditional methods of production. Thus it was no longer necessary to distinguish the output of modern industry from that of the handicraft industry. Alternatively, one might ascribe the abandonment of the distinction to a desire to show a more rapid growth of the industrial sector. Furthermore, from 1961 to 1963,

---

    c. Other oil-bearing crops: peanuts, rapeseed, sesame, cottonseed
    d. Plant fibers: cotton and hemp
    e. Other industrial crops: sugar cane, sugar beets, tobacco, tea
    f. Vegetables
    g. Fruits
  2. Animal products: cattle, horses, mules, donkeys, sheep and goats, hogs, poultry
  3. Forest products: timber, tung nuts, general forest products
  4. Fishery products
  5. Miscellaneous agricultural products

The gross value output of industry is the sum total of the gross value output of three categories of industrial enterprises: modern industry, handicraft workshops, and the non-workshop handicrafts, the last including handicraft cooperatives and individual handicraftsmen. Industry is defined to include manufacturing, mining, utilities, lumbering, and fishing.

A modern industrial enterprise is one employing relatively modern equipment in its major production process, which, in China, means the employment of equipment driven by mechanical power. A handicraft workshop is an industrial establishment where work is carried on primarily by manual labor and has more than three workers, including apprentices. Smaller establishments and cooperatives are not handicraft workshops, but belong to the last category.

The gross value of industrial production is computed on the basis of the "factory method," which excludes intra-enterprise sales, but includes inter-enterprise sales.

For further elaboration of these points, see Ta-chung Liu and Kung-chia Yeh, *The Economy of the Chinese Mainland-National Income and Economic Development, 1933–1959*, II (Santa Monica, Calif.: The RAND Corporation, 1963), Appendices E and F.

no official statistics on the aggregate industrial output, either modern or handicraft, were published.

OFFICIAL STATISTICS OF GROSS
INDUSTRIAL OUTPUT
(In billions of 1952 yuan)

| | All industry | Modern industry | Handicraft industry | |
			Factory	Cottage
1952	34.3	22.1	7.3	5.0
1957	78.4	55.6	13.4	9.4
1960	214.2ᵃ	. . . *	. . .	. . .

ᵃ Estimated from 1957 price base.
SOURCE: *Wei-ta ti Shih-nien*, pp. 75, 80, 83.
* Throughout this volume, . . . will indicate "no information" while - - - will mean "nil."

As the statistics above clearly indicate, there was a substantial growth in 1952–57, regardless of the output series employed. However, modern industry registered a higher rate of increase, namely, 152 per cent for the five-year period, or an annual average of 20.3 per cent. On the other hand, factory handicraft production increased by nearly 84 per cent during 1952–57, and cottage handicraft production by 88 per cent, i.e., 13 per cent and 13.5 per cent per annum respectively. If a comparison is made between 1957 and 1960 in terms of the gross value output of *all* industry, the annual growth rate would average 39.5 per cent, a sharp increase over the 1952–57 record of 17.9 per cent.

There are, however, a number of reasons why these statistics are unsatisfactory and why alternative estimates should be used. In the words of one recent discussion on this subject, "The official series can be criticized on at least two principal counts. First, being a measure of the gross industrial output based on the 'factory method,' there is a certain degree of double counting in the reported output. Increased industrial output may come about merely as a result of increasing frequency of reports following changes in the organization of production. In the same category, we may include distortion of the series due to changes in the coverage of reporting industrial output. Secondly, the official series are subject to exaggeration because after 1952, they included an increasing volume of new products. These products were priced at experimental cost levels, which are much higher than the normal production costs. This may be described as the 'new product effect.' "[3]

The alternative estimates of Western scholars fall into two categories. There are (a) aggregative value output series, which are essentially similar to the official data in construction, differing from them only in so far as the component physical production series and their value weights are expressly given and are, one may safely assume, different from those used in the official statistics; and (b) estimates of modern-industry production deduced from the consumption of inputs of electricity and steel. The first set of estimates made by Chao Kang, and, in an earlier attempt, by Fred C. Hung, excludes the output of the machine industry in which the "new-product effect" was concentrated. The (b) estimates, on the other hand, are derived from a series of modern industry output which has been "adjusted" for the "new product effect." All these estimates, therefore, result in lower growth rates than the official series.

However, since the (a) estimates are still indices of output weighted by values, their adequacy is directly affected by the quality of the physical-output series and the nature of the value weights.

First, the reported output series from official statistics does not take into account changes in quality. This is especially true between 1958 and the institution [in 1961] of the new policy of quality improvement. . . . Second, if the value weights consist of commodity prices, the industrial-output series would then reflect the relative weights or prices used. [In the case of Communist China, the prices were biased in favor of producer goods.] . . . Third, inasmuch as the industrial-output series built up in this manner rests upon only a selected number of commodities, it is a true reflection of the general situation only in so far as the sample selected is an accurate reflection of the entire industrial sector. Since the output statistics are confined to a small number of commodities, primarily producer goods, which are fast growing, the industrial-output series drawn up in this way inherently has an upward bias. . . . Lastly, the use of prices as weights does not allow for changes in the cost of production, especially if constant prices are used and if performance does not remain at the same level over a period of time. . . . [Even] if [the] weights refer to value added or factor cost in any one period (1952, for instance), while they would take into account

[3] Fred C. Hung and Yuan-li Wu, "Conceptual Difficulties in Measuring China's Industrial Output," *The China Quarterly,* London, January–March, 1964, pp. 56–64.

cost differences among individual commodities included in the over-
all series, they would still not be able to meet the objection of possible changes in efficiency and in production cost over a period
of time.[4]

Furthermore, the (a) estimates are restricted to the period for
which physical output data are available, that is, in most cases,
to 1959.

The (b) estimates can be extended over a greater number of years
and can thus afford us a better view of the Great Leap period
and its aftermath. On the other hand, they implicitly assume
relatively constant production functions—that is, unvarying relationships between industrial output and the power and steel inputs
employed—as well as fairly stable compositions of the industrial output, at least as far as the proportions between products
requiring grossly disparate input coefficients in steel and power
are concerned. These assumptions are most precarious in any
long-term projection, although in the "composite series" of estimates cited below, which are based on electric power and finished-
steel inputs, attempts were made by the authors to allow for

ALTERNATIVE ESTIMATES OF THE GROSS OUTPUT OF MODERN INDUSTRY
Values in billions of yuan at 1952 prices

	Official statistics adjusted for "new-product effect"		"Composite series" of estimates based on functions of electricity and finished-steel input		Chao Kang's estimates
	Value	Index (1952 = 100)	Value	Index (1952 = 100)	Index
1952	22.0	100	22.4	100	100
1953	28.4	129.1	27.8	124.1	124.7
1954	33.0	150.0	32.7	146.0	141.6
1955	35.6	161.8	36.4	162.5	146.9
1956	45.0	204.6	44.7	199.6	182.2
1957	49.7	225.9	50.0	223.2	195.9

Source: Fred C. Hung and Yuan-li Wu, *op. cit.,* p. 61. The estimates by
Chao are taken from Chao Kang, "Indices of Industrial Output in Communist China," *Review of Economics and Statistics,* August, 1963. For a full
discussion of the method of construction of the "composite series" and the
regression equations employed, see Yuan-li Wu, *et al., The Economic Potential of Communist China,* chapter x.

[4] *Ibid.,* pp. 57–58.

changes in the "production function" and the "product mix." The projections also were made for a few years only.

A striking comparison may be made between the growth rate based on the official estimates of the gross output of modern industry in 1952 and 1957 and the corresponding rates based on the alternative estimates. The apparently large upward bias in the official record, which we have tried to explain in the preceding, somewhat technical, discussion, serves to indicate the difficulties one encounters in trying to arrive at a true quantitative measurement of the performance of the industrial sector.

	1952	1957	Average annual rate of growth (in per cent)
Index of official estimate of modern industry output	100	251.6	20.3
Adjusted official estimate	100	225.9	17.7
"Composite series" index	100	223.2	17.4
Chao Kang's index	100	195.9	14.4

The statistical difficulties are inherent and are by no means dependent upon any deliberate falsification of data. Of course, exaggerated output statistics, particularly in 1958–60, would tend to enhance the upward bias. Furthermore, the difficulties are no less real for Chinese planners even though they are not hampered by any deliberate restriction of information. As we shall see in Chapter VIII, when planning is based on such exaggerated output data, a major source of error and a "destabilizer" are incorporated into the planning system.

Characteristics of the Industrial Sector in the Pre-Communist Period

That the rate of growth of the modern industrial sector in Communist China was very rapid prior to the failure of the Great Leap cannot be denied. But what has the rapid growth meant to the Chinese economy? Has it been beneficial to further growth? Has it been worth the cost? In order to answer these questions, even in a very cursory fashion, we turn now to an examination of how the enlargement of the industrial sector has altered its pre-

Communist character, whether rapid expansion has been at the expense of qualitative improvement, and in what manner the long-term prospect of economic growth has been affected by the rate and pattern of industrial development.

In summary, the character of the industrial sector of the pre-Communist Chinese economy may be outlined under the following headings:

1. Sectoral structure. "Light" industries and consumer-goods industries were relatively more developed than the so-called "heavy" industries and producer-goods industries such as the metallurgical industry, machine building, etc. Power supply and transportation facilities were also inadequate and tended to be a constraint to rapid economic development.

Chinese domestic industry was unable to produce many industrial raw materials and finished products. Even in the case of agricultural raw materials, such as wheat, cotton, and tobacco for the flour milling, textile, and tobacco industries, foreign supplies were relied upon to a large extent. An important consideration was the relative reliability of imports in terms of quality and delivery. Thus, the foreign market was called upon to resolve bottlenecks and deficiencies which might otherwise have developed. In other words, the external sector provided the solution of the "conversion problem" in Chinese economic development, as it usually does in all economies not subject to a strictly autarkic policy.

In the case of many machine products, domestic facilities in existence before World War II were often able only to do some repair and assembly work. Although this situation was significantly altered in Manchuria during the war, and to a lesser extent in the southwest in unoccupied China and in some areas of North China under Japanese occupation, postwar damages because of the Soviet despoliation of Manchuria,[5] civil-war activi-

[5] See Edwin W. Pauley, *Report on Japanese Assets in Manchuria to the President of the United States* (Washington, D.C., 1946). According to the report, "The value of the properties removed by the Soviets is probably one-tenth of the amount of damage and economic collapse resulting from the same removals. Many of the items removed were key installations. . . . At least one-third of the original Japanese investment would be required to restore the damaged and destroyed plants to their original productive level. This does not take into account further deterioration and the loss of production before the old level is reached. These would probably double the cost. Taking all this into consideration, two billion U.S. dollars is considered to be a conservative estimate of the damage to Manchuria resulting from the

ties, and disrepair and disuse during a period of hyperinflation and economic chaos again set the industrial sector back considerably.

In a partial census of 27 cities in mainland China (and Taiwan) in 1947, in terms of employment, textiles, food processing, chemicals, apparel manufacturing, and paper manufacturing and printing, listed in descending order, ranked above such industries as machinery, metallurgical products, metal working, and electrical equipment and supplies. The textile industry also possessed by far the largest amount of equipment in terms of motive power.[6] Another indication of the industrial structure may be found in the relative proportion of producer-goods output to that of consumer goods. According to estimates by T. C. Liu and K. C. Yeh, the proportion of modern industrial output (including modern manufacturing, modern mining, and utilities) in 1933 accounted for by consumer goods was 81.1 per cent, while the share of producer goods was 18.9 per cent.[7]

2. The extent of the "dual" economy. Furthermore, in 1933, the handicraft industry, which used little mechanical power and was carried on in small workshops and homes, contributed 2.04 billion yuan at 1933 prices to the national output as measured by the net domestic product, in comparison with 0.64 billion yuan

---

Soviet occupation." (Pp. 36–37.) The degree of damage to specific industries may be seen from the following:

Industry	Estimated per cent reduction in productive capacity resulting from Soviet occupation
Electric power	71
Coal	90
Iron and steel	51–100
Railroads	50–100
Metal working	80
Nonferrous mining (coal excepted)	75
Liquid fuels and lubricants	75
Chemicals	50
Cement	50
Textiles	75
Paper and pulp	30
Radio, telegraph, and telephone	20–100

[6] Yuan-li Wu, *op. cit.*, p. 37.
[7] Ta-chung Liu and Kung-chia Yeh, *op. cit.*, pp. 215–17 and Appendix H.

by modern manufacturing.[8] The existence of a traditional sub-sector and a modern subsector side by side in manufacturing was closely paralleled by similar dualistic existence in mining and transportation. The simultaneous existence of enterprises that exhibit gross disparity in size, methods of production, product quality, costs, and prices is probably a common phenomenon in most countries still in an early phase of modernization.[9] It was certainly characteristic of the pre-Communist Chinese economy. As a matter of fact, a common and persistent complaint in the pre-World War II period was the inability of the traditional handicraft industry to hold its own in the face of the superior competitive strength of the modern enterprises. The result was a form of technological unemployment, brought about by the reduction of the size of the traditional sector rather than the replacement of labor by machinery in enterprises which continued to exist as separate entities.

3. Industrial location. Before World War II, modern industry was concentrated in a few treaty ports in China proper and Manchuria. As Wang Foh-sheng reported in 1946,[10] slightly more than 50 per cent of the country's modern industrial output in 1933 was derived from Shanghai, while Manchuria accounted for 12 per cent, and a small number of industrial centers in North China, Central China, and South China were responsible for the remainder. As a result of greater rates of industrial expansion in southwest China, parts of North China, and Manchuria, the relative importance of Shanghai declined during the war. This geographical pattern was further complicated by Soviet removals of industrial equipment from Manchuria at the end of World War II. The locational pattern of industrial development immediately before the establishment of the Communist regime was marked by spotty and uneven development. In an industrial survey published in 1948, outside of Manchuria only eighteen cities located in thirteen provinces had enough manufacturing enterprises to earn the designation of "principal" industrial centers, however modest the meaning of "principal."[11] On the other hand, ten provinces or re-

[8] *Ibid.*, chapter ii, Table 8, p. 94.

[9] For a discussion on the various aspects of "dualism," see chap. ii, in Gerald M. Meier, *Leading Issues in Development Economics* (New York: Oxford University Press, 1964), and the bibliography on pp. 88–89.

[10] Wang Foh-sheng, *China's Industrial Production, 1931–46* (Nanking: Institute of Social Sciences, 1948), p. 4.

[11] For a fuller discussion of the pre-Communist spatial characteristics of the Chinese economy, see the author's forthcoming study on *The Spatial Economy of Communist China.*

gions (based on the later Communist administrative divisions) reported no "principal" industrial centers at all. In fact, with the exception of the Fukien and Chekiang provinces, both industrial and agricultural development was concentrated in the coastal provinces whereas northwest and southwest China (with the exception of Szechwan Province) were the most underdeveloped regions. This lopsidedness in industrial development was also reflected in a corresponding imbalance in the development of railways, the country's principal long-distance carrier other than coastal shipping.

4. Ownership. The concentration of modern industry in certain areas was not unrelated to the nature of ownership. In 1933, for instance, one half of all industrial workers in Shanghai were in the employ of foreign firms. In Manchuria, Japanese investments dominated the field. During and immediately after World War II, state ownership of industrial enterprises was given a strong boost through the wartime expansion of government industry in unoccupied China and the confiscation of Japanese-owned firms at the end of the war. According to one Communist source, 74 per cent of total industrial capital in 1936 was foreign-owned.[12] Because of heavy Japanese investments during the Sino-Japanese War (1937–45) and their later confiscation, Wu Ch'eng-ming has put the share of state-owned industrial capital in 1946 at 67.3 per cent, as against the private share of 32.7 per cent.[13]

The predominance of foreign firms was characteristic of the beginning of modern Chinese economic development. Their concentration in treaty ports and areas of strong foreign political influence helped to create "external economies" at these centers, thus leading to the initial concentration of all modern industry, both foreign and native-owned, in the same few places. Furthermore, the association of foreign ownership of productive enterprises with political extraterritoriality enjoyed by foreign powers until the end of World War II contributed to the popular acceptance of the political slogan that foreign capital and imperialism went hand in hand. The predominance of foreign capital was also often regarded as the reason why Chinese industry had been confined to raw-material production and, insofar as manufacturing was developed at all, to the production of consumer goods. The thesis that foreign manufacturers did not wish to create local competi-

[12] *People's Daily*, May 21, 1953.
[13] Wu Ch'eng-ming, "Chung-kuo Kung-yeh Tzu-pen ti Ku-chi ho Fen-hsi" (Estimate and Analysis of China's Industrial Capital), *Hsin-hua Yüeh-pao* (*New China Monthly*), I, Peking, November, 1949, pp. 108–11.

tion with their own imported products was generally accepted by the Chinese public, even though the growth of foreign- as well as domestic-owned textile manufacturing in China before the Communist period would seem to contradict such a simplified interpretation.

5. The capital market and management. Lacking a well-organized capital market and having poor business organization and management, particularly with regard to marketing and cost and quality controls, the pre-Communist industrial sector of China suffered from the usual shortcomings of an underdeveloped country. Capital was often tied up in fixed assets, leaving insufficient working capital for operations. The corporate form of organization based on public issues was still much less common than private enterprises financed by a single family or a small group of persons. Thus, in addition to the shortage of savings, economic development was handicapped by problems of organization and mobilization of capital.

Significant Changes Under the Communist Regime

The principal changes in the industrial sector under the Communist regime may be examined against the historical background described above.

First, as a result of the pattern of resource planning and investment allocation within the sector of modern output, official reports put the share of producer goods at 43 per cent in 1952,[14] as compared with 18.9 per cent in 1933. It rose steadily in the course of the First Five-Year Plan, reaching 57 per cent in 1957. Very sharp increases were then registered in 1958 and 1959.[15] According to the same sources, as much as 69 per cent of total industrial production consisted of producer goods in 1959, prior to the 1960 crisis. Looking at the sectoral structure in a different manner, we see that the output of the food-processing and textile industries, which, although they include some producer goods, consist predominantly of consumer goods, constituted 63.5 per cent of the production of modern industry in 1952, while the ratio fell to 49.1 per cent in 1957.[16]

[14] Liu and Yeh, *op. cit.*, II, App. F, p. 654.
[15] Yuan-li Wu *et al.*, *The Economic Potential of Communist China*, I (Menlo Park, Calif.: Stanford Research Institute, 1963), Table 46, p. 224.
[16] Yuan-li Wu *et al.*, *op. cit.*, Vol. I, 1963, Table 24, p. 131.

Second, the share of handicraft production in the entire industrial sector declined during the First Five-Year Plan. Official estimates of gross industrial output showed handicraft production
and the output of modern industry in 1952 at 12.3 billion and 22
billion yuan (at 1952 prices) respectively.[17] The corresponding
values in 1957 were 22.8 billion and 55.6 billion yuan respectively.
The relative ratios shifted from 1:.56 to 1:.41 in favor of modern
industry. In terms of the net value-added, the ratio between the
handicraft sector and modern manufacturing changed from 1:.75
to 1:.35, as compared with the 1:3.19 ratio in 1933.[18] Furthermore,
as one might expect, during 1953–57, a higher proportion of the
handicraft-industry sector was devoted to consumer-goods production rather than that of producer goods in comparison with
the modern industry sector. During 1958–59, however, when the
small-industry movement was still in full swing, the composition
of the industrial output using traditional methods was probably
altered, with producer goods accounting for a much larger share,
inasmuch as the production of pig iron and crude steel was made
the core of the movement. However, the distinction between the
handicraft and the modern subsectors became rather blurred.

Third, with respect to the relocation of industry, a recent study
shows that greater emphasis has been given to the establishment
of industrial centers in the more developed regions of the country
(Manchuria, east China, and north China) in comparison with
the less developed regions. This relative emphasis favoring the
developed regions is also more pronounced than the corresponding relatively greater industrial importance of the coastal provinces vis-à-vis the inland provinces. In other words, there has been
a decided movement of industry away from the coast, but industrial expansion has continued to stress the more developed regions. In the less developed regions, particularly northwest and
southwest China, industrial development has been slow despite
some outstanding accomplishments in isolated cases, such as the
oil fields in Kansu and Tsinghai.[19]

Lastly, as noted in Chapter IV, the nationalization of industry
was virtually complete by the end of 1956. Together with the
collectivization of agriculture, the stage has been set for the effective pre-emption of resources for investment. The institutional lag

[17] Official statistics quoted in Yuan-li Wu *et al.*, I, 1963, p. 130.
[18] Wu, *et al.*, *op. cit.*, I, 233, and Liu and Yeh, *op. cit.*, chap. ii, Table 8.
[19] See Wu, *The Spatial Economy of Communist China* (unpublished
study).

hampering the marshaling of savings for economic development has ceased to be a major problem. Similarly, the continuing emphasis on economic accounting has created a greater awareness of the importance of cost and productivity and of the truism that economic efficiency is a prerequisite of rapid development.

An Optimal Course of Industrial Expansion

The break with the past was quite decisive in several ways, particularly in the speed of the expansion of the modern sector, the emphasis on producer goods, and the geographic shift away from coastal areas. On the other hand, the geographic change was not as radical as it might have been. Stress on the establishment of small enterprises employing traditional methods of production during the Great Leap added to the dualistic character of the industrial sector. In a sense, both of these developments have served to make the modification of the industrial economy less radical than it might have been. Both have been results of the planners' realization of the shortage of capital, which discourages new industrial development in remote and backward areas while pointing to the apparent advantage of less capital-intensive methods of production on the assumption that the quality of the products would be acceptable. The crucial question is whether the nevertheless large departures from the past are conducive to optimal industrial development.

Given the over-all rate of investment relative to current consumption, the rate of industrial development depends of course on the allocation of funds to the industrial sector, the intrasectoral allocation of investment in industry, the capital intensity of the production processes used, and the efficiency or productivity with which inputs, including services from newly invested capital goods, can be translated into output. Since the economy does not stand still technologically, the rate and nature of industrial development also depend upon the propensity of introducing innovations (including new products, new methods of production, and new organizational forms) and the rate of expenditure of resources in research and development that would generate the flow of innovations.

Perhaps one of the most important long-term effects of the Communist regime's energetic drive to industrialize the country has been the propagation of a receptive and even enthusiastic attitude toward economic and technological change. Concomitant with this attitude is the sense of individual participation in a nationwide movement toward modernization. The small-industry drive during the Great Leap period may have contributed significantly to these developments, even though its complacent belief in the unlimited efficacy of labor-intensive methods in all branches of industrial production bordered on naïveté. Furthermore, the early establishment of the Academy of Sciences and, later, of the State Scientific and Technological Commission, was supported by an official awareness of the importance to coordinate the effort in scientific research and development with production.[20] The research tasks outlined by Kuo Mo-jo, Director of the Academy, for the First Five-Year Plan period were all invariably geared to production planning. A system of rewards, both in public honors and in materialistic terms, has also been established in order to promote inventions and innovations on a more practical plane.[21]

On the other hand, as pointed out in Chapter III, Chinese economic planning is not as efficient as it seems. The practice of economic accounting has not always been faithfully carried out. Often it has suffered because of the emphasis on production in quantity. Furthermore, because of the limited role played by the pricing system and the inadequate inclusiveness of the cost concept, there are inherent difficulties in the efficient management of enterprises. For the same reasons, proper investment criteria are lacking in the allocation of investment funds both within the industrial sector and between sectors.

Within the rapidly developed steel industry, for instance, in spite of the fast growth of over-all output up to 1960, intra-industry balance was not attained between the successive stages of production, such as pig iron, ingot steel, and finished steel products. As of 1960, there was an excess of ingot capacity relative to the other stages. Although a lesser imbalance existed in terms of production, the seemingly better performance was only a result of the inadequate supply of quality steel, which could be converted into suitable finished products that were in demand. The accumulation of unwanted inventory, in part a result of the undue stress on quantity and the emulation campaigns in production based on it, while shortages continued to plague other sections of the steel industry, may therefore be regarded as a typical

---

[20] *People's Daily*, Peking, June 12, 1955.

[21] *Fa-kuei Hui-pien* (*Compendium of Laws and Regulations*), I, September, 1954–June, 1955, pp. 427–34, and II, July–December, 1955, pp. 753–55.

example of faulty planning in an industry that underwent exceptionally rapid growth in recent years.[22]

Another example of poor planning may be found in the development of energy resources. Commenting on developments in 1949–60, one recent study noted: "Industrial consumption of electricity has been maintained only at the expense of other sectors, particularly the households. The planners have failed to make adequate allowance for structural changes that have increased the relative size of industries of high power consumption and changes in production methods that have increased electricity input." Furthermore,

> a proper balance has not been maintained within the sector of energy resources. Coal production has been developed beyond the level that was immediately necessary, and by expanding the number of native mines in the first three years of the Second Five-Year Plan, coal production has been increased with great wastefulness of available deposits and of manpower badly needed elsewhere. . . . [There] is some question whether the proper proportion between hydro and thermal power plants has been maintained. The need felt by the planners to shorten the construction period and the confusion about the relative investment costs of the two types of plants has caused a certain degree of indeterminateness in policy. . . . [Finally], the exploitation of water and coal resources so far has done little to reshape the regional pattern of production to correspond more closely to the geographical distribution of energy resources.[23]

Given intrasectoral and intersectoral imbalances in the development of industry, planning errors are reflected in specific shortages and unintentional accumulation of inventories, the latter including products of substandard quality. As long as output is valued at constant prices—possibly the planned prices of a certain date—a fundamental question may be raised as to the meaningfulness of the reported value-output statistics. The same question would apply to the possibility of employing investment-output ratios as a basis of comparison for the relative advantage of investment in different sectors of the economy. In the short run, high growth rates may conceal planning errors. When these errors are rectified, the recorded growth rates would have to be revised. In the meantime, however, the quantitative record of industrial

[22] See Yuan-li Wu, *The Steel Industry in Communist China* (New York: Frederick A. Praeger, Forthcoming).

[23] Yuan-li Wu, *Economic Development and the Use of Energy Resources* (New York: Frederick A. Praeger, 1963), pp. 200–201.

expansion is misleading and must be subjected to a more searching qualitative analysis.

Reorientation of Industrial Policy

A reorientation of industrial policy took place in 1961 following the withdrawal of large numbers of Soviet technical experts from China in 1960. It took place along with a drastic cut-back of investment, especially industrial investment. (See Chapter V.) While the new economic policy gave priority to agricultural recovery, the new industrial policy stressed (1) the development of those branches of industry the output of which would serve as input in the agricultural sector, and (2) the importance of maintaining product quality and of keeping production cost under control. This means that the machine-manufacturing industry must change its product mix in favor of such items as farm machinery and implements, including water pumps and tractors, while the chemical industry must expand its fertilizer production, and the fuel and power industries must maintain an increasing output at adequate quality. Furthermore, the machine-tool and construction industries must strive to produce more plants for the manufacture of these end products. The requirement that quality be improved and that only profitable production be permitted implies stricter enforcement of the principles of economic accounting and re-examination of its concepts.

During 1962–63, the results of this new policy were reasonably satisfactory in terms of the changes in the product mix envisaged. Preliminary estimates have put the output of steel at 7 million tons in 1962, and that of chemical fertilizers at 2.05 million tons in the same year.[24] These compare favorably with the corresponding reports for 1957, when industrial production had not yet been thrown into confusion by the Great Leap and the subsequent crisis. Other preliminary estimates have put the aggregate output of modern industry at 72 billion yuan in 1962, which would be equivalent to 76 per cent of the 1960 output of 94.5 billion yuan, or 144 per cent of the 1957 output of 50 billion yuan.[25] Inasmuch

[24] *China Weekly*, XLII, No. 11, June 3, 1963, p. 12, and "Communist China's Industry in the Past Year," *Fei-ching Yen-chiu* (*Research on Communist China*), No. 12, December 25, 1962, pp. 89–99.

[25] According to an official report attributed to Chou En-lai, there was a 15 per cent increase in industrial output during 1964 in comparison with the 1963 level. This put the 1964 figure "far higher than in 1957." *Peking Review*, VIII, No. 1 (January 1, 1965), p. 8.

as industrial production may have fallen to a low of 39.1 billion yuan in 1961,[26] a substantial recovery would seem to have taken place following the reorientation of industrial policy.

However, even with the new industrial policy (still in force in 1964), which has abandoned the "big push" and "small industry" approach of the Great Leap, only the gross errors of resource allocation have been corrected. Adequate investment criteria remain wanting. Nor can one be certain of the duration of the new policy.

Trends and Fluctuations in Industrial Output

Finally, a comparison may be made between the growth trend and fluctuations of modern industry output in the Communist period and the corresponding data of the pre-Communist period. The relevant data are presented in Figures VI-1–4. Figure VI-1 shows the industrial output index in 1931–46, with 1931 = 100, together with a linear trend computed by least squares. Figure VI-2 does the same for the years 1952–62 under the Communist regime. Figures VI-3 and 4 present the annual data as per cents of the corresponding trend values.

The year 1931 is the first year of Wang Foh-sheng's industrial-output index series, which ends in 1946. Although the period covered is shorter than the entire period of Nationalist rule on the Mainland before the establishment of the Communist regime (1927–49), it spans virtually the entire period. The flood of 1931, the world-wide depression of the early 1930's, and the war years were all significant sources of distortion of the trend. Given the data available, there is no real solution by means of which these distortions might be corrected. On the whole, the net effect is probably an underestimate of the slope of the trend line in 1931–36.

Bearing this consideration in mind, we must nevertheless note the sharp difference in the slopes of the two trend lines. An explanation of this difference should be sought both (1) in the different approaches to industrial development during the two periods, and (2) in the large investments made during the war years, which did not produce full observable effects at the time. Furthermore, allowance must be made for the methodological questions of measuring industrial output raised in the beginning of this

[26] Yuan-li Wu *et al., op. cit.,* I, 1963, p. 224.

FIGURE VI-1.   INDEX OF MODERN INDUSTRY OUTPUT, 1931-1946
(1931 = 100)

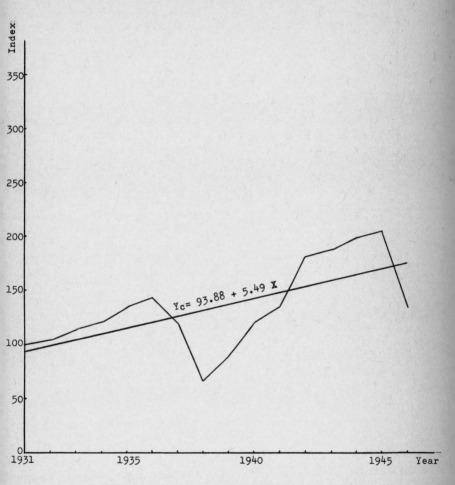

SOURCE: WANG FOH-SHEN, CHINA'S INDUSTRIAL PRODUCTION, 1931-1946,
INSTITUTE OF SOCIAL SCIENCES, NANKING, 1948, p. 12.

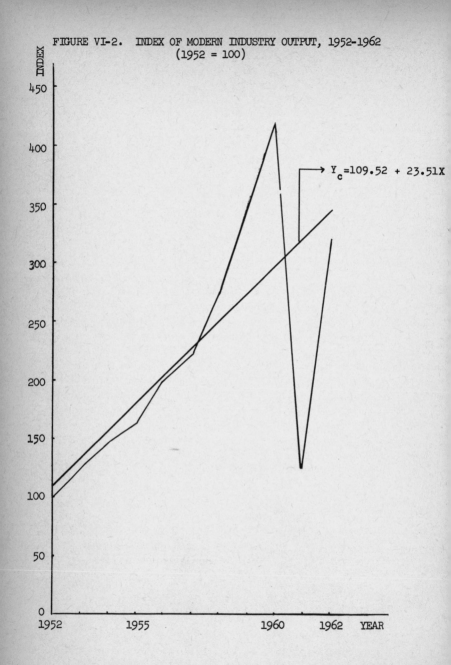

FIGURE VI-2. INDEX OF MODERN INDUSTRY OUTPUT, 1952-1962
(1952 = 100)

$Y_c = 109.52 + 23.51X$

SOURCE: FRED C. HUNG & YUAN-LI WU, "CONCEPTUAL DIFFICULTIES IN MEASURING CHINA'S INDUSTRIAL OUTPUT", THE CHINA QUARTERLY, JANUARY---MARCH, 1964, p. 61.

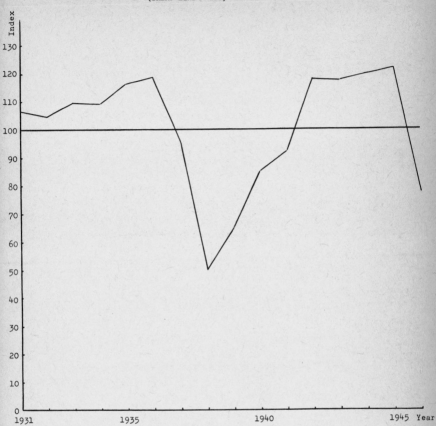

FIGURE VI-3. FLUCTUATIONS IN MODERN INDUSTRY OUTPUT, 1931-1946
(TREND LINE = 100)

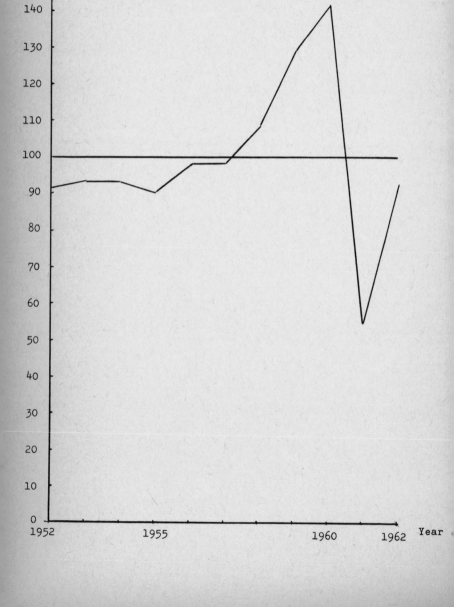

FIGURE VI-4. FLUCTUATIONS IN MODERN INDUSTRY OUTPUT, 1952-1962
(TREND LINE = 100)

chapter. On the other hand, one is nevertheless faced with the seemingly compelling conclusion that the higher trend in 1952–62 may indeed mark a new departure in Chinese economic development.

Finally, we see from Figures VI-3 and -4 that in spite of the discrepancy in the trends, the industrial output in the two periods nevertheless showed fluctuations about the trend that were not grossly dissimilar in amplitude. As mentioned earlier, however, the pre-Communist data incorporate the experience of the war years, while the later data include the effects of the Great Leap Forward and its aftermath. While one can regard the war as an extra-economic factor, there is some question as to whether the Great Leap Forward, together with the ensuing crisis, was not in the main an endogenous factor. This will be discussed further in Chapter VII.

Performance in the Agricultural Sector

The Relative Importance of the Agricultural Sector

If a large proportion of the labor force of any country is employed in a particular economic sector, working on the exploitation of a resource (such as land) that is fixed in amount, and if the resultant ratio of resource per capita is exceedingly small, one can in general infer that output and income per capita in this sector will be low and that the country as a whole is economically underdeveloped. If the sector in question is agriculture, one has a typical agrarian economy characterized by overpopulation on the land, a low output per farm worker, and, usually, a heavy concentration of the agricultural, as well as total, labor force in the production of the bare essentials to support life.

A priori, the following observations are also likely to be true in such an economy. First, to a considerable extent, production in the nonagricultural sectors will be dependent on agricultural products as inputs, so that the relative over-all importance of the agricultural sector in the country's GNP and aggregate employment will exceed the ratios of the "value-added in agriculture" to the GNP and of agricultural employment to total employment. Second, as a corollary, goods of agricultural origin are likely to constitute a high proportion of the country's exports. In the absence of any significant foreign-capital inflow, the availability of such exports would play a critical part in determining the volume of imports and, indirectly, in all likelihood, the production of goods to which the imported input components are indispensable. Third, although a high relative proportion of agricultural output in the GNP does not necessarily imply insufficient diversification in the economy as a whole, the fact that agriculture is particularly susceptible to the vagaries of nature imparts considerable uncertainty to the size of the agricultural sector's output and the country's over-all economic well-being in any given year. The high degree of uncertainty as to the result of the productive effort makes the agricultural sector a potentially destabilizing factor in the economic development of the country and a disruptive influence in its economic planning. Finally, it is especially difficult to implement rigorous government controls of production in agriculture for technical reasons. Since production is not concentrated under one roof, supervision is far more difficult than in industrial operations, and greater reliance must be placed upon the provision of adequate positive incentives to the farmer. Moreover, because of the susceptibility of agricultural production, especially crop cultivation, to unexpected changes in local conditions—the influence of the "microclimate" for instance—success in agricultural production is likely to be predicated upon a high degree of decentralization in decision-making. In fact, both the consideration of adequate incentive and this technical factor would seem to require decentralization in decisions affecting the manner of production as well as the distribution of output.

It follows from the above that an underdeveloped, predominantly agricultural country must depend upon the agricultural sector as a major source to finance its investment program and to produce a large part of its current output. Under such conditions, it is entirely logical for the government and its economic planners to want assured control over the agricultural sector, including the determination of the size and composition of its production and the disposal of the output. Yet it is precisely the rigidity that such controls are likely to assume which tends to affect agricultural production adversely. Thus the planners may be confronted with a dilemma that cannot be readily resolved.

To what extent conditions in Communist China correspond to the above hypothetical model may be gleaned from the following remarks:

In the first place, during 1953–57, according to one estimate, the proportion of the gross domestic product originating in agriculture fell gradually from 45 per cent to 38 per cent. In 1960, it fell still further, reaching a low of 26 per cent. However, possibly because of the overestimate of industrial production in 1960 and the depth of the then agricultural crisis, the relative share of 26 per cent registered by agriculture in 1960 was somewhat misleading. Following the sharp decline in industrial production during 1961–62, the trend was reversed and the proportion once more reached 43 per cent in 1962. Furthermore, because of the lower rate of depreciation in agriculture, which in Communist China is much less "capital-intensive" than industry, the proportion of the net domestic product originating in the agricultural sector was somewhat higher. It varied from 46 per cent in 1953 to 39 per cent in 1957, with a low of 27 per cent in 1960, and 47 per cent in 1962.[1] Thus the agricultural sector may be said to account *directly* for at least 40 per cent of the country's total output.

The proportion of agricultural workers in total employment approximated 77–78 per cent in 1952–57. In 1952, 199.9 million workers in the agricultural sector produced 35.9 billion yuan (at 1952 prices) of the gross domestic product.[2] In 1957, 215.8 million agricultural workers produced 38.1 billion yuan. In the nonagricultural sectors, the corresponding figures were 59.4 million workers and 39.7 billion yuan in 1952, and 64.2 million workers and 61.9 billion yuan in 1957. The per-capita figures would show a decrease of 1.7 per cent in agriculture during the five-year period, while the increase in the nonagricultural sectors was 44 per cent. The per-capita output in terms of gross value-added in the nonagricultural sectors was 3.7 times that of the agricultural sector in 1952, and 5.5 times in 1957. That agricultural production lagged behind advances in the nonagricultural sectors during the First Five-Year Plan is beyond doubt.

Thirdly, official statistics show that during 1952, 59 per cent of Communist China's exports consisted of agricultural products[3] (including subsidiary agricultural products[4]), plus another 23 per cent representing manufactures of agricultural origin. In 1957, the corresponding ratios were 40 per cent and 31.5 per cent respectively. The reader can refer to Chapter IX in order to appreciate fully the approximate effect of any curtailment of agricultural export on the balance of payments. The effect of any serious curtailment of agricultural exports or of any large import of agricultural goods due to failures in domestic farm production can be easily visualized.

In the fourth place, it has been estimated that nearly 48 per cent of Communist China's state budget in 1952–57, net of foreign

---

[1] Yuan-li Wu *et al., op. cit.,* I, 1963, Table 51, 241.
[2] *Ibid.*
[3] *Wei-ta ti Shih-nien (Great Ten Years),* 1959, p. 156.
[4] According to official practice, as of 1958, "subsidiary agricultural production" includes (1) fishing, hunting, and gathering of wild (including marine) live animals, plants and ores, (2) preliminary processing by producers of self-produced agricultural products, (3) handicraft products produced for own consumption and use, and (4) handicraft processing for other consumers. See *T'ung-chi Yen-chiu (Statistical Research),* No. 5, 1958, p. 22.

loan receipts, was, either directly or indirectly, borne by the peasants.[5] This "total burden," including both the agricultural tax
itself and the peasants' estimated share of other taxes, public
bonds, and profit of state enterprises, was probably around 30
per cent of the agricultural sector's income. Since a major portion
of the state budget was earmarked for investment, it follows that
the peasants were responsible for a large portion of the investments financed through the state budget, in addition to investments carried out by unpaid labor or undertaken on the peasants'
own account.

According to Liu's estimate, approximately 75 per cent of the
gross domestic product within the agricultural sector in 1952–57
was accounted for by crop cultivation.[6] Furthermore, within the
crop cultivation subsector, a little more than 70 per cent of the
gross domestic product originated was attributable to food crops.[7]
Still other statistics indicate that the production of cereals and
potatoes ("food grain" in Chinese statistics) accounted for 56 per
cent of the gross domestic product originating in the agricultural
sector in 1952, and that the relative share stood at 53 per cent in
1957,[8] when they accounted for more than 70 per cent of hectares
planted. The production of staple "grains" would thus directly
account for 20 per cent (50 per cent of 40 per cent) or more of
the total output of the country. The effect of fluctuations in the
output of a few commodities on the national product and the
consequent vulnerability of the economy can thus be readily
imagined.

Production versus Distribution—the Crux of the Chinese Agricultural Problem*

Opinion was divided in pre-Communist China on how to increase agricultural production and farm income. One school of

[5] Mah Feng-hua, "The Financing of Public Investment in Communist China," *The Journal of Asian Studies*, XXI, No. 1 (November, 1961), 45.

[6] T. C. Liu and K. C. Yeh, *The Economy of the Chinese Mainland—National Income and Economic Development, 1933–1959*, I, 212.

[7] *Ibid.*, II, p. 557.

[8] Yuan-li Wu *et al.*, *op. cit.*, I, Table 38, p. 193.

* Much of this and the following sections in the present chapter is taken
from an essay contained in a joint study by the author with Professor John Lossing Buck and Mr. Owen L. Dawson, whose comments have been most helpful.
The reader may find it useful to refer to the entire monograph, *Food and
Agriculture in Communist China*, published by the Hoover Institution. The
author is grateful to the Hoover Institution for permission to draw on this
material.

thought placed the principal emphasis on increase in per-capita production, which, according to studies of farm operation, was considered a function of farm size rather than one of land ownership. It was recognized that mass poverty could be alleviated only through increase in production, provided of course that the beneficial effect would not be offset by greater inequality in the distribution of farm income. This would necessitate control of usurious interest and of high land rent. But the real solution had to be sought in an increase in the land-labor ratio and the expansion of farm holdings. However, given the relatively inelastic supply of land and the gradual population growth, this condition could not be fulfilled without developing alternative forms of employment for the agricultural population. Such alternatives could of course be provided either in industry (away from the rural areas) or, if technologically and institutionally possible, on the spot.

Others in pre-Communist China were more concerned with the distributive aspect of farm income. Theoretical support of their position could be found in the argument that high land rent and usury would preclude borrowing for investment purposes. Instead, they would lead to "waste" of the savings of land owners in the form of consumption loans, and, because of the inability of the poor farmers to meet their obligations, the increasing concentration of land ownership in fewer and fewer hands. Consequently, the first step toward the solution of China's agrarian problem would have to be the redistribution of land or "land reform." Rent and interest controls would of course be preliminary to redistribution.

That industrialization, interpreted here broadly as the development of alternative forms of nonagricultural employment, constitutes the fundamental solution of China's agrarian problem cannot be denied. For the limited land available constitutes a real constraint on agricultural expansion. In spite of varying estimates of the amount of arable land in mainland China, no one has put it at more than 20 per cent of the total land area, and some at considerably less. The highest estimate of cultivated land to be found in *Land Utilization in China* was 108.2 million hectares, while the highest claim under the Communists was 112 million hectares, in 1956. The economic feasibility of increasing the cultivated area and the speed at which this can be done are both subject to serious doubt. If not much new land can be brought under cultivation, the question, then, is how to expand the size of the farm as an operating unit. One alternative would be to allow the more efficient farmers to expand their scale of operation and to have the displaced farmers absorbed into other forms of employment. A second alternative would be to merge the individual farms into cooperatives, leaving the surplus farmers in a state of underemployment or, as in the first case, absorbing them into other forms of employment. In each case, of course, in order to avoid undesirable political and social consequences, there would be the problem of regulating the speed at which surplus farm labor would be separated from farming and of matching this release of labor with an appropriate rate of absorption into other employments.

The Communist Party of China adopted the solution of collectivization as a means of increasing the size of the operating farm unit, because it was, and still is, ideologically opposed to the emergence of a "rich peasant" economy. However, for political reasons, it went about collectivization in a roundabout manner, first advocating and then carrying out a land-redistribution program. The advocacy of land reform earned the Communists the reputation of being agrarian reformers, which was exceedingly helpful in foreign as well as domestic propaganda. The implementation of the land-reform program, carried out in most parts of the country during 1950–52, was instrumental in redistributing wealth as well as political and economic power in rural areas. The process of collectivization or formation of cooperatives, carried out largely in 1954–56, was spearheaded by the formation of "mutual aid" teams. In 1958, the cooperative farms were further merged into communes, although the operating unit was the "production brigade," which corresponded to the cooperative farm in size.

Some of the Outstanding Questions

How effective has the Communist solution been? Has production increased with the successive institutional changes? If this has not always been true, what other underlying reasons can account for the institutional changes undertaken, apart from the political consideration which prompted the initial "land reform"? In particular, what accounted for the transition from the cooperative farm to the commune? What technical factors have affected the course of development of agricultural output? What conditions would seem to be necessary for the recovery and expansion of agricultural output in the light of the experience of the first decade and a half of Communist rule, particularly of the period since 1958?

Need for a Reappraisal of Official Communist Statistics

Before one can evaluate the accomplishments of Communist China in the agricultural sector, an attempt must be made to determine certain quantitative records. In this connection, using the official series of the gross value of agricultural output, an annual rate of increase of 4.5 per cent would be indicated during the First Five-Year Plan. However, this claim is subject to dispute. The principal point at issue lies in the questionable output statistics of major subsectors in agriculture. In particular, attention should be focused on the official food-grain output estimates.

That Communist China's food-grain production statistics may be highly unreliable was first brought into sharp focus in 1958–59. In 1958 and early 1959, grain production in the first year was reported as 375 million metric tons, compared with 185 million tons in 1957. Some Western observers considered the alleged doubling of grain output in the space of one year as virtually impossible, although it was generally agreed that a considerable increase in production could be brought about over a longer period of time. Subsequently, in August, 1959,[9] this official claim underwent a rather sharp reduction, to 250 million tons—i.e., one-third smaller than the original estimate. This revision, the need for which was attributed to statistical inexperience of the reporting personnel, cast rather serious doubt on the accuracy of the entire statistical series, including both the revised estimate for 1958 and the reports of earlier years.

A number of reasons might be advanced to explain the unreliability of the grain statistics and to suggest possible means of adjusting the estimates. The several possible sources of error may be outlined as follows: (1) The discrepancy between the original estimate and the revised estimate for the year 1958, released in 1959, may be accounted for by a confusion in the estimate of unit area yield and inconsistency between the yield estimate and the acreage estimate employed in arriving at the total output. (2) A second source of error contained in grain output statistics before 1958 might well be the underestimate of planted acreage in the earlier years resulting from an underestimate of cultivated land.

[9] Reported in *The Wall Street Journal,* August 27, 1959.

(3) For the period from 1958 on, especially in 1958–62, an over-estimate of grain production may have occurred because of the unusually large discrepancy between "biological yield" and "barn yield" due to the inability of the communes to harvest all the crops and a sharp increase in wastage. Furthermore, gross inaccuracy in reporting output probably accentuated the overestimate during the Great Leap.

Depending upon how the adjustments are made, the revised grain-output statistics would differ considerably from the official output data. The result of one series of such adjustments is presented in Tables VII-1 and VII-2 below. As a consequence of the adjustments, the rate of growth of grain production during the period prior to the sharp decline which began in 1959 would be reduced to below the official claim. If the adjusted estimates are correct, it would follow that the long-term trend of grain production in mainland China is quite modest. Inasmuch as the trend, based on the adjusted estimates for 1950–57, spanned a period during which there was little technological change in the agricultural sector, one may take the trend as representative of what can be normally expected of grain production given only some gradual improvements in farm technology. It follows further that should such a long-term trend fail to meet the grain requirements of an increasing population determined on an autarkic basis, the estimated deficiency would have to be met through technological changes not previously allowed for in the derivation of the trend. A methodology may then be developed to evaluate the future prospect of Chinese agriculture and its principal determinants.

The Yield and Acreage Estimates

The source of the statistical error which gave rise to the large overestimate of the 1958 crop was first suggested in a 1958 article by Wang Kuang-sheng in *Statistical Research*.[10] This explanation was also pointed out by the present author at a meeting of the Association for Asian Studies in 1960.[11] According to Wang, the standard method adopted by the Statistical Bureau in 1956 for computing unit area yield for food grains is as follows: (1) Aggre-

[10] *T'ung-chi Yen-chiu*, No. 1, January, 1958, pp. 33–38.
[11] Yuan-li Wu, in *Land Tenure, Industrialization, and Social Stability: Experience and Prospect in Asia*, ed. Walter Froehlich (Milwaukee: The Marquette University Press, 1961).

TABLE VII-1. FOOD BALANCE SHEET BASED ON OFFICIAL PRODUCTION STATISTICS
(In million metric tons)

Year of Consumption	Production of Cereals and Potatoes in Preceding Year (in grain equivalent) (1)	Accumulated Stock (2)	Waste (3)	Seeds (4)	Feed (5)	Manufacture (6)	Net Export (7)	Total Available for Human Consumption and Stock (8)=(1)+(2)−[(3)+(4)+(5)+(6)+(7)]	Estimated Human Consumption (9)	Net Remaining as Stock (possibly fictitious) (10)=(8)−(9)	Net Remaining for Addition to Stock at End of Year (11)=(10)−(2)
1950	108.1	...	3.9	5.6	8.6	2.9	–	87.1	133.9	−46.8	−46.8
1951	124.7	...	4.6	6.4	10.4	3.8	–	99.5	136.6	−37.1	−37.5
1952	135.1	...	5.0	6.9	10.8	4.0	+0.9	107.5	139.3	−31.8	−31.8
1953	154.4		5.8	7.9	12.9	4.7	+0.9	122.2	142.4	−20.2	−20.2
1954	156.9	6.3[a]	5.9	8.0	12.8	4.7	+1.1	130.7	145.7	−15.0	−21.3
1955	160.5	9.5[a]	6.0	8.4	12.6	4.7	+1.3	137.0	148.9	−11.9	−21.4
1956	174.8	16.0[a]	6.6	9.0	14.0	5.2	+1.2	154.8	152.1	+2.7	−13.3
1957	182.5	15.5[a]	7.0	9.5	14.3	5.3	+1.1	160.8	141.8	+19.0	+3.5
1958	185.0	22.9[a]	7.1	9.5	14.3	5.3	+1.2	170.5	160.2	+10.3	−12.6
1959	250.0	32.9[a]	10.7	12.9	20.6	7.4	+1.7	229.6	140.4	+89.2	+56.3
1960	220.0[b]	89.2	9.4	11.4	18.1	6.5	–	263.8	108.1	+155.7	+66.5
1961	185.0[b]	155.7	7.9	9.6	15.2	5.5	−5.6	308.1	101.1	+207.0	+51.3
1962							−3.2				

Notes to Table VII-1:

Col. (1): Source: Wei-ta ti Shih-nien (Great Ten Years) (Peking, 1959), p. 105. [b] Unadjusted estimates based on official sources

Col. (2): Government cumulative stock plus nongovernment cumulative stock. For 1953–56, the former is given in T'ung-chi Kung-tso (Statistical Work), No. 19 (1957), p. 32. [a] Government stock only

Notes to Table VII-1 (Continued on facing page)

Notes to Table VII-1 (*Continued from facing page*)

Col. (3): 3 per cent of gross output of paddy rice, wheat, and other cereals; 10 per cent of gross output of tubers. T. H. Shen, *Agricultural Resources of China* (Ithaca, N.Y.: Cornell University Press, 1951), Appendix.

Col. (4): Paddy rice, 2.9 per cent of gross; wheat, 9.5 per cent; other cereals, 6 per cent; tubers, 6.9 per cent. These are weighted means derived from the 1931–37 data for twenty-two provinces and 1937–38 data for Manchuria given by Shen, *op. cit.*

Col. (5): 1 per cent of gross wheat output; 18.5 per cent of miscellaneous cereals; 19.4 per cent of tubers; none for rice. Columns 5 and 6 are both derived from Shen, *op. cit.*

Col. (6): Paddy rice, 1 per cent of gross production; wheat, 2 per cent; other cereals, 5.5 per cent; tubers, 5 per cent.

Col. (7): Estimated as follows: 1953–56, derived from *T'ung-chi Kung-tso,* 1957 (see reference under column 2); 1958–59, *Tsu-kuo* (*China Weekly*), No. 423, pp. 3–4, Hong Kong, 1961; 1952, same as 1953; 1957, average of 1953–56; 1961–62, derived from *Far Eastern Economic Review* (Hong Kong), XXXIV, No. 2 (October 21, 1961), 128.

Col. (9): Unit consumption of unprocessed grain (kg. per adult per year) X adult equivalent population at mid year (millions) ÷ 1000 = total consumption of unprocessed grain in M.T.

1950–56	In 1955, rationing regulations were promulgated by Communist China. The ration amounted to 201 kg. a year for a person doing light work in rice-eating and wheat-flour-eating regions. The corresponding ration for a person doing heavy work was 252 kg. per year. Weighted in accordance with the 1954–56 urban (14 per cent) and rural (86 per cent) population respectively, the national mean grain consumption per adult would work out at 245 kg. of processed grain.
1957	210 kg. of processed grain per adult per year.
1958	Same as 1950–56 period—245 kg.
1959	202 kg. per adult per year.
1960	150 kg.
1961	145 kg.
1962	145 kg.

SOURCES: "Chukoku no Shokuryo Jijo," *Ajia Keizai Jumpo* (*Asian Economic Thrice-Monthly* (Tokyo), No. 450 (November 20, 1960), pp. 1–10; *Shih-shih Shou-ts'e* (*Current Events*) (Peking), No. 15 (1957), p. 18; additional sources cited in the author's article "Farm Crisis in Red China," *Current History,* September 1959, p. 192.

Unit consumption of processed grain ÷ 0.86 (milling factor) = unit consumption of unprocessed grain (except for 1957, 1959, and 1960, due to slight differences in the grain mix).

Adult equivalent population = total mid-year population X 0.86 (conversion factor derived from age composition given in *Jen-min Pao-chien* (*People's Health*) (Peking), I, No. 5 (May, 1959), p. 463. Through 1957, the data are based on official estimates. For 1958–59, the estimates are based on an annual growth of 2.2 per cent. The 1960–62 estimates are at a slightly lower rate of increase. The original data of mid-year total population in millions are: 1950, 547; 1951, 558; 1952, 569; 1953, 581; 1954, 595; 1955, 608; 1956, 621; 1957, 637; 1958, 654; 1959, 668; 1960, 682; 1961, 693; 1962, 702; 1963, 711.

TABLE VII-2. An Adjusted Model Food Balance Sheet
(In million metric tons)

Year of Consumption	Adjusted Production of Cereals and Potatoes in Preceding Year (1)	Estimated Production Deducted from Waste, Seed, Feed, and Manufacturing (1) × 0.8 = (2)	Net Export (3)	Total Available for Human Consumption and Stock (4) = (2) − (3)	Estimated Human Consumption (5)	Net Remaining for Addition to Stock (6) = (4) − (5)	Cumulative Amount of Col. (6) (exclusive of initial stock at 1950 year end)
1951	179.8	143.8	—	143.8	136.6	+7.2	+7.2
1952	182.9	146.3	+0.9	145.4	139.3	+6.1	+13.3
1953	184.2	147.4	+0.9	146.5	142.4	+4.1	+17.4
1954	180.0	144.0	+1.1	142.9	145.7	−2.8	+13.6
1955	177.1	141.7	+1.3	140.4	148.9	−8.5	+5.1
1956	184.1	147.3	+1.2	146.1	152.1	−6.0	−0.9
1957	182.5	146.0	+1.1	144.9	141.8	+3.1	+2.2
1958	185.0	148.0	+1.2	146.8	160.2	−13.4	−11.2
1959	175.4	140.3	+1.7	138.6	140.4	−1.8	−13.0
1960	154.4	123.5	—	123.5	108.1	+15.4	+2.4
1961	130.0	104.0	−5.6	109.6	101.1	+8.5	+10.9
1962	140.0	112.0	−3.2	115.2	103.5	+11.7	+22.6
1963	160.0	128.0	−4.7	132.7	113.0[a]	+19.7	+42.3
					143.6[b]	−10.9	−11.7

Notes to Table VII-2:

Column (1): 1950–55—The cumulative total of withdrawals from stock in 1950–56 in Table VII-1 amounted to 192.3 million tons (Table VII-1, Col. 11). At the end of 1956, the minimum value of government stock was 15.5 million tons. However, the initial stock in 1950 could not possibly approach the total of these two figures—about 208 million tons. To allow for any possible overestimate of consumption as well as for the initial stock at the beginning of 1950, we disregard the 40.8 million tons in 1950 and assume the cumulative total of withdrawals in 1951–56 to be 145.5 million tons. The last figure is treated as a reflection of the total extent of underestimation of net supply derived from the production of 1950–55. 145.5 million tons, plus 20 per cent of the gross output allotted to seeds, feed, waste, and manufacturing, leads to a total underestimate of about nearly 181.8 million tons for 1950–55. The 181.8 million tons cumulative total underestimate of grain production during 1950–55 is then distributed over the individual years in the same proportion as the assumed underreporting of equivalent planted area during the same period.

Notes to Table VII-2 (Continued on facing page)

Pro- duction Year	Official Estimated Production (in million tons) (1)	Estimated Percentage Under-reporting of Equivalent Area Planted to Grain (1955–57 mean=100) (2)	(3)=(2)× 100÷44.6	Under- estimate of Grain Production (4)	Esti- mated Pro- duction
1950	124.7	13.5	30.3	55.1	179.8
1951	135.1	11.7	26.3	47.8	182.9
1952	154.4	7.3	16.4	29.8	184.2
1953	156.9	5.7	12.7	23.1	180.0
1954	160.4	4.1	9.2	16.7	177.1
1955	174.8	2.3	5.1	9.3	184.1
Total		44.6	100.0	181.8	

1957–60—The cumulative addition to stock in 1957–61 was 165 million metric tons (Table VII-1, Col. 11). The 165 million tons less the 8.8 million tons purchased from abroad in 1961 and 1962 yields 156.2 milion tons. This figure is regarded as representing the cumulative overestimate of net supply during 1958–60. In order to reduce the net supply by 156.2 million tons, the gross production should be reduced by 195.2 million tons if 20 per cent of the gross was wasted in processing or devoted to uses other than food. This assumed overestimate of 195.2 million is distributed as follows:

	Production Reported	The Production Reported as per cent of 655 (three-year total)	Million Tons	Estimated Production
1958	250	38.2	74.6	175.4
1959	220[a]	33.6	65.6	154.4
1960	185	28.2	55.0	130.0
Total	655			

[a] Adjusted from an earlier claim of 270 million tons by multiplying the unrevised total of 375 million tons of 1958 by a factor of 41/70. This is the ratio of 1958 unrevised yields to 1959 yields in four provinces. *People's Daily*, October 15 and 20 and November 2, 1958; October 6, March 7, April 14, and June 18, 1959; *The Red Flag*, No. 18 (1959).

1961—The 1961 production is estimated at not more than 10 million tons greater than that of 1960.

1962—The 1962 output is estimated at 14 per cent higher than in 1961, or 160 million tons. Both the 1961 and the 1962 figures are based on Hong Kong and other Far Eastern reports.

Column (2): 20 per cent of the total estimates of production is used for feed, seed, waste, and manufacturing.

Column (3): Same as Table VII-1, Col. 7.

Columns (5) to (7): [a] Preliminary, based on 1960 per adult consumption
[b] Preliminary, based on 1961 per adult consumption

gate of area planted (excluding land for green manure) ÷ total cultivated area = the general index of multiple cropping. (2) Aggregate of area planted to grain (i.e., the crop hectare area) ÷ the general index of multiple cropping = area of cultivated land taken up by grain (i.e., the crop area under grain). (3) Total output of grain ÷ the area of cultivated land taken up by grain = the average yield of grain per unit area. In other words, the average yield of grain corresponds to yield per unit crop area; it is not yield per crop hectare. This means that the yield per unit of crop area would be higher than the yield per crop hectare since the crop hectares in food grains are greater than the crop area in grains. In estimating the total grain output on the basis of sample unit area yield (i.e., yield per unit crop area under grain), one should of course multiply the unit area yield by the crop area under grain. If by any chance one were to multiply the yield per hectare of crop area by the number of crop hectares planted, the estimate would exceed the correct total by a factor equal to the multiple cropping index. Furthermore, any extension of double cropping of any crop would increase the general multiple cropping index and correspondingly raise the unit area yield of grain.

Notwithstanding Wang Kuang-sheng's discussion, the official *Handbook of Agricultural Statistics*[12] issued in 1956 stated that various types of yields could be compiled on the basis of sown acreage, harvested acreage, and cultivated acreage for different categories of crops. Furthermore, for agricultural planning, the instruction was to compute yields on the basis of sown acreage, although whether output was to be the actual harvest or the expected harvest was not clear. Finally, actual practice tends to lag behind the official instructions. Thus, there may be a considerable difference between any two of the following concepts, namely, the actual harvested yield per hectare sown, the expected yield before harvest per hectare sown, and the expected yield before harvest per hectare cultivated (or harvested). Whatever may be the concept of yield employed, if it is based on a sample, and if the sample is biased in favor of high yield farms—perhaps small experimental plots—there would be an added source of upward bias.

In the case of the 1958 initial estimate of 375 million tons, the corresponding unit area yield reported at the time was a rounded figure of 3 tons per hectare. If we take this unit area estimate as

[12] *Handbook of Agricultural Statistical Work* (Peking: Statistical Publishing House, 1956).

yield per hectare of crop area and divide it by the general multiple cropping index of 1.45 reported for 1958, the unit yield per crop hectare would be approximately 2,070 kilograms. If this figure is then multiplied by the 1958 grain hectare area reported in 1959, or 121 million hectares, the estimated output would be equal to approximately 250 million tons. This was precisely the revised figure reported in 1959.

The preceding operation would seem to substantiate the hypothesis that the initial official claim of 1958 erred in the application of the formula for computing the grain yield. That such an error could take place can only be explained by the dilution of the statistical staff in the Bureau and its field offices and by the insistence of the Communist Party to allow politics to "take command" even in such matters as statistical reporting.

Underestimate of Grain Output Statistics Before 1958

Turning next to the pre-1958 output estimate, there is reason to believe that the earlier figures underestimated actual output. This hypothesis is based on the view that if consumption estimates were made for the years 1950–56, withdrawals from stock during 1950–56 would reach a cumulative total of nearly 200 million tons. Furthermore, there was a minimum of 15.5 million tons of government stock at the end of 1956. The initial stock in 1950 could not possibly have approached such a phenomenal volume. Inasmuch as food was not rationed at the beginning of the 1950's, and inasmuch as the consumption estimates used in this hypothetical food balance sheet (Table VII-1) would yield a per-capita calorie intake (about 2,350 calories per adult per day) below the level of the normal prewar diet, it would seem that the computed heavy withdrawal of stock was in fact a fictitious one. In other words, there must have been a serious underestimate of current production. Allowing for such uses as animal feed, seed requirements, and raw material in manufacturing, plus some waste in processing, the underestimate of net supply of food grain available for human consumption during the year must be raised by approximately 25 per cent in order to arrive at the underestimate of gross output.

According to official statistics, the area of cultivated land in Communist China increased steadily from 100.4 million hectares in 1950 to 112 million hectares in 1956. The mean for 1955–57 would amount to 111.2 million hectares, which happens to correspond fairly closely to Buck's highest estimate in *Land Utilization in China*, combined with estimates for Manchuria, Jehol, Sinkiang, and Sikang—108.8 million hectares. Parallel to the rising trend of cultivated land, the crop hectare area planted with cereals and potatoes rose in official statistics from 104.8 million hectares in 1950 to 124.3 million hectares in 1956. The mean for 1955–57 is 121.2 million hectares. A hypothesis can therefore be advanced to the effect that up to 1956, the reported increase in cultivated land, as well as in hectares planted, was essentially a statistical increase due to better reporting coverage. That 1956 should be the terminal year for this statistical phenomenon would not be surprising in view of the fact that the program of collectivization was completed in 1956 and that land statistics probably became more accurate in that year. Of course, one may raise the question why the land statistics had not been better in the earlier years in view of the land reform program carried out in 1950–53. The explanation may lie in the fact that the State Statistical Bureau was not established until the end of 1952; furthermore, the statistical reporting system, especially in the rural areas, was not fully established and the returns were not standardized until several years later. Table VII-2 presents a possible model of adjustment on this basis.

Overestimate of Grain Output Statistics in 1958–60

It is generally known that the curtailment of personal consumption of the staple foods began in 1959 and that it became quite serious in 1960–62. It is also common knowledge that Communist China's policy of autarky in grain supply was reversed for the first time in 1961, and grain imports have continued up to this writing (1964–65). Consequently, one would assume that the existence of any sizable stock at the end of 1961 may be safely precluded. Yet if the grain output statistics in Table VII-1 were employed for the years 1958–60, there would emerge a cumulative addition to stock between 1957 and 1961 equivalent to some 165 million tons. This inconsistency implies that an overestimate of production still existed in the revised official claims. As an approximation, this overestimate can be taken out of the data for 1958–60. Such an adjustment is made in Table VII-2. The result is a discount of 38 per cent for 1958 and a minimum discount of 28 per cent for 1960.

Reference may be made at this point to two interesting comparisons. In the first place, according to reports in late 1959 and early 1960 pertaining to substantiated grain-output figures for three provinces (Kwangtung, Shantung, and Kansu), the corrected figures were 40 to more than 50 per cent smaller than the unrevised reports of 1958.[13] If the unrevised 375 million ton total were subjected to a 50 per cent discount, the result would be 187.5 million tons, or the same as in 1957. This would be slightly higher than the adjusted estimate in Table VII-2.

In the second place, according to Naum Jasny, the Soviet official crop estimate in 1935–39 should be subjected to a discount of 16.5 per cent in 1935, 28 per cent in 1936, 20.2 per cent in 1937, 20.0 per cent in 1938, and 22.8 per cent in 1939 in order to arrive at barn yield.[14] According to reports in 1957,[15] methods of estimating crops in Hopei and Heilungkiang indicated that the crops were estimated in terms of biological yield. It may be presumed, therefore, that the official production estimates were virtually all based on biological yield. During 1958 and the subsequent years, labor shortage at harvest time, greater incidence of sabotage, negligence, and theft under the commune system, and additional difficulties in harvesting large potato crops grown on hillsides may have accounted for a larger than usual discrepancy between the sown area and the harvested area and, therefore, between the biological and the barn crops. Furthermore, the apparently very large discount in 1958 was probably in part merely a compensation for inaccurate and exaggerated reports of the "biological crop" because of the field agents' inclination to report unusually high yields in the spirit of the Great Leap in order to impress their superiors with their ideological rectitude.

A Hypothetical Growth Trend of Grain Production and the Prospect of Food Deficiency

On the basis of the adjusted figures for 1950–57 in Table VII-2, a linear trend can be fitted by least squares. The trend equation is $Yc = 180.644 + 0.373X$ ($X = O$ in 1950 as base). Based on the projected trend values, an estimate of the deficiency between the trend value and any projected consumption requirement can then

[13] *People's Daily,* October 6, November 2, and December 21, 1958; October 7 and 20, 1959; February 6, 1960.

[14] Naum Jasny, *The Socialized Agriculture of the U.S.S.R.* (Stanford, Calif., 1949), pp. 548 and 744.

[15] *T'ung-chi Kung-tso (Statistical Work),* No. 19, 1957.

be made. Similarly, one could ascertain the gap between the trend value and actual grain production, which fell considerably below the trend during the years of agricultural crisis.

TABLE VII-3. COMPARISON BETWEEN ADJUSTED ESTIMATES OF GRAIN PRODUCTION AND TREND VALUE

Production Year	Adjusted Estimate of Grain Production (1)	Estimated Trend Value (2)	Total Hypothetical Consumption Requirement of Following Year (3)	Deviation of Estimated Production from Trend[a] (2)—(1)	Shortfall of Trend Below Consumption Requirement (3)—(2)
1950	180	180.6	172.6	+.6	—8.0
1951	183	181.0	175.9	—2.0	—5.1
1952	184	181.4	179.2	—2.6	—2.2
1953	180	181.8	181.7	+1.8	—.1
1954	177	182.1	184.3	+5.1	+2.1
1955	184	182.5	188.9	—1.5	+6.4
1956	182	182.9	194.9	+.9	+12.0
1957	185	183.3	200.0	—1.7	+16.7
1958	175	183.7	204.4	+8.7	+20.7
1959	154	184.0	208.7	+30.0	+24.7
1960	130	184.4	212.1	+54.4	+27.7
1961	140	184.8	214.8	+44.8	+30.0
1962	160	185.2	217.6	+25.2	+32.4
1963	183[b]	185.6[b]	220.0	+2.6	+34.4

[a] Indicates actual production falling short of trend value.

[b] Preliminary. The 1964 harvest has been reported at about 200 (probably rounded) million tons. See Edgar Snow's report of his interview with Mao Tse-tung in *The New Republic,* February 27, 1965.

Col. 1: Table VII-2.

Col. 2: Computed from equation.

Col. 3: 1950–55, Cols. (1)—[(6)+(3)] in Table VII-2.

1956–63, estimated at 245 kg. of processed grain per adult and 20 per cent of gross output for uses other than direct consumption as food.

As for the future, the growth of the consumption requirement would depend largely upon the rate of population increase and the obvious need to maintain a minimum level of consumption, plus a certain degree of steady improvement. From the point of view of increasing production above the estimated 1962 barn crop of 160 million tons, the required increase may be treated as the net result of a two-part effort—first, recovery to the trend level, and, secondly, increase over and above the trend value, or what is tantamount to a revision of the trend. The latter part of the increase in production would have to be predicated upon a new departure in farm technology.

Competing Uses of Land

The preceding discussion has concerned itself with the problem of measuring the actual and reported gain in the production of food crops. Superimposed upon the problems attending food production is the related issue of allocating land among different competing claims. A special case of the problem is the allocation of land between food-grain production and cotton production. Up to 1955 at any rate, when collectivization was not yet complete, adjustment in allocation was accomplished by manipulating the parity ratio between individual food crops, on the one hand, and cotton, on the other. The parity ratio was employed in determining the rate at which cotton farmers should pay the agricultural tax computed in terms of grain and in exchanging cotton for grain through the government-sponsored marketing agencies. With the end of the First Five-Year Plan and the onset of the Great Leap Forward, Communist policy stressed the production of food crops at the expense of other crops. Thus the problem of whether the cotton acreage should be radically changed has been largely obscured.

However, in the light of the large imports of food since 1961, one may legitimately raise the question of the available alternatives. Would it be better to produce more food at home at the expense of cotton? The cotton might then be imported, or it might be replaced by artificial fibers, plants for the production of which might in turn be imported. Or would it be better to produce more cotton at the expense of food, export cotton textiles, and import more food? Would the principle of autarky rule out the latter alternative even if it should prove to be more advantageous, since self-sufficiency in food is regarded as being of transcendental importance? How would one determine the relative advantage of any activity unless all costs and prices are given? The last point then raises the question of the determination and use of land rent and the degree of flexibility permitted in regulating prices according to supply and demand. It is doubtful that the Communist

Chinese planners have fully appreciated this particular manifestation of the problem of resource allocation in agriculture.

Productivity and Institutional Change

Returning to the contention that institutional change would increase labor productivity and therefore output per man *as well as* per unit area, one may now inquire whether actual experience has borne out this hypothesis. The redistributed land and the small owner cultivators created during the land-reform period constituted such a brief and transitory stage that there was no basis for a real comparison with the previous record. However,

TABLE VII-4. COMPARATIVE DATA ON CROP YIELDS
(*In kilograms per hectare*)

	1952 Communist China	1955 Communist China	1931–37 Average China Proper	1929–33 Most Frequent Yields Mainland China
Paddy	2,445	2,674	2,532	3,273–3,384
Wheat	735	858	1,078	1,077–1,213
Corn	1,343 ⎫		1,379	1,321
Kaoliang	1,178 ⎬	1,047[a]	1,366	1,279
Millet	1,140 ⎭		1,178[b]	1,178[b]
Tubers (original weight)	7,500[c]	7,516[c]	7,900	5,837

SOURCES: 1952, *K'o-hsüeh T'ung-pao* (*Science Bulletin*), No. 5 (1954); 1955, computed from *Jen-min Shou-ts'e* (*People's Handbook*), 1957, pp. 470–71; 1931–37, T. H. Shen, *op. cit.*; 1929–33, John Lossing Buck, *Land Utilization in China*, 1937, pp. 224–25.

[a] Miscellaneous grains
[b] Weighted average of millet and proso millet
[c] Mostly sweet potatoes

available estimates of yield per hectare in 1955, when a considerable number of cooperative farms were already in existence, showed that the results were generally unfavorable in comparison with the average yields of 1931–37 for China proper (with the exception of paddy rice), and that it was uniformly unfavorable in comparison with the most frequent yields in 1929–33.

In terms of the farmer's income, Liao Lu-yen, Communist China's Minister of Agriculture, stated in early 1958 that about 30 per cent of the agricultural cooperatives in China (46 per cent of the cooperatives in some provinces) had by then *caught up* with local "well-to-do middle peasants" in their production level and that 20 per cent of the cooperatives in China had caught up with the local "well-to-do middle peasants" in income standard.[16] It should be noted in passing that in pre-Communist China the "middle peasants" were the little farmers whose farms were too small to be efficient. As a whole, according to Liao, by early 1958 (before the establishment of the communes), 20–30 per cent of the cooperatives in China had reached the level of the "well-to-do middle peasants." Furthermore, according to a November, 1957, study, surveys of agricultural cooperatives of different types in various places showed that the grain output per unit area of the "well-to-do middle peasants" was generally about 20 per cent higher than that of the newly established cooperatives, and that the former's per-capita income was about 30 per cent higher than the corresponding figure in the cooperatives.[17]

Inasmuch as statistics of yield and income under the commune became exceedingly unreliable, and inasmuch as the sharp decline in agricultural, and particularly grain, output began in 1959, any comparison of yield and labor productivity based on these statistics with corresponding data under the cooperative system would be misleading. However, because of the undeniable agricultural crisis, one would assume that the communes definitely failed to evoke any real increase in output, even though there may have been a large rise of labor input during the early phase of the commune movement in 1958–59. The prodigious expenditure of labor in irrigation, deep-plowing, and the application of fertilizers is well known and may be obtained from a number of sample studies.[18]

Apparently the cooperative farm did not succeed in raising unit area yield. On the other hand, from the point of view of the Communist authorities, it did offer two advantages over the individual farm. First, the formation of the cooperative farm thwarted any tendency toward the emergence of a new "rich peasant" class, which probably would have occurred had the

[16] *Hsüeh-hsi (Study)*, No. 3, February, 1958.
[17] *Cheng-chih Hsüeh-hsi (Political Study)*, No. 11, November, 1957.
[18] See, for instance, the report on the Hung-kuang people's commune in the *People's Daily*, April 18, 1959.

owner-cultivators created under the land reform been left to their own devices.[19] Ideologically and politically, this was a significant advantage from the point of view of the Communist Party. In the second place, on the basis of an income study undertaken in 1957 covering 228 agricultural cooperatives in 24 provinces, it was found that communal accumulation (including possibly proceeds from the government's compulsory purchases applied to reduce existing indebtedness to the government), together with additions to share capital in the cooperative, and work performed on construction projects without pay constituted some 15 per cent of income (i.e., the sum of the same items and personal income distributed to the commune members).[20] This relatively high, though perhaps still inadequate, rural saving-income ratio in the cooperative was probably one of the reasons why the Communist authorities decided to accelerate the completion of the cooperative-farm movement in 1956 (although it had originally been scheduled for 1958) and to maintain an even higher ratio. At the same time, according to the same survey, the per-capita personal income was probably around 48 to 56 yuan a year. This may be compared with a per-capita rural income of 58 yuan in 1931–36 at prewar prices.[21] Thus one may assume that the accelerated transition to the cooperative farm was due to the desire to increase the rate of saving in the agricultural sector, while the failure for production to rise in spite of the larger operating units (compared with the individual farm) was a result of inexperience, poorly directed production planning, and adverse effects of the cooperative form of organization on incentive.

The formation of the cooperative farm meant that persons who had hitherto been underemployed but had been supported by other members of their households could no longer be so supported in the cooperatives because of the latter's need for stricter cost accounting. In the circumstances, there was a large-scale population movement from the villages to the cities. Accordingly, increased pressure was felt by the authorities to accelerate the creation of alternative forms of employment. It is quite possible that this consideration may have contributed to the subsequent

[19] The March 22, 1957, issue of the *People's Daily* reported a number of instances of the disbanding of cooperative farms and of peasant withdrawals. For a discussion on this phase of collectivization, see Cheng Chu-yüan, *Communist China's Economy, 1949–1962* (Seton Hall, 1963), p. 36.

[20] See also the section on the investment-income ratio in Chapter V.

[21] Yuan-li Wu, *op. cit.*, 1961, p. 25.

decision to develop rural industry in the commune as a part of the small-industry movement.

The commune in its turn was significant as a form of organization of the labor force. It increased labor mobility and expanded the size of the labor force, which could now be engaged in agricultural as well as nonagricultural activities on an around-the-clock, full-employment basis. However, as mentioned earlier, the operating unit of farming in the commune was the "production brigade," which corresponded roughly to the cooperative farm in size. Thus the economic justification of the commune did not lie in any expected increase in farm size, but rather in the expansion of labor-intensive, nonagricultural projects and the much higher saving-income ratio which the commune made possible.

In practice, however, because of poor cost-accounting practices in the communes, the employment of unpaid labor, and the high mobility of labor, many of the industrial and agricultural projects begun in the commune were not completed.[22] Labor was shifted from one type of work to another, and the administrators failed to realize that such shifts, though entailing no monetary expenditure, did incur "opportunity costs," consisting of the unfinished work elsewhere. Deep-plowing, irrigation work, collection and application of manure, collection and transportation of ore for the "backyard iron furnaces," and many other demanding tasks were all extremely costly in terms of labor input. At the same time, direction of farm work by centralized directives proved to be not only ineffective but actually damaging. While poor weather conditions may have played their part in the reduction of agricultural output in 1959 and the later years, mismanagement under the commune and an incentive crisis attributable equally to the communal form of organization and the high saving-income ratio were the true culprits. This explains why the major effort—which began in 1961 and was redoubled in 1962—to revitalize agriculture has essentially consisted of some radical modifications of the commune system.

Reorganization of the Commune and the Production and Distribution System

As a result of subdivision, the number of communes increased from 24,000 to nearly 100,000 in 1962, while the number of pro-

[22] See also Chapter VIII below.

duction brigades rose to 500,000.[23] This resulted in changing the average size of the commune to 1,150 households each and that of the production brigade to 230 households each. The decrease in the size of the commune is symptomatic of some very radical and far-reaching changes which took place during 1961–62.

First, in May, 1961, a new set of regulations governing the organization of the commune was promulgated by the authorities. These regulations were introduced to bring some degree of uniformity to the diverse developments which had occurred in communes in different parts of the country since the winter of 1960. In the last quarter of 1961, both the commune and the production brigade were further downgraded. Finally, in September, 1962, the decision was handed down from the Communist Party of China to continue its new policy of emphasizing the "production team" while at the same time calling for the consolidation of the spirit of collectivization in the agricultural sector.

In order to understand the significance of these changes, the mid-1961 regulations with respect to ownership of property, control over the use of the means of production, decision-making in implementation, and the principles and methods employed in distributing output should be studied. In summary, these regulations provided for the concentration of decision-making on production in the hands of the peasants below the commune level, the curtailment of the powers of the commune, which had led to the abuse of labor mobility and frequent changes in production plans, restoration of some private production for their own account by the peasants, the determination of the peasants' compensation more closely in line with the amount of work performed, and an increase in the ratios of consumption to income and of monetary compensation to rations in kind. However, as the *People's Daily* stated in August, 1961,[24] as of that time, the production brigade still remained as the independent accounting unit, in contrast to the smaller production team which had again assumed its precollectivization role as the basic unit in organizing production.

A further step was taken in January, 1962, when the official press took the line that agricultural recovery depended upon the "productive activism" of the masses and that this could be accomplished only through the Communist Party's policy to employ

[23] *New China Yearbook*, Tokyo, July 1962, pp. 19–20.
[24] *People's Daily*, August 29, 1961.

the production team as the accounting unit.[25] The same paper then spoke of the overexpansion of the production brigade that had led to "egalitarianism" in distributing output to the detriment of incentive. Apparently, following this further revision of policy, distribution becomes vested in the hands of the production team. The team now owns both the land and the greater part of the equipment and draught animals it uses. These changes are said to be desirable because, until mechanization can become the rule, the smaller production and distribution units would be more adapted to the present stage of development of Chinese agriculture. Thus the reversal of policy really represents an effort to return to a production unit corresponding more closely to the larger farm of the pre-Communist period while attempts are made to preserve the necessary ideological framework and government control required. Except for a small number of areas, the production team became the basic accounting as well as production unit in 1963.

Unfortunately for the Communist planners, a dilemma between incentive and government control remains. As the *Southern Daily* of Canton stated on April 6, 1963, "Some well-to-do middle peasants have said, 'The government needs only to control the collection and purchasing of grain; it should not bother about how agricultural production is done.' . . . The new and old upper middle peasants have a comparatively strong spontaneous tendency toward capitalism." If such a spontaneous tendency is to be combated, would the need for ideological control interfere with the provision of adequate incentives and the restoration of production?

Technological Improvements in Agriculture

During the 1958–59 commune movement and the concomitant drive to increase crop production, emphasis was placed on the more intensive application of labor input in the form of more irrigation works, more deep plowing, more application of natural fertilizer and compost, closer planting, and continuous field supervision. While some of these measures were efforts to improve the methods of cultivation, they rested on the traditional technological base. In contrast, the effort to bring about agricultural recovery since 1961 has been concentrated on more radical tech-

[25] *People's Daily*, January 1, 1962.

nological improvements, particularly the electrification of irrigation facilities, a greater degree of mechanization, and more
intensive use of chemical fertilizers.

One estimate puts the size of irrigated land in 1962–63 at about
50 million hectares.[26] Of these, the total area that could be irrigated by electrically operated pumping facilities in 1962 would
probably amount to 4.8 million hectares, as compared with 3.3
million hectares at the end of 1961.[27] The 1962 estimate is based
on a utilization rate of 3.2 hectares per kilowatt of pumping
facility and 1.5 million kilowatts of electrical pumping equipment. In 1963, the area of irrigated land possessing electrically
operated pumping facilities was probably around 6.4 million
hectares.[28]

A so-called mechanization program in agriculture has thus far
consisted of an increase in the number of tractors available. In
terms of 15-horsepower standard units, the number increased
from 59,000 units in 1959 to 81,000 in 1960, 90,000 in 1961, and
approximately 100,000 at the end of 1962.[29] A number of these
were operated by tractor stations, 390 of which were set up during 1953–57.[30] As of 1960 year end, 28,000 tractors were employed
in the 2,490 large state farms, which averaged 2,100 hectares
each.[31]

Since, according to Chinese reports, a standard tractor can
cultivate only about 100 hectares of land, the increment in hectares that can be machine-cultivated during the 1961–62 period
was extremely small. Some of the large state farms, where the
degree of mechanization is higher, have reported an increase in
labor productivity as high as 70 per cent when the comparison

[26] *Kung-jen Jih-pao (The Worker's Daily)*, Peking, March 8, 1961, reported
an increase in irrigated area of 20 million hectares in 1958–60, which, when
added to a total of 34.7 million hectares in 1957, gives a new total of 54.7
million hectares.

[27] *People's Daily*, October 23, 1961.

[28] NCNA, April 12, 1963.

[29] *Far Eastern Economic Review*, Hong Kong, XXXIX, No. 7 (February
14, 1963), 309–10, and *China Weekly*, Hong Kong, No. 515, November,
1962, pp. 175–82.

[30] Leslie T. C. Kuo, "Agricultural Mechanization in Communist China,"
The China Quarterly, No. 17, 1964, London, pp. 134–50.

[31] See Wang Cheng, "Chia-ch'iang Kuo-yin Nung-ch'ang ti Chien-she"
("Strengthen the Construction of State Farms"), *Hung-ch'i (Red Flag)*, No. 7,
1961, p. 1.

is made between "semimechanization" and the employment of traditional farm implements, and another 150 per cent more if the comparison is between "semimechanization" and "mechanization." On the other hand, by far the most important role of the machine-manufacturing enterprises, many of which have been assigned to the specific task of aiding agriculture, has been the production of simple farm implements, although some of these may be of improved design. The same enterprises have been kept busy in repair work. Reports from different parts of the country often tell of unskilled handling of machinery and indifferent maintenance and high replacement requirements, complicated by the existence of machines of many different makes.

Finally, domestic production of chemical fertilizers in 1958 was less than 1 million tons, while import at the time amounted to about 1.5 million tons. Production in 1962 was approximately 2 million tons, while output in 1963 was probably 2.6 million tons. Imports were 1.2 million tons in 1962, and 1.7 million tons in 1963.

These tentative and sketchy statistics would seem to show that the ascertainable quantitative effect of the "technological revolution" on the 1962 and 1963 harvests was not particularly significant. The 10–15 per cent increase in grain output during 1961–62 and the probably greater increase in 1962–63, both of which fell well below the trend values, could not therefore be attributed to the beneficial effects of the technological improvements. On the other hand, any large increase above the trend values in the future would have to be predicated upon technological improvements. On the basis of projected population increments, it should then not be too difficult for Communist China's planners to forecast the demand for investment in chemical fertilizers, fertilizer plants, other farm chemicals, and electric and other equipment necessary for the continued expansion of mechanization and electrification. What this would mean in terms of foreign-exchange requirement and the country's residual import capacity for other purposes can thus be derived.

It is entirely conceivable that because of the needs of the agricultural sector, the availability of exchange may become the effective constraint to the import of industrial equipment and raw materials other than those destined for the agricultural sector. Consequently, success in agricultural recovery may become a prerequisite of economic growth in general. The alternative of importing food would be even more expensive unless large non-

agricultural exports can be developed. Such a development, however, cannot be expected to take place without further industrial
expansion, which is precluded by assumption in the absence of
greater growth in agriculture.

CHAPTER VIII

Fluctuations and Growth

Fluctuations in Income and Employment

A fundamental criticism often leveled by Marxists and others against the market economy and the system of private enterprise is the latter's susceptibility to economic instability. The recurrence, if not regular periodicity, of these fluctuations and the tendency for unemployment and shrinking profits to become increasingly severe will, according to the protagonists of central planning and socialism, eventually bring about the collapse of the capitalist economy. Furthermore, according to the Marxists, the tendency for the profit rate to decline underlies the frenetic drive of capitalist economies to seek external markets, a development which inevitably leads to colonial expansion and war.

Once a centrally planned, socialist economy has been established, it is generally assumed by the planners that unemployment will cease to exist. For the planning boards would never plan for anything less than full employment, although today "full employment" tends to mean something different from the absence of involuntary unemployment at the going wage rate. Instead, there might be involuntary employment. An implicit assumption is that there would never be any divergence between the realized and the planned state of affairs. However, even if we were to grant the greater ease with which effective demand can be sustained in a command economy, is it really true that divergence between the plan and the actual state of the economy can never be such as to cause significant fluctuations in income and employment?

Estimates of the gross domestic product of Communist China in 1952–62 have shown an increase from 75.6 billion yuan in 1952 to 120.7 billion in 1960, followed by a decline of 82.1 billion in

1961. From 1961 to 1962, there may have been a substantial recovery, which occurred especially during the latter part of 1962. A preliminary estimate of the gross domestic product on the basis of one study has placed it at 109 billion yuan in 1962. The sharp decline in 1960–61 was in the neighborhood of 31 per cent—that is, on a scale comparable to the 30 per cent decline of the GNP of the United States in 1929–33 during the Great Depression. There were indeed two principal differences between the Chinese "Great Slide" and the Great Depression of the United States. The latter was less precipitate. The 30 per cent decline of the U.S. GNP spread over a period of four years, whereas the Chinese output fell similarly in perhaps a little over one year. Second, the decline was much greater in investment than in consumption in the United States, whereas, in Communist China, it was consumption that suffered most.[1]

Furthermore, even official reports from Communist China have related from time to time stories of large population movements from one sector of the economy to another. The intensified collectivization process in 1955–56 coincided with one such major migratory movement of peasants to the cities in search of food and employment. The collapse of the Great Leap Forward brought on another massive population flight. The first could probably be interpreted simply as the conversion of disguised unemployment to open unemployment.[2] The second was plainly not an example of ordinary "frictional unemployment" that could not be readily averted under conditions of economic change. Thus, it would seem, depressions do occur even in a planned, Communist society.

The next question is whether we can go beyond such a simple statement. Is it conceivable that the Chinese "depression" of 1960–62 was "inevitable" in the sense that it was a necessary outcome of what had transpired earlier? Is there a "business cycle" that would fit the development model of Communist China?

[1] Yuan-li Wu *et al., The Economic Potential of Communist China,* I (Menlo Park, Calif.: Stanford Research Institute, 1963), Tables 51 and 90.
[2] The number of urban employed of "workers and staff" at the end of 1956 was reported at 24.7 million persons. Of the latter, 640,000 were ordered to return to the villages in 1957. Ministry of Justice, Bureau of Investigation, *Kung-fei Ti-i-ko Wu-nien-chi-hua chih Yen-chiu* (A *Study on the Communist First Five-Year Plan*) (Taipei, 1958), pp. 321–22. The scale of forcible migration or relocation from urban to rural areas in 1961–62 reached many millions.

The Rates of Growth, Planned versus Feasible

As we have pointed out in Chapter I, all economic planners, including those of Communist China, tend to have some preconceived ideas of what constitutes a desirable rate of growth. Since in the initial stage of the evolution of economic plans the scope of planning is usually limited to a few sectors of the economy, this planned rate of growth tends to be a "partial rate." As economic development proceeds, additional sectors of the economy are usually brought under the framework of planning and closer control. The process is marked by an increase in the number of products or industrial branches for which control figures are issued.

In the case of Communist China, the First Five-Year Plan was not really completely formulated until 1955, and it was decidedly limited in scope at the beginning. Even as late as 1956, when the Second Five-Year Plan was submitted to the Eighth National Congress of the Communist Party, Chou En-lai was still rather imprecise about the degree to which Communist China's national income would be increased by the time the Second Five-Year Plan was completed. Yet at the same time he was able to indicate a doubling of the industrial output by 1962 above the 1957 planned level as the target for the Second Five-Year Plan. This would seem to mean that the planners envisage a fairly definite desired rate of expansion for the industrial and related sectors but that they have only an imprecise conception of the minimum desirable rate of growth for the entire national output.

Again, as discussed earlier, the planned rate of growth is determined by (1) what the planners regard as feasible and (2) what they deem to be desirable. Their conception of the feasible rate of growth is in turn determined by what has been accomplished in the past both in the domestic economy and in other countries in comparable circumstances. At the time of the Second Five-Year Plan, the desired rate of industrial expansion was doubtless influenced by the actual rate of expansion during the first five-year period as perceived by the planners. Furthermore, the experience of the Soviet Union during its first few five-year plans was also a source of reference for the Chinese. On the other hand, what is regarded as desirable is often conceived in terms of overtaking a rival. Such a rival must be represented by a country which could conceivably be overtaken. Thus in 1958, Communist

China strove to overtake the United Kingdom in aggregate (not per capita) output in the industrial sector in a period of fifteen years. This target was employed by Chinese planners in the same way as the overtaking of the United States has been used by Soviet planners, that is, as a remote objective and as a point of political exhortation.

The target-setting process described above has two implications. In the first place, the higher the rate of growth attained in the past, the higher tends to be the future planned rate of growth. There is almost an irresistible inducement to set a future rate of growth that is at least as high as before, if not higher. The ideological and nationalistic ambitions that demand rapid industrialization conspire to bring about an acceleration of the planned rate of expansion. In the second place, once a foreign rival has been chosen, there is also the tendency to try to overtake him at an accelerated rate. The existence of these built-in tendencies to speed up the planned rate of growth was amply demonstrated in Communist China by the frequent and continual upward revisions of production and investment targets.

In the absence of perfect foresight or coincidence, there is no reason why the planned rate of growth would necessarily equal the maximum feasible rate that can be attained and sustained under "normal" conditions. In fact, the higher the planned rate of expansion, the greater is the danger that it would exceed the maximum feasible rate and the more likely it is for the actual or realized rate of expansion to fall below both the planned rate and the maximum feasible rate.

Several factors should be included under the assumption of "normal conditions." First, under "normal conditions" are implied certain specific expectations about the availability of foreign aid which does not have to be paid for out of the current output. In the case of Communist China, the total amount of foreign aid has been relatively modest, and Chinese planners would at any rate prefer to achieve development with self-sufficiency. Following the curtailment of Soviet technical and material assistance in 1960, self-reliance has been the dominant theme of Chinese economic planning. Secondly, under "normal conditions" is assumed the maintenance of a consumption level that, while consistent with the rate of investment envisaged and with government consumption plans, is at the same time high enough to obviate any serious loss of incentive which might result in a reduction of production or in political and social unrest. In the third place, "normal conditions" imply that the "product mix" in the national output would be such as to enable the planners to realize their specific investment and production plans. As a minimum, this condition would be satisfied if the different sectors of the economy would develop in reasonable balance within the framework of certain planned targets based on a system of preconceived but enforceable priorities, so that shortage in any sector could be accommodated by substitution or minor readjustments in the production plan. Where capital goods that are not produced at home are concerned, this condition would be satisfied if exportable goods and services are always available and can be disposed of externally at appropriate prices, so that the necessary imports could be obtained. Where goods can be and are produced at home, the same assumption would imply the existence of a sufficiently high degree of substitutability of various factors of production, so that a shortfall in any one sector could be met by substitution with a different product or input withdrawn from a less important industry or sector. Conversely, there must be sufficient stocks of goods in existence which could be drawn upon to meet shortfalls in current production without seriously impairing the future potential of the economy.

Under these so-called "normal conditions," the maximum feasible rate of growth of the entire economy would be defined by the availability and quality of the labor force, the existence of natural resources in adequate quantities, the technical production functions, and the possibility of maintaining a desired rate of aggregate investment. These general determinants of the rate of growth are further supplemented by such factors as increase in labor productivity, technological improvements, and the increasing skill of labor. Furthermore, the maximum feasible rate of growth may be altered as a result of changes in the primary determinants.

Deviations Between the Actual and the Planned Rates of Growth

In the normal course of things, investment plans are sometimes delayed and production may fall behind schedule. Other unexpected contingencies that would delay production may also occur. Furthermore, where planning is limited to a few sectors of the economy, failure to realize the plan may occur as a result of disproportion originating in the sectors left outside of the plan. Whatever the cause of the failure, such failures are bound to occur from time to time in a world of uncertainty. When the original planning is based on an exaggerated conception of what is feasible, possibly because of built-in upward biases in the statistical reports of past accomplishments, plan failures are all the more likely. When they do occur, new ways have to be found to readjust the plan.

Import of goods to substitute for products that have not been produced is one possible method of readjustment. A second one is the withdrawal from inventory where stocks are available. A third alternative is to pass the shortfall to a less important sector of the economy by redirecting the supply of inputs. Where disinvestment of foreign assets is not practicable either because of difficulties encountered in rearranging import schedules under bilateral trade agreements or because of shortage of foreign exchange, only the other two alternatives can be considered.

Where stock withdrawal can be employed to meet a production shortfall, the planners would have certain advantages. If the planners are able to use *surplus* inventory over and above the minimum amount required for a given level of output, while the consumption of such surplus inventory in production would amount to disinvestment and, therefore, a reduction of the total output of the period, the inventory reduction would nevertheless not necessitate a reduction of the capacity to produce in subsequent periods. That is to say, the planners are under no obligation to rebuild inventory to the previous surplus level. The expansion plans for subsequent periods can therefore be carried out without any alteration of the original planned rate of growth even though, because of the reduction of inventory in the preceding period, the economy would be more vulnerable from now on to further shocks of the same kind. Since a shortage that occurred in a preceding period was absorbed by inventory reduction, surplus inventory has been eliminated, and in the absence of such surplus, it might become necessary to withdraw resources from other activities.

There are, however, certain specific limitations which tend to reduce the possibility of employing inventory withdrawal as a corrective measure. First, certain services and products cannot normally be stockpiled. One of the most important factors is electric power, which in most cases is an indispensable input in industrial production. In the second place, faulty data may create shortages. Stocks that are available on paper may turn out to be nonexistent or they may not be available at places where they are supposed to be according to records. In the third place, in underdeveloped countries which are intent on maintaining as high a rate of production as possible, "goods in process" in the "production pipeline" are usually kept at a minimum so that the ratio of working capital to output is usually kept as low as possible. Lastly, available inventories may be inappropriately distributed geographically, so that deficits at some places cannot be met by surpluses located elsewhere.

What has been said of the ratio between inventory of raw materials and production would also apply to the ratio of equipment held in reserve to total available equipment. The constant demand for the full utilization of existing equipment has the effect of making the economy more vulnerable to the emergence of specific shortages. If lack of surplus inventory or of excess capacity or the inability to hold a commodity in stock or poor geographical and interplant distribution should lead to an inflexibility of response in those sectors of the economy which suffer from sudden shortages, the planners would be forced to resort to imports or to shifting the shortage and the readjustment problem to other, less important, sectors. The case of the underdeveloped economy is particularly marked by the small number of its modern industrial branches and therefore the limited substitutability it enjoys of industrial goods of the same nature. Its shortage of foreign exchange also limits its recourse to imports. Thus the emergence of a serious shortage in an important sector of the economy is often resolved by shifting the adjustment to the least important sector. More frequently than not, the least important sector in an economy bent on industrialization and economic expansion is the sector of the consumer.

However, the level of consumption, especially when it is barely sufficient to provide for minimum maintenance, may have a direct relationship to labor productivity. Any reduction of consumption below the minimum, or even the failure of an anticipated increase in consumption, may result in a reduction of output in the subsequent period. Thus, it is entirely possible for the disruption of the production plan in any one sector to lead to a drop in productivity and output, not only in the given period, but also in subsequent periods.

Even with the possible reduction of consumption as a result of the transfer of resources from the consumption sector to the economic sector or sectors that suffered the initial shortfall, it may nevertheless be impossible to maintain output in the latter. This means that the curtailment of consumption as a part of the adjustment process would still be accompanied by a decline of investment below the planned level. Thus production in subsequent periods would suffer not only because of the adverse effect on productivity due to the decline of consumption, but also because of the failure to maintain investment and expansion plans as originally conceived.

Once a slowdown of the rate of expansion has occurred, there would be a strong inducement for the planners to raise the rate of investment in subsequent periods in order to make up for lost time. Such a decision would tend to add to the stress and strain of the economic system. It would tend to enhance the vulnerability of the system through possible miscalculation, mismanagement, and external shocks. The adverse incentive effect, together with errors of other types, may then create even more serious shortages and thus aggravate the decline of the rate of growth. In case of a further decline in the rate of growth or of an actual downturn of the absolute level of output, the gap between the planned and the actual rates of growth would widen. How long this disequilibrium (or failure to achieve the "plan of balances") would last would depend partly upon the speed with which the planners might (1) realize their error and (2) act upon this realization by readjusting the planned rate of growth downward to correspond to the actual rate. Here the lack of an adequate statistical collection and communication apparatus, including computing tools, of underdeveloped countries such as Communist China would accentuate the difficulty and generally prolong the time which must elapse before a correction can be made.

The downward adjustment of the planned rate of growth toward the actual rate would usher in a period of readjustment and consolidation and offer the economy a breathing space. During this time, bottlenecks and shortages would be resolved and incentive lags remedied. Once this process has been completed, it is then possible for the rate of expansion to be resumed at a higher level, preceded of course by the arrest of the decline. In adjusting the planned rate of growth downward toward the actual rate, the planners may bring it to below the maximum feasible rate of growth. In the short run, this may be unavoidable and necessary because of the temporary reduction of the maximum feasible rate during a crisis. If the original planned rate was set accurately at the potentially feasible rate as we have defined it, reduction of the planned rate would necessarily bring it to below the potential rate. Thus an overcorrection occurs, and a reversal of the decline would follow once the initial difficulties have been resolved. If, on the other hand, the original planned rate was set at a level above the potential rate, reduction of the planned rate to the level of the actual rate which has by now fallen to below the potential rate would also cause the planned rate to be lower than the potential rate.

Another reason for a renewed expansion is that some of the initial shock that occurs because of the sudden emergence of the shortfall may have been caused simply by delays in the completion of certain construction projects. Once the delays have been eliminated and the investment projects come to fruition, we might find the economy entering into a phase when the realized rate of expansion actually exceeds the planned rate. The same kind of discrepancy must also arise as a result of occasional "favorable shocks" or "windfalls," such as bumper crops. If the actual rate of growth should exceed the planned rate, in the short run, even an unplanned increase in consumption may result. Should this occur, there might be an increase in productivity, leading therefore to a cumulative increase in the rate of growth in subsequent periods. Such a process would then increase the gap between the actual rate of growth and the readjusted planned rate until an upward revision of the latter takes place. Increase in the planned rate would bring about an increase in investment, raising the latter to a level above that which would correspond to the potential rate sustainable at the level of output obtained prior to the windfall. If the windfall does not lead to an enduring increase in productivity or some favorable and permanent shift of the production function, the emergence of plan nonfulfillment in the future would again become inevitable. In this manner, it is possible to build an economic model of continual instability in which the actual rate of growth fluctuates around the planned rate while the planned rate is shifted periodically, but almost always with some delay, thus making the fluctuations so much the greater.

Conditions Underlying Cyclical Fluctuations in Communist China

The preceding cyclical model has been constructed on the basis of Chinese experience in 1952–62, although it may be of more general applicability. Specifically, to recapitulate, the conditions that have brought the experience of Communist China in line with the model requirements are (1) an increasingly rising planned rate of economic development, (2) a partial approach toward economic planning in which the sector of output devoted to consumption has been treated as a residual, (3) built-in biases in statistical information on agricultural as well as modern industrial output which resulted in exaggeration of the realized rate of growth perceived by the planners, thus causing the latter to raise the planned rate of growth repeatedly, (4) the absence of an adequate and properly distributed inventory, aggravated by transportation difficulties and inaccurate accounting, in order to cushion shortfalls that occur in the economic system, (5) the inadequate development of certain industries, such as the generation of electric power, the output of which could not be stored, (6) the existence of relatively few modern industries and industrial enterprises, as is characteristic of most underdeveloped economies in their early phases of development, to provide for greater flexibility in substitution when an unexpected plan failure occurs in any one sector, (7) the low level of personal consumption maintained under the Communist regime which makes any decrease in consumption a very serious matter with adverse effects on labor incentive and productivity, (8) the emergence of a number of shocks to the economic system which occurred during the Great Leap, (9) a delay in the collection and processing of statistical data, which led to the postponement of the recognition of the economic crisis and the subsequent plan revision, and (10) the unlimited confidence of the Chinese planners and their belief that ideology and faith were a substitute for balanced economic growth and modern technology. Among the shocks to the economic system that occurred were (a) faulty planning due to the failure to account for opportunity cost under the commune, which in turn led to an abuse of labor mobility and nonfulfillment of production plans in many sectors, (b) an exaggerated estimate of grain production in 1958, leading to an erroneous downward revision of the production plan in 1959, (c) the adverse incentive effect of the method of income distribution and reorganization of family life in the commune, (d) the naïve and exaggerated hope that the small-industry drive could technically be a substitute for modern technology, (e) Soviet withdrawal of technical assistance and delayed Soviet shipments of machinery needed for Chinese construction projects, and (f) the deliberate policy of Mao Tse-tung to adopt the "big-push" approach during the Great Leap in order to accomplish what he thought was a wavelike progression, which might resemble the process of historical change envisaged in the Marxist-Hegelian theory of history.

Finally, it should be noted that there are certain elements of asymmetry which would prevent the opposing phases of the cycle from being an exact replica of each other. First, during an upswing, there is a tendency to accelerate the planned rate of growth on the part of the planners. On the other hand, when a downswing threatens, no corresponding psychological compulsion exists to adjust the planned rate downward in order to head off the downturn. On the contrary, the tendency is to delay and eventually to make adjustments that are not quite sufficient to restore sectoral balance. Secondly, while any decrease in consumption below the bare maintenance level may promptly reduce incentive and productivity at the upper turning point, an increase in consumption from an exceedingly depressed level may have a salutary effect only after the passage of considerable time. The passage of time is required in order to permit any increase in consumption to achieve credibility and to correct the debility and resentment of the workers. In the third place, during a downswing, various sectors of the economy would be affected in different degrees. Disinvestment may take place in some sectors even though the net investment may be positive. The subsequent upswing may therefore be delayed until a protracted period of relative stability has passed during which the sectoral disinvestments are made good. This would seem to apply especially to the agricultural sector of the Chinese economy. Thus the duration of the two major phases of the cycle would not necessarily be the same. Last but not least, the intensity of the decline in a downswing may become so great that political stability would be threatened, thus making recovery under the same regime indeterminate. That is to say, long-term equilibrium at a low level of employment and output may become extremely difficult.

Once the downswing has been arrested, it is of course possible for windfalls to speed up the recovery process. Such windfalls may consist of the completion of investment plans that had been cut off as a result of overcorrection. A second factor may be the unexpected availability of external credits. A bumper crop would constitute a third category of windfalls. An unexpected, important technological innovation may be another. These are some of the positive factors that may regenerate an upswing of the economy.

Factors Underlying Long-term Growth

From the above it should be possible to deduce some of the basic conditions under which cyclical fluctuations might be averted. Perhaps a key to these conditions would be the selection of a planned rate of growth more in line with the maximum feasible rate. Some of the additional implications are: (1) scrupulous avoidance of overacceleration of the planned rate of growth, (2) better collection and processing of statistics that would not exaggerate the accomplished rate of expansion, (3) deliberate and careful maintenance of sectoral balance through, for instance, the use of input-output tables, (4) the treatment of the consumption sector as one of the major plan targets rather than as a residual, (5) maintenance of high quality in production, so that the products of any sector can really be depended upon as effective inputs of other sectors, and (6) enlargement of the range of substitution between inputs in order to cushion shortfalls in production by greater reliance on imports and the improvement of research and development, and (7) maintenance of an effective incentive system to prevent the adverse effect on production of a sharp decline in labor productivity.

Notwithstanding the new economic policy adopted after 1961, the principal obstacle to a policy like the one outlined above is, of course, Communist ideology, aggravated by the nationalistic desire to promote rapid economic development. Communist ideology may continue to hamper the adoption of an incentive system that would work in the long run. It may preclude the employment of pricing and costing measures that would provide adequate criteria for investment. It may prevent the acceptance of sufficient decentralization and efficient local control that would help reduce serious planning errors. Nationalism and xenophobia, on the other hand, may stand in the way of greater reliance upon import, a more moderate rate of growth, and the abandonment of military and other political adventures that tend to threaten steady economic growth and reduce the availability of foreign trade and credit.

According to Chou En-lai, the Third Five-Year Plan is now officially scheduled to begin in 1966, the period between 1961 and 1965 having apparently been relegated to "consolidation and readjustment"—what we might regard as the downswing and the lower turning point of the Chinese cycle. It remains to be seen whether an anti-instability policy will be adopted during the Third Plan.

CHAPTER IX

Communist China in the World Economy

General Principles of Policy

What is the role of the outside world in the economic development of Communist China? What part does Communist China play in trade and other economic relations with the rest of the world?

The first thing a student accustomed to conditions in a market economy unhampered by foreign-exchange and quantitative-trade restrictions must realize is that the imports of Communist China are not decided by the preferences of individual buyers on the basis of simple price comparisons between domestic and foreign goods. The decisions on what and how much to import are made centrally by state trading offices on the basis of the national economic plan. Price comparisons are made between potential imports from one country and another. But such price comparisons are often superseded by other political and economic requirements, such as the need to balance imports from one country against exports to the same country because of stipulations in some trade agreement, or the political expediency in using trade as a means of achieving foreign-policy objectives. Furthermore, price comparisons between domestic and foreign goods are meaningless because the exchange rate,[1] not being subject to the requirement of equating the supply and demand of foreign exchange

---

[1] There is no official yuan-dollar rate. If the cross rate between sterling and the dollar is computed at $2.80 per pound, the nominal rate would be 2.46 yuan per dollar. If the cross rate between the Hong Kong dollar and the U.S. dollar is computed at 5.5 Hong Kong dollars to the U.S. dollar, a rate of 2.35 yuan per U.S. dollar would be obtained.

on a free exchange market, is really little more than an arbitrary arithmetical ratio for conversion purposes. One cannot even ascertain whether it is worthwhile to import commodity A or to produce it at home by comparing the cost of producing A at home with the cost of producing the necessary exports to pay for the import of A. Unless exactly the same physical resources are used in producing A and the exports in question, the cost comparison between the two would have to be predicated on given factor prices. This step would then take us back to the difficult question of pricing in general, which was discussed in Chapter III.

An understanding of the manner in which decisions relating to imports in Communist China are arrived at must therefore be sought by examining the nature of the economic plan and the "national goals" it serves. Export decisions, on the other hand, are made principally in order to pay for imports, and secondarily for political reasons. Since self-sufficiency is a major national goal, as a rule goods are imported only if they cannot be produced at home in the quantities envisaged by the plan, perhaps at any cost, or if they cannot be produced according to the necessary quality specifications. Since rapid economic development based on a high rate of capital formation is another major national goal, it follows that as a rule, consumer goods would not be imported. Imports, therefore, would normally consist of capital goods and industrial raw materials.

These general rules are naturally subject to modifications. For instance, goods may be imported as a means of meeting contingencies and assuaging plan failures although, barring special circumstances, production failures in the consumer-goods sector are less likely to call for imports than corresponding failures in the producer-goods sector. The continued import of food grains since 1961 and up to this writing represents a very notable exception. Imports may also be made in order to facilitate exports of greater value. For instance, cheaper foods such as barley may be imported while rice, a more expensive grain, is exported. Sometimes imports may take place only to be re-exported as a part of multilateral trade deals. For instance, rice imports from Burma may be contracted for re-export to Ceylon in exchange for rubber;[2] similarly, imported rubber from Malaya may be re-exported to the

[2] See Yuan-li Wu, "The Soviet 'Economic Offensive' in Asia and Its Effect on United States–Asian Trade," *American Trade with Asia and the Far East,* ed. Robert J. Barr (Milwaukee: The Marquette University Press, 1959), pp. 291–317.

Soviet Union. Under particular conditions, imports may take place because, for reasons of foreign policy, it is considered expedient to import from a certain country, e.g., the large importation of Cuban sugar. Or goods may be imported as a part of a barter arrangement under which other goods had been exported earlier. However, as far as "economic principles" are concerned—even though these may not be the best economic principles under a different economic system—the principal guidelines are "self-sufficiency" and "producer goods only."

While the preceding remarks may help explain why certain goods are imported, additional factors must be considered in understanding China's planning of trade balances between exports and imports. The key to the understanding of foreign-trade policy may be found in the regime's need to earn foreign exchange to finance external expenditures other than imports (both goods and intangibles). If past loans have to be serviced, additional foreign exchange receipts must be earned. This means that exports must be larger than imports not financed by new loans, if we abstract from nonexport earnings of foreign exchange.[3] This requirement is complicated by two further conditions: First, external expenditures such as the maintenance of diplomatic missions, subversive and propaganda operations, and various contingency payments can be financed only by means of convertible currencies, which must be earned from Western countries. Second—although information on this point is scanty—it may be necessary to service foreign loans, at least in part, by cash payments in convertible currencies. Consequently, it is necessary for Communist China to create an export surplus in trading with Western countries while its trade with the Soviet Union and other bloc countries would be governed in general by the principle of bilateral trade balance, modified only to the extent that loans are made and may be serviced by current exports.

As for the relative size of trade with the Soviet bloc and trade with the non-Communist countries, this is influenced by political conditions. On the one hand, China's external alignment has thus far precluded the extension of long-term loans and grants by the West, although this situation has undergone some change since 1963. Up to the early 1960's, therefore, Soviet-bloc credit was all that Communist China was able to get. On the other hand, after the Communist regime's entry into the Korean war, the United

[3] The principal source of nonexport exchange earnings consists of remittances from Chinese residents overseas.

States imposed a total embargo on exports to the Chinese mainland, and this embargo is supported by the exclusion of goods of mainland Chinese origin from the U.S. market. A number of European countries, plus Canada and Japan, have joined the United States in a Coordinating Committee—these are the COCOM countries[4]—which regulates exports to Communist China. On the whole, regulation by the COCOM countries, in spite of vociferous complaints by some European and Japanese traders, has succeeded in reducing the volume of exports of certain "strategic items" to Communist China. These political facts have contributed to China's much greater trade with the Soviet bloc than with the West prior to the failure of the Great Leap. As the political environment changes, it is entirely possible that another reorientation may take place. The principal difficulty will probably lie in Communist China's export capability.

Finally, a word should be said of trade relations with other underdeveloped nations. Communist China has assiduously cultivated economic relations with countries in Asia and Africa and, more recently, with Latin America. Political reasons dominate these activities. First, exports to these countries under arrangements of foreign aid given by Communist China would enhance Chinese prestige and influence. These political relations may be useful in helping Communist China line up votes for her admission into the United Nations or gain the support of local Communist parties in the Sino-Soviet dispute. Second, some of these countries may be able to supply goods that China has to import for purely economic reasons, such as rubber from Malaya and oil from Indonesia. In the third place, to the extent that earnings from exports to any of these countries are in convertible currencies, it would pay to expand exports to them. Some of them may constitute potential markets for Chinese manufactures, whereas the developed Western countries are more interested in importing agricultural goods, crude materials, and the traditional handicrafts. There are also special circumstances which make it relatively easy for Communist China to expand exports to some of the areas in this category. By virtue of their large populations of Chinese descent, Hong Kong and Malaya offer two such examples where Chinese export of ordinary consumer goods can be sold without the usual marketing problems in export promotion.

[4] The COCOM countries are: The United States, Canada, Japan, Belgium, Luxembourg, Denmark, France, the Federal Republic of Germany, Greece, Italy, the Netherlands, Norway, Portugal, Turkey, and the United Kingdom.

Composition of Imports

The greatly altered composition of Chinese imports under the present regime may be easily illustrated as a reflection of the role of imports in the national economic plan. Before the Communist takeover, in 1947, more than 19 per cent of Chinese imports consisted of consumer goods, more than 18 per cent of capital goods, and the remaining 62 per cent of raw materials and fuel, particularly petroleum products and cotton.[5] As early as 1950, the composition of Chinese imports had changed as follows: capital goods, nearly 31 per cent; consumer goods, less than 9 per cent; raw materials and fuel, nearly 61 per cent.[6] For the period 1955–57, imports from the Soviet Union consisted of machinery and equipment, 37.2 per cent; transportation equipment, 2.5 per cent; crude materials, 2.2 per cent; chemicals, 1.7 per cent; manufactures, 19.8 per cent; other, 36.7 per cent.[7] During the same period, Chinese imports from the West were composed of machinery and equipment, 7.6 per cent; transportation equipment, 1.9 per cent; crude materials, 34.6 per cent; chemicals, 24.4 per cent; manufactures, 22.9 per cent; other, 8.6 per cent.[8] Only a very small portion of the manufactures and of the "other" items were consumer goods. The smaller proportion of machinery and equipment in imports from the West, in comparison with imports from the Soviet Union, and the larger proportion of chemicals imported from the West were results of Soviet aid to Communist China, coupled with export controls on the part of the COCOM countries, and chemical fertilizer imports from the West.

An outstanding example of the effect of the policy of self-sufficiency was the elimination of grain imports early under Chinese Communist rule and the transition to grain export.[9] The same applies to the curtailment of cotton imports. Both are in sharp contrast to the pre-Communist state of affairs. Some cotton

[5] Yuan-li Wu, *An Economic Survey of Communist China* (New York, 1956), p. 469.

[6] *Ibid.*

[7] U.S.S.R., *Veneshniaia Torgovlia*, statistical supplements (Moscow, 1956–57).

[8] The Mutual Defense Assistance Control Act of 1951, 11th, 12th, and 13th Annual Reports; U.S. Department of Commerce, International Trade Analysis Division, "Free World Exports to Soviet Bloc Countries by Commodity Groups," 1958, 1959, 1960.

[9] See Chapter VII.

imports are always carried on, but they are generally of the long-staple variety needed for the manufacture of fine piece goods, some of which are exported. Cotton is also imported because of politically motivated bilateral trade agreements with Egypt and Pakistan. The more striking deviation from this established policy came in 1961, when large food imports were made, and the same practice has been continued up to this writing (Winter 1964–65).[10] As noted before, food would not have been imported in order to offset plan failures if the regime had not faced dire need. Disaffection in the armed forces, severe shortage in the cities, and depletion of emergency stocks were among the causes of this radical change in policy, a change which the Communist authorities no doubt hope is temporary.

Direction of Trade

Because of its political orientation, Communist China first altered the direction of trade in favor of the Soviet bloc. While trade with the Soviet bloc had been altogether negligible before, the percentage of bloc trade in Communist China's total foreign trade increased to 26 per cent in 1950 according to Soviet statistics, or 33.5 per cent according to Chinese trade returns. Toward the end of the First Five-Year Plan, it stood at the level of 75 per cent. Two-thirds of the latter, or 50 per cent of the total trade, was with the Soviet Union.[11] Because of the possibility of re-exports—goods consigned to a European port or sold to another bloc country may be redirected or resold to Communist China, while Chinese exports to a bloc country may be re-exported to the West—these statistics in all likelihood underestimate mainland

[10] A recent report states: "Including shipments to be delivered by the end of 1964, the Communist regime has imported over 22 million metric tons of grain since 1960 at an estimated cost in excess of $1.5 billion. If contracted deliveries are fulfilled, imports of grain into China in 1964 will top all previous years. With the recent negotiations for additional wheat shipments by Argentina, deliveries of grain in 1964 will be in excess of 6 million tons. Large amounts of grain are to be delivered by Canada in 1965 and 1966, according to the agreement of 1963." See Marion R. Larsen, *The Agricultural Situation & Crop Prospects in Communist China, 1964* (Foreign Agricultural Economic Report No. 20, Economic Research Service, USDA, Foreign Regional Analysis Division, October, 1964).

[11] Yuan-li Wu, *et al.*, *The Economic Potential of Communist China,* I, 307, and Yuan-li Wu, *The Economic Impact of the Rise of Communist China* (Santa Barbara, Calif.: General Electric Company, 1962), p. 49.

China's trade with the West. But the preponderant share of the bloc in Communist China's foreign trade was unmistakable.

A. TRADE WITH THE SOVIET UNION

As far as trade with the Soviet Union is concerned, the published foreign trade statistics show (1) rising imports from the Soviet Union from 1950 to 1956, dipping slightly in 1957–58, then rising again in 1959, followed by a small dip in 1960 and a sharp decline in 1961–63; (2) generally rising exports to the Soviet Union through 1959, followed by a drop and a sharp fall in 1961–63; (3) as a result of these changes, the existence of an annual trade deficit in 1950–55, followed by the transition to annual trade surpluses from 1956 on in spite of the curtailed volume of trade beginning in 1960 (Figure IX-1). Generally speaking, the earlier

TABLE IX-1. SINO-SOVIET TRADE
(*In million rubles*)

Year	Soviet Exports (Chinese Imports)	Soviet Imports (Chinese Exports)	Soviet Imports (Chinese Exports) Surplus (+)
1950	350	172	−178
1951	431	298	−133
1952	499	373	−126
1953	628	428	−200
1954	684	521	−163
1955	674	579	−94
1956	660	688	+28
1957	490	664	+174
1958	571	793	+223
1959	859	990	+131
1960	735	763	+28
1961	331	496	+166
1962	210	465	+255
1963	169	372	+203

Note: All data in *new* rubles. Data for 1959 and earlier have been converted to new rubles at the rate of 1 old ruble = 0.225 new ruble.

SOURCE: U.S.S.R., *Vneshniaia Torgovlia*, Statistical Supplements (Moscow, 1950–63).

trade deficits were a reflection of the inflow of Soviet long-term loans and trade credit under the current trade arrangements. On the other hand, the trade surpluses beginning in 1956 represented loan services and repayments. Apparently, China was for a time not able to keep up with the payment schedule, for by 1961, according to a Soviet announcement, Communist China was in arrears to the tune of 1.3 billion yuan, which had to be refinanced. It was then agreed that Communist China would repay her indebtedness to the Soviets by 1965, although accelerated repayment in 1963 may succeed in clearing the outstanding debt by the end of 1964. If no new debt is incurred, one should expect Sino-Soviet trade to be conducted on a strictly balanced basis from year to year.[12]

B. TRADE WITH THE WEST[13]

Communist China's trade with the West is characterized by (1) a consistent deficit on the part of China in favor of the COCOM countries, Japan being a notable exception; (2) a surplus in favor of China in her trade with the West as a whole; (3) concentration of the surplus noted in (2) in trade with a few areas only, in particular Hong Kong and Malaya. Recent exceptions to the normal trade surplus with the West as a whole are a reflection of Communist China's large food purchases from abroad.

The most significant point to be deduced from the above is apparently the existence of relatively small markets for Chinese products in Europe, in contrast to the large markets in such places as Hong Kong and Malaya. The latter are distinguished from other parts of Asia by their large Chinese population and their ability to pay.

As one can see from Figures IX-2 and -3, the trend of exports from the COCOM countries to Communist China has headed downward since 1958, although imports of food grains since 1961 have helped boost the volume, especially if we include exports from all the free world countries, some of which are not in the COCOM group. On the other hand, Chinese exports to both the COCOM group and all free world countries have fluctuated from year to year, rising to a peak in 1960, followed by a decline

---

[12] See note 23, p. 190.

[13] The "West" is used here interchangeably with the term the "free world," which is understood to include the entire world excluding the "bloc countries." Included in the "bloc" are Albania, Bulgaria, Czechoslovakia, the Soviet Zone of Germany, Hungary, Poland, Romania, the U.S.S.R., Outer Mongolia, North Korea, North Vietnam, and Communist China.

FIGURE IX-1. FREE WORLD AND SOVIET

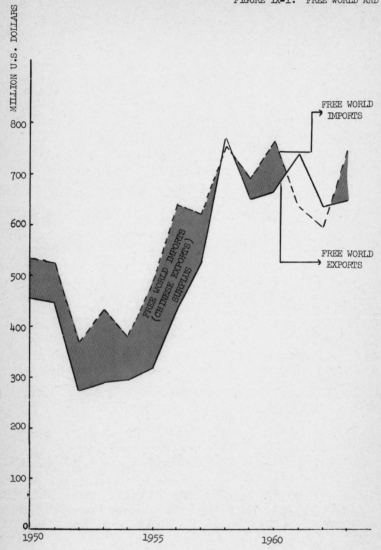

MILLION U.S. DOLLARS

FREE WORLD
IMPORTS

FREE WORLD IMPORTS
(CHINESE EXPORTS)
SURPLUS

FREE WORLD
EXPORTS

800

700

600

500

400

300

200

100

0

1950   1955   1960

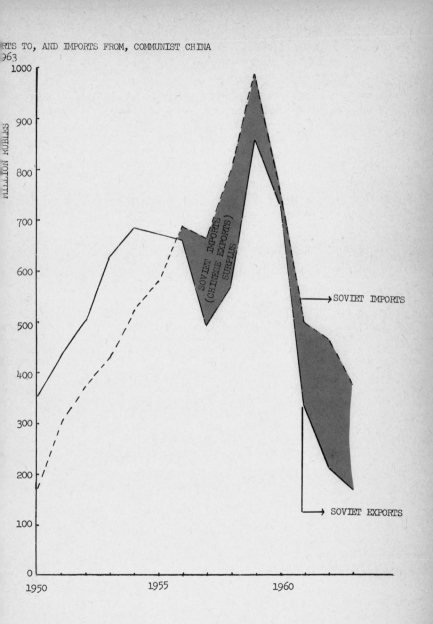

to 1962 and recovery thereafter. The fluctuations are clearly in conformity with fluctuations in domestic production.

One of the effects of the fluctuations is felt in the changing trade surplus in Communist China's commerce with the free world countries. On the basis of the general principles governing Chinese foreign trade developed earlier in this chapter, and as long as large external credits from the West are not available, any decline of the surplus would be a clear sign of strained foreign-exchange positions and possibly a reflection of domestic economic difficulties. Such periods of external and domestic economic difficulties were seen in 1961–63 (Figure IX-1). In contrast, 1952–57 was a period of relative growth.

C. TRADE WITH OTHER ASIAN COUNTRIES

Apart from earning foreign exchange to finance expenditures in other countries, Communist China's trade with Asian countries is dominated by an admixture of various political considerations and economic designs. Trade is often dangled as a lure to foreign exporters, some of whom, as in the case of Japan, may look upon the high level of past trade with nostalgia. The prospect of trade expansion is then used as a weapon to gain political concessions. This is true especially in the case of Japan, whose participation in the much-maligned selective-export embargo sponsored by the United States and whose trade with and recognition of Nationalist China are constant targets of Communist China's political maneuvers.

Secondly, underdeveloped countries which have export surpluses of primary products for sale, such as Burma's rice, Ceylon's rubber, and Indonesia's oil, may be encouraged through offers of long-term contracts and bulk purchase. Often these lures are accompanied by Chinese offers of industrial goods, machinery, and even technical assistance. These offers serve also as window-dressing of successes in economic development on the Chinese mainland, although the credibility of the Communist developmental model was seriously tarnished in 1961–62. Not infrequently, China may resort to the dumping of exports in competing with third countries, such as Japan and India, or, in an opposite twist, withhold shipments to force buyers to adjust their purchases or resort to other economic-warfare measures in order either to enhance Communist China's future bargaining position or her political influence.

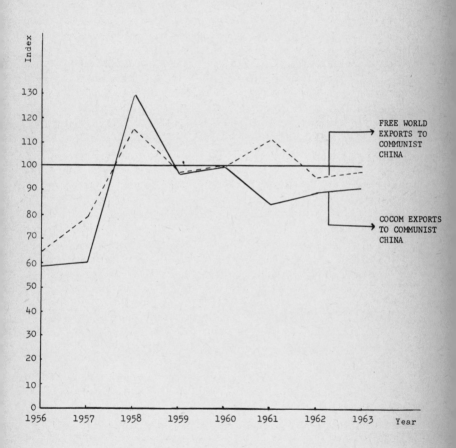

FIGURE IX-2. INDEX OF FREE WORLD AND COCOM COUNTRIES'
EXPORTS TO COMMUNIST CHINA
(1960 = 100)

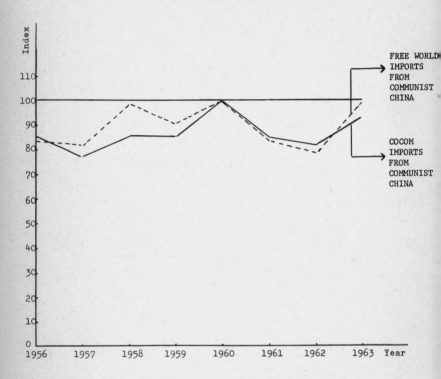

FIGURE IX-3.   INDEX OF FREE WORLD AND COCOM COUNTRIES'
IMPORTS FROM COMMUNIST CHINA
(1960 = 100)

Considerable progress was made by Communist China in
expanding her trade with other Asian countries during the period
of the First Five-Year Plan and through the first phase of the
Great Leap Forward. Since then, however, Chinese trade with
the Asian countries has maintained a fairly stable level. Some
growth was experienced only in the case of a few countries,
notably Hong Kong, Malaya, Indonesia, and Japan. These typical
examples serve to illustrate the underlying purposes of Chinese
trade: (1) to earn convertible exchange, (2) to cultivate political
and economic ties, and more recently in the case of Japan, (3) to
use the lure of trade and its possible expansion for the solicitation
of external credit.

TABLE IX-2. FREE-WORLD COUNTRIES' TRADE WITH COMMUNIST CHINA,
1950–63[a]
(*In millions of U.S. dollars*)

Year	Free-world Exports (Chinese Imports)	Free-world Imports (Chinese Exports)	Free-world Imports (Chinese Exports) Surplus (+)
1950	452.1	534.7	+82.6
1951	446.2	524.7	+78.5
1952	272.5	367.9	+95.4
1953	287.4	432.7	+145.3
1954	294.2	379.7	+85.5
1955	317.3	487.1	+169.8
1956	434.2	641.4	+207.2
1957	527.8	624.0	+96.2
1958	770.9	755.8	−15.1
1959	651.6	693.4	+41.8
1960	669.0	766.7	+97.7
1961	742.2	637.5	−104.7
1962	637.2	598.5	−38.5
1963	653.5	754.1	+100.6

SOURCES: Mutual Defense Assistance Control Act of 1951, 16th Report to Congress, U.S. Department of State, 1963, p. 52; and International Trade Analysis Division, Bureau of International Commerce, U.S. Department of Commerce, March and May 1964.

[a] Through 1962, Cuba was included in the free-world trade statistics: The volume of trade was:

	Cuban Exports to Communist China	Cuban Imports from Communist China
	(*In millions of U.S. dollars*)	
1960	32.1	. . .
1961	95.6	. . .
1962	85.3	. . .

If Cuba were excluded, the free-world figure would be:

	Free-world (*less Cuba*) Exports to Communist China	Free-world (*less Cuba*) Imports from Communist China
	(*In millions of U.S. dollars*)	
1960	636.9	. . .
1961	646.6	. . .
1962	551.9	. . .

However, because of the lack of data on Chinese exports to Cuba, a full adjustment cannot be made in the figures and tables in this chapter. Since 1963, Cuba has been excluded from the free world in the Department of Commerce trade statistics.

TABLE IX-3. COMMUNIST CHINA'S TRADE WITH FREE-WORLD AND COCOM COUNTRIES, 1956–63

| | Exports to Communist China | | | | Imports from Communist China | | | |
| | Total Free-world | | COCOM Countries | | Total Free-world | | COCOM Countries | |
Year	Value (millions of U.S. dollars)	Index (1960 = 100)	Value (millions of U.S. dollars)	Index (1960 = 100)	Value (millions of U.S. dollars)	Index (1960 = 100)	Value (millions of U.S. dollars)	Index (1960 = 100)
1956	434.2	64.9	203.6	58.6	641.4	83.7	225.1	85.3
1957	527.8	78.9	209.8	60.4	624.0	81.4	204.3	77.4
1958	770.9	115.2	447.4	128.8	755.8	98.6	225.8	85.6
1959	651.6	97.4	336.3	96.8	693.4	90.4	225.7	85.5
1960	669.0	100.0	347.4	100.0	766.7	100.0	263.9	100.0
1961	742.2	110.9	294.3	84.7	637.5	83.1	223.0	84.5
1962	637.2	95.2	309.4	89.1	598.5	78.1	215.4	81.6
1963	653.5	97.7	316.1	91.0	754.1	98.4	245.4	93.0

SOURCES: Same as Table IX-2.

D. TRADE WITH OTHER COUNTRIES

As of 1963, Communist China is said to have trade relations with about eighty countries and trading areas. As of the end of 1961, the geographical distribution of trade agreements with other countries or areas, including both bilateral governmental agreements and agreements concluded with foreign private trade groups, was as follows: Bloc countries, ten (including Cuba); Europe, fifteen; Asia, eleven; Latin America, three; North America, one; Near East, ten;[14] Africa, nine; Oceania, one. Agreements with the African and Latin American countries are mostly of recent origin. Reported purchases of sugar from Cuba and cotton from Mexico are among the more recent forays in trade with Latin America. Agreements with the nascent African countries are often related to political and subversive activities.

However, the existence of trade agreements does not mean the automatic conclusion of contracts under which the actual exchange of goods takes place. On the basis of available statistics, most of such trade is extremely small in value.

Apart from the Soviet Union, the COCOM countries (which are mostly European countries, plus Canada, Japan, and the United States), and the Asian countries, few other countries really have any significant volume of trade with Communist China. Aside from the Soviet bloc and the COCOM groups, the largest trade partners are Hong Kong, Indonesia, and Malaya, but special demographic and political conditions prevail in these cases, as will be explained later. Within the bloc, the more important trade partners are Czechoslovakia, East Germany, Hungary, Poland, and Romania. Although some trade data are available,[15] the lack of meaningful exchange rates unfortunately precludes a real country-by-country comparison.

Scale and Significance of Soviet Aid

It is exceedingly difficult to evaluate the relative importance of Soviet aid to Communist China for a number of reasons.

The first is the conceptual difficulty in defining "aid." For frequently, Soviet aid is taken in a very broad sense to include imports from the U.S.S.R. that were paid for by current Chinese

[14] Excluding countries otherwise included in Asia and Africa.
[15] "Communist China and the Soviet Bloc," *The Annals of the American Academy of Political and Social Science,* CCCXLIX, September, 1963.

exports. Thus both trade and aid in the narrower sense are included. To the flow of goods one might add technical assistance as an important factor contributing to the recipient country's economic development. In a narrower sense, aid proper is understood to include only goods that are financed in such a way as not to require current payment by Communist China. Obviously, whatever the scope of Soviet aid, goods destined for the civilian economy as a whole must be further distinguished both from military supplies and from the import components of capital-investment projects in Communist China.

A second difficulty stems from the fact that the Soviet Union considers the transfer of assets located in mainland China from Soviet to Chinese ownership as a part of aid. It is possible that some of these assets had previously been imported into China. On the other hand, it is unlikely that all of them were, and there is always the thorny question of valuation. Joint ownership of the former Chinese Changchun Railway in Manchuria and development corporations for the exploitation of nonferrous and rare metals in Sinkiang were set up under early agreements between the two countries. Together with Soviet military establishments at Lü-shun (Port Arthur), these Soviet interests were later transferred to Communist China. The estimated value of the assets has been put at 1.66 billion yuan.[16] In speaking of Soviet aid to Communist China, one must be wary of the manner in which this item is treated.

Still another difficulty stems from the fact that a common gauge for measuring the scope of Soviet aid is the number of investment projects in which Soviet aid goods play an important part. First, the manner of counting—that is, what should be regarded as a project—is never clearly defined, so that even if the method of measurement is constant, the data over the years would only indicate the trend of change rather than its absolute scale. Second, the term "aid goods" still begs the question, previously posed, of what "aid" is. Third, the degree of completion of the projects cannot be determined. Lastly, whether it is legitimate to measure the contribution of aid goods in terms of the total production capacity of the investment projects in which they are used depends, of course, upon the ratio of the import components to domestic goods employed.

On the basis of available statistics, fifty projects constituted the initial group of Soviet aid projects agreed to between the two countries in 1950. Another 91 projects were added in 1953, making

[16] Yuan-li Wu *et al., op. cit.,* I, 263.

a total of 141 projects. During the First Five-Year Plan, the number was again increased, first to 156, in 1954, and then to 211, in 1956. Finally, during 1958–59, aid in the construction of an additional number of projects, including some large power plants, was negotiated, the reported additions being 47 in 1958, and 78 in 1959,[17] making the cumulative grand total 336. However, many of the 125 projects negotiated in 1958–59 were probably disrupted or abandoned, following the curtailment of Soviet assistance in 1960.

The role of Soviet aid may be examined from both the Soviet and the Chinese points of view. The time of the appraisal would also make a considerable difference. The Soviet point of view is clearly illustrated in a number of publications of which the following is a typical example. Writing in the *Red Star* of February 14, 1964, M. Kapitsa described the scope of Soviet assistance as most comprehensive and generous.

> The industrial potentials created in China with the cooperation of the U.S.S.R. are of considerable importance in the total industrial capacity of the country. In 1960, they produced 30 percent of the pig iron smelted in China, 39 percent of the steel, 51 percent of the rolled products, 91 percent of the tractors, 80 percent of the trucks, 30 percent of the output of synthetic ammonia, 25 percent of the electric power output, and 55 percent of the steam and hydraulic turbines. . . .
>
> In the period between 1954 and 1963, the Soviet Union turned over to the Chinese People's Republic over 24,000 sets of scientific and technical data including over 1,400 blueprints covering entire enterprises. About 10,000 Chinese engineers, technicians, and qualified workers underwent a course of industrial education and practical training at Soviet enterprises and institutions. . . . Over 10,000 Soviet specialists [were engaged in work in China].[18]

Until the curtailment of Soviet aid in 1960, China's leaders would have agreed heartily with the above statement. As the pre-1960 literature shows, there was no lack of expressions of appreciation and of Chinese obeisance to the "selfless" and "boundless" generosity of the Soviet Union in the name of "Marxism-Leninism," "internationalism," and the "solidarity of the proletariat." As the dispute between Peking and Moscow deepened, however, Communist China's appraisal of the role of Soviet aid changed

---

[17] *Chūgoku Seijikeizai Sōran (Political and Economic Views on Present Day China)* (Tokyo, 1962), p. 731.

[18] M. Kapitsa, "A Significant Date in the Life of Two Great Peoples," *Krasnaya Zvezda (Red Star)*, February 14, 1964.

radically. A sharp contrast to the "milk-and-honey" tone of appreciation is provided by a letter addressed to the Central Committee of the Soviet Communist Party by its Chinese counterpart on February 29, 1964.[19] Referring to a Soviet offer of November 29, 1963, to send technical experts back to China, the Chinese letter stated bluntly: "To be frank, the Chinese people cannot trust you. They have just healed wounds caused by your withdrawal of experts. These events are still fresh in their memory. With the leaders of the CPSU pursuing an anti-Chinese policy, the Chinese people are unwilling to be duped." Referring to Soviet loans, the Chinese Communists assumed the plaintive role of the injured, for "it must be pointed out that China used them mostly for the purchase of war material from the Soviet Union, the greater part of which was used up in the war to resist United States aggression and to aid [North] Korea." The letter also pointed out, "China has paid and is paying the Soviet Union in goods, gold, or convertible foreign exchange for all Soviet-supplied complete sets of equipment and other goods, including those made available on credit plus interest."

As for Soviet technical assistance, Communist China accused the Soviet Union of having "unscrupulously" withdrawn the 1,390 Soviet specialists working in China, "torn up 343 contracts and supplementary contracts concerning experts, and scrapped 257 projects of scientific and technical co-operation, all within the short span of a month." Communist China said in the letter of February 29, 1964, that the peremptory withdrawal of Soviet experts posted in more than 250 enterprises and establishments in many fields had damaged production, construction, designing work, and research, and that this "perfidious action disrupted China's original national economic plan and inflicted enormous losses upon China's socialist construction."

As for the approximate value of Soviet loans to Communist China, an official statement by Li Hsien-nien, Communist Minister of Finance, put the total amount at 5.294 billion yuan for the period of 1949–57.[20] Of this amount, 2.174 billion were spent dur-

---

[19] The letters exchanged between the Soviet Union and Communist China in 1963–64 are found in the *Peking Review*, VII, No. 19 (May 8, 1964), pp. 7–27.

[20] Li Hsien-nien, Report on 1956 Final Accounts and 1957 State Budget (Delivered at the Fourth Session of the National People's Congress on June 29, 1957), and *Hsin-hua Pan-yüeh-k'an* (*New China Semimonthly*) (Peking), No. 14, July, 1957, p. 21.

ing 1949–52, leaving 3.12 billion for 1953–57. On the basis of Soviet trade statistics, the cumulative total of China's import surplus in 1950–52 inclusive amounted to 1.936 billion old rubles, while the corresponding total for 1953–55 was 2.034 billion rubles. According to a recent study by Mah and Chao, the effective exchange rate up to late 1957 was probably around 1 old ruble to 1 yuan, rather than the 2 to 1 ratio which has since been disclosed as the trade ruble rate.[21] This would mean that the cumulative trade deficits on the part of Communist China were 1.936 billion yuan in 1950–52 and 2.034 billion in 1953–55, making a total of 3.970 billion yuan.

Apart from the trade deficit in 1949, not included in the above statistics, what accounts for the difference between the 3.97 billion yuan and the total Soviet credit in 1949–57 estimated at 5.294 billion yuan? One interpretation would be to treat the plant and other asset transfers as a part of the total credit. If the 1.66 billion yuan mentioned earlier is taken to be the correct figure, the accumulated import deficits plus this amount would reach 5.63 billion yuan, which is reasonably close to Li Hsien-nien's 5.294 billion. Other interpretations are also possible, of course.

From January, 1956, to January, 1958, Communist China had an export surplus with the Soviet Union equal to 902 million old rubles or 902 million yuan at the same rate of 1 to 1. The corresponding surplus in 1958–60 was 1.696 billion old rubles, or the equivalent of 3.392 billion yuan at the new rate of 1 yuan to 2 rubles. The total export surplus in the five-year period would therefore amount to 4.294 billion yuan. If the total debt is assumed to have been 5.294 billion yuan, not allowing for interest charges, the remaining balance in 1961 would be 1 billion yuan. The reported payment in arrears at the time was 1.279 billion yuan.[22] According to the result of negotiations in 1961, Communist China was to repay the outstanding balance by the end of 1965. Realized export surpluses in trading with the Soviet Union

[21] Kang Chao and Feng-hwa Mah, "A Study of the Ruble-Yuan Exchange Rate," *The China Quarterly* (London), No. 17, January–March, 1964, pp. 192–204.

[22] Yuan-li Wu, *et al., op. cit.,* I, 309 and 330. This would be equivalent to 2 billion old rubles or .909 billion new rubles. According to the *Peking Review* of January 1, 1965, p. 9, "The sum total of the principal plus interest we owed the Soviet Union was 1,406 million new rubles; we have paid 1,389 million new rubles on schedule and have proposed to the Soviet side to pay off the remaining 17 million rubles ahead of schedule from the favorable balance in our trade with the Soviet Union in 1964."

in 1961 and 1962 were at the rate of 166 and 255 million new rubles, or 368.5 and 566.1 million yuan respectively.[23] The rate of repayment in 1963 was said to be accelerated—the reported Chinese export surplus was, however, only 203 million rubles, or 451 million yuan—so that the debt may be cleared up during 1964.

The Potentials of a Reorientation of Trade

The sharp decline of trade with the Soviet Union in 1961 was partly a reflection of the deepening economic crisis in Communist China, which was itself in part a result of the curtailment of Soviet technical assistance and equipment shipments. The intensification of the doctrinal dispute with the Soviet Union was not unrelated to the economic causes. Thus the interaction between political considerations and economic necessity has raised the question whether Communist China would not reorient her external trade away from the Soviet bloc and toward the West. One might examine this question in several parts.[24]

First, to what extent has such a reorientation actually taken place?

If 1960 is taken as the base year with an index of 100, the index of Soviet exports to Communist China would be 45 in 1961 and 23.0 in 1963. During the same period, the index of exports from the West to Communist China was 110.9 in 1961 (1960 = 100), 95.2 in 1962, and 97.7 in 1963. If comparison with the trend of Soviet exports to China were made on this basis, one would obtain a distinct impression of a substantial reorientation of Chinese purchases away from the Soviet Union as a matter of deliberate policy (Figure IX-4).

The same impression would be obtained if we examine the direction of Chinese exports. With 1960 as 100, the index of Chinese exports to the Soviet Union would be 65 in 1961, and 48.8 in 1963. On the other hand, Chinese exports to the West declined from an index of 100 in 1960 to 83.1 in 1961, 78.1 in 1962, and 98.4 in 1963. Although lack of Soviet trade statistics for 1964 so far again precludes a complete comparison, the impression of a deliberate policy change would be unmistakable (Figure IX-5).

[23] 1 yuan = .45 new ruble. See Kang Chao and Feng-hwa Mah, *op. cit.*, p. 199.

[24] A trade agreement concluded in 1965 reportedly calls for an increase in Sino-Soviet trade above the 1964 level. The 1964 statistics were not yet available at this writing.

TABLE IX-4. INDEX OF SOVIET AND FREE-WORLD EXPORTS
TO COMMUNIST CHINA
(*1960 value = 100*)

Year	Soviet Exports to Communist China (Chinese Imports)	Free-world Exports to Communist China (Chinese Imports)	Free-world Exports to Communist China (Excluding Food Grains)
1956	89.8	64.9	64.9
1957	66.7	78.9	78.9
1958	77.7	115.2	115.2
1959	116.9	97.4	97.4
1960	100.0	100.0	100.0
1961	45.0	110.9	60.1
1962	28.6	95.2	44.7
1963	23.0	97.7	54.3

SOURCE: Tables IX-1 and IX-3.

TABLE IX-5. INDEX OF SOVIET AND FREE-WORLD IMPORTS
FROM COMMUNIST CHINA
(*1960 value = 100*)

Year	Soviet Imports from Communist China (Chinese Exports)	Free-world Imports from Communist China (Chinese Exports)	Free-world Imports from Communist China (Excluding Hong Kong and Malaya)
1956	90.2	83.7	83.0
1957	87.0	81.4	74.5
1958	103.9	98.6	89.1
1959	129.8	90.4	91.9
1960	100.0	100.0	100.0
1961	65.0	83.1	79.9
1962	60.9	78.1	67.3
1963	48.8	98.4	84.9

SOURCE: Tables IX-1 and IX-3.

However, a distinction should be made between the degree of
reorientation that has already taken place and a change in policy
that would lead to long-term shifts in the direction of trade. Such
a distinction can be made if the same statistics are analyzed
with some adjustments. First, inasmuch as food grain imports
were made by Communist China during this period as an emergency measure, and inasmuch as such imports were available

FIGURE IX-4. INDEX OF SOVIET AND FREE WORLD EXPORTS TO COMMUNIST CHINA
(1960 VALUE = 100)

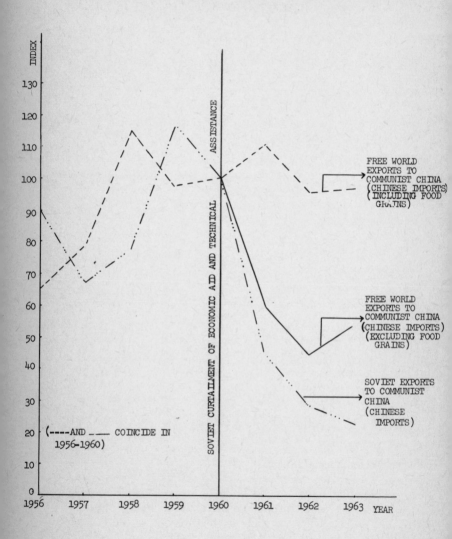

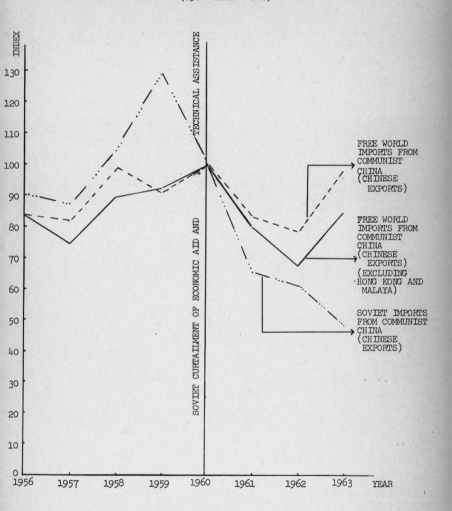

FIGURE IX -5. INDEX OF SOVIET AND FREE WORLD IMPORTS FROM COMMUNIST CHINA
(1960 VALUE = 100)

from the West only, it would be more appropriate to compare the exports of the West to Communist China, excluding food, with Soviet exports to China. If the food-grain data are excluded, with 1960 as 100, the index of the West's exports to China would be 60 in 1961, 44.7 in 1962, and 54.3 in 1963. While these adjusted figures would still constitute a slower decline of non-food imports from the West in 1960–62 than Soviet exports to China, the discrepancy from the trend of Soviet exports up to 1963 would no longer be so startling. Similarly, if Chinese exports to Hong Kong and Malaya are excluded from Chinese exports to the West, inasmuch as both places are heavily populated by persons of Chinese descent and thus constitute special markets for Chinese exports, the corresponding index would be 79.9 in 1961, 67.3 in 1962, and 84.8 in 1963. The gap between the trend of Chinese exports to the Soviet Union and that of exports to the free world would again be narrowed. Moreover, even following the recovery of Chinese exports to the West in 1963, it would still be below the level reached in 1956.

If the more important Western trading partners of China are examined individually,[25] it can be seen that so far as exports to Communist China are concerned, the percentage decline of exports from the Soviet Union in 1960–63 exceeded the relative decline of exports from the United Kingdom, Italy, Egypt, Ceylon, Denmark, and Hong Kong (Group A). In the case of Canada, Japan, Australia, France, Argentina, and the Netherlands, exports to Communist China actually increased in 1960–63 (Group B). The decline was, however, larger, in the case of exports from Belgium and Luxembourg, Malaya, and West Germany (Group C). In examining imports from China during the same period, the following groups of countries can also be distinguished from each other: (D.) Countries whose imports from Communist China underwent a smaller percentage decline in 1960–63 than Soviet imports from Communist China—Canada, France, the Netherlands, Belgium and Luxembourg, West Germany, the United Kingdom, and Italy; (E.) Countries whose imports from Communist China increased during the period—Japan, the U.A.R., Ceylon, Malaysia, Australia, Argentina, and Hong Kong; (F.) Countries whose imports from Communist China underwent a larger percentage decline than Soviet imports from Communist China—Denmark.

[25] Mutual Defense Assistance Control Act of 1951, 16th Report to Congress, Department of State, 1963, pp. 55–64.

If we disregard the countries from which large food-grain exports to Communist China took place (i.e., Canada, Australia, Argentina, and France), as well as Hong Kong and Malaysia, which have large Chinese populations, there are seven countries in groups A and B, as against three countries in group C, and nine countries in groups D and E, as against one country in group F. The degree of trade reorientation toward the non-Communist countries had become noticeable by the end of 1963.

However, even if Chinese external grain purchases should cease as a result of the expansion of domestic production, and if the export surplus in trading with the Soviet Union should no longer be necessary after the completion of Soviet loan repayments, the potential of trade reorientation would remain rather limited. The limitations lie in Communist China's ability to expand exports outside of the traditional markets, such as Hong Kong and Malaysia, where Chinese produce enjoys a special advantage. The availability of these markets would be a function of Communist China's ability to develop new exports. While Chinese efforts may be met with easier success in finding suitable exports to some of the less-developed countries, development of markets in Europe and other more advanced economies would be considerably more difficult. If export promotion cannot be crowned with success, at least not immediately, the prospects of Communist China's trade with the West, and indirectly of Chinese economic growth, would be greatly influenced by the possibilities of Western credit. It is in this connection that Chinese credit discussions with Japan and some of the Western European countries in 1963–64 have assumed particular significance.

Relative Importance of Communist China to the World Economy

The preceding discussion shows that by 1963, despite some evidence of resumed expansion of trade with the West, China had not yet regained the peak level of her imports from the same countries, which for the Communist period was attained in 1958. In the case of Chinese exports, the previous peak for the Communist period was attained in 1960. It was approximated, but again not yet reached, in 1963. If we take the respective peak years for Chinese imports (1958) from the West and Chinese exports (1960) to the West, and compare the figures with the total

exports or imports of the partner countries, the relative importance of Chinese trade to the latter can be seen.

If the largest eleven trading partners of Communist China are
considered, the results are as follows:

In 1960, of the seventeen countries, eleven imported from Communist China goods of a total value ranging from negligible to 0.9
per cent of their respective imports from the world.[26] The individual percentages were: the United Kingdom, .54; West Germany, .69; France, .36; Canada, .10; Italy, .51; the Netherlands,
.47; Japan, .46; Belgium and Luxembourg, .25; Australia, .50;
Denmark, 0.94, and Argentina, negligible.[27] Only Hong Kong derived 20.22 per cent; Malaya, 8.11 per cent; the United Arab Republic, 3.02 per cent; Indonesia, 9.93 per cent; Ceylon, 6.75 per
cent; and Burma, 9.49 per cent of their respective imports from
Communist China. The cases of Indonesia, Burma, Ceylon, and
the United Arab Republic are to be explained by their political
sympathy toward China and their bilateral trade agreements with
her. The cases of Hong Kong and Malaya were the result of the
large local Chinese population. In general, therefore, Communist
China was a rather insignificant supplier of goods on the world
market in 1960, as she still is today.

In 1958, of the seventeen principal Western trading partners of
China, twelve exported to that country from .01 to 1.84 per cent
of their respective world exports.[28] The individual figures were:

[26] The 17 countries selected had an annual import from (or export to)
Communist China greater than $15 million in at least one of the years in
1960–62 inclusive. These 17 countries account for 85% of total free-world imports from Communist China.

[27] The countries are listed in order of their total imports from the world.
Their total imports accounted for 58.9 per cent of total imports of the free
world countries (excluding the United States) from the world. 1. United Kingdom, 2. Federal Republic of Germany, 3. France, 4. Canada, 5. Italy, 6. the
Netherlands, 7. Japan, 8. Belgium and Luxembourg, 9. Australia, 10. Denmark, 11. Argentina, 12. Hong Kong, 13. Malaya, 14. the United Arab Republic (Egypt), 15. Indonesia, 16. Ceylon, 17. Burma.

[28] The 17 countries together account for 82 per cent of total free world
exports to Communist China in 1958. The order in which they appear in the
text is determined by the value of their respective exports to the world. Together they account for 60.1 per cent of the exports of the free world countries (excluding the United States) to the world. Data are derived from
United Nations, *Yearbook of International Trade Statistics, 1961,* New York.
1. United Kingdom, 2. Federal Republic of Germany, 3. France, 4. Canada,
5. the Netherlands, 6. Belgium and Luxembourg, 7. Japan, 8. Italy, 9. Australia, 10. Denmark, 11. Argentina, 12. Indonesia, 13. Malaya, 14. Hong
Kong, 15. the United Arab Republic, 16. Ceylon, 17. Burma.

TABLE IX-6. EXPORTS OF SELECTED FREE-WORLD COUNTRIES TO COMMUNIST CHINA, 1960–63
(In millions of U.S. dollars)

Country	1960 Value	1960 Index	1961 Value	1961 Index	1962 Value	1962 Index	1963 Value	1963 Index
Canada	8.9	100	120.9	1,358.0	137.0	1,538.0	96.9	1,088.8
Japan	2.7	100	16.6	614.8	38.0	1,425.9	62.4	2,311.1
Belgium/Luxembourg	44.6	100	10.2	22.9	8.0	17.9	9.5	21.3
France	52.8	100	36.4	68.9	43.3	82.0	58.4	110.6
Federal Republic of Germany	95.4	100	30.5	32.0	31.1	32.6	15.4	16.1
Italy	39.7	100	29.7	74.8	19.0	47.9	19.3	48.6
United Kingdom	89.8	100	36.6	40.8	24.1	26.8	37.4	41.6
United Arab Republic (Egypt)	44.5	100	14.6	32.8	19.1	42.9	16.4	36.9
Burma	7.9	100	37.2	470.9	18.9	239.2	2.0[a]	—
Ceylon	25.3	100	17.4	68.8	28.0	110.7	21.1	83.3
Indonesia	35.4	100	36.4	102.8	34.4	97.2	7.3[a]	—
Malaya	28.4	100	3.8	13.4	0.8	2.8	5.4	19.0
Australia	23.5	100	161.5	687.2	97.8	416.2	207.8	884.3
Argentina	1.4	100	4.2	300.0	26.4	1,885.7	3.1	221.4
Denmark	2.1	100	4.2	200.0	3.7	176.2	0.6	28.6
Netherlands	6.9	100	4.1	59.4	3.6	52.2	12.9	187.0
Hong Kong	2.3	100	1.4	60.9	1.5	65.2	1.4	60.9
Total	511.6		565.7		534.7		577.3	

SOURCE: Same as Table IX-2; Mutual Defense Assistance Control Act of 1951, 17th Report to Congress, U.S. Department of State, 1964, pp. 65–70.
[a] First quarter only.

TABLE IX-7. IMPORTS OF SELECTED FREE-WORLD COUNTRIES FROM COMMUNIST CHINA, 1960–63

(In millions of U.S. dollars)

Country	1960 Value	1960 Index	1961 Value	1961 Index	1962 Value	1962 Index	1963 Value	1963 Index
Canada	5.8	100	3.2	55.2	4.3	74.1	4.8	82.8
Japan	20.7	100	30.9	149.3	46.0	222.2	74.6	360.4
Belgium/Luxembourg	9.9	100	3.4	34.3	4.8	48.5	8.2	82.8
France	22.7	100	15.9	70.0	16.9	74.4	21.1	93.0
Federal Republic of Germany	69.4	100	39.7	57.2	39.3	56.6	40.8	58.8
Italy	24.1	100	12.3	51.0	14.1	58.5	19.1	79.3
United Kingdom	69.2	100	86.4	124.9	64.8	93.6	51.9	75.0
United Arab Republic (Egypt)	19.5	100	18.9	96.9	19.3	99.0	19.9	102.1
Burma	24.7	100	20.6	83.4	28.6	115.8	6.9[a]	—
Ceylon	27.8	100	7.3	26.3	8.6	30.9	29.0	104.3
Indonesia	57.0	100	39.9	70.0	30.4[b]	53.3	...	...
Malaya	57.1	100	56.3	98.6	65.9	115.4	94.0	164.6
Australia	10.3	100	6.9	67.0	11.1	107.8	14.5	140.8
Argentina	c		c		c		c	
Denmark	17.0	100	13.5	13.5	9.4	55.3	6.7	39.4
Netherlands	21.4	100	15.2	15.2	13.9	65.0	15.8	73.8
Hong Kong	207.5	100	180.0	180.0	212.3	102.3	260.2	125.4
Total	664.1		550.6		589.9		667.6	

SOURCE: Same as Table IX-2; Mutual Defense Assistance Control Act of 1951. 17th Report to Congress, U.S. Department of State, 1964. pp. 71–76.

a First quarter only

b January–June only

c $50,000 in 1960; $200,000 in 1961 and 1962; $100,000 in 1963.

United Kingdom, .82 per cent; West Germany, 1.84 per cent; France, .86 per cent; Canada, .16 per cent; the Netherlands, .37 per cent; Belgium and Luxembourg, 1.71 per cent; Japan, 1.76 per cent; Italy, 1.27 per cent; Australia, 1.50 per cent; Denmark, .30 per cent; Argentina, .01 per cent, and Burma, 1.54 per cent; Indonesia, 5.49 per cent; Malaya, 6.17 per cent; Hong Kong, 5.21 per cent; the United Arab Republic, 7.42 per cent; and Ceylon, 4.54 per cent were again the exceptions. In general, Communist China was not a large purchaser of exports from the West in 1958, nor is she today. This general situation has not been altered despite some reported increases in trade between Communist China and Western countries in 1964.

On the other hand, when Soviet exports to Communist China were at their height in 1959, prior to the Sino-Soviet dispute, they were responsible for 17.54 per cent of total Soviet exports. In the same year, when Soviet imports from Communist China were also at their peak, the value was equivalent to 21.69 per cent of total Soviet imports. Thus the decline of trade with Communist China in 1961–63 was probably not without its problems of adjustment to the Soviet Union, although the effect may have been much less painful than it has been to China.

Finally, the role of Communist China in the world economy must also be evaluated from the point of view of some of the underdeveloped countries which receive aid from Communist China. During the 1950's, such aid, frequently given as outright grants, was provided to thirteen countries,[29] including North Korea, Outer Mongolia, North Vietnam, Hungary, Albania, Burma, Cambodia, Ceylon, Nepal, Indonesia, Egypt, Guinea, and Yemen. Laos, Cuba, Ghana, Mali, and Nigeria are among the countries to which additional aid has been extended in the 1960's. Political motivation has predominated, while the estimated total of 3.7 billion yuan for the period between 1953 and 1960 inclusive was relatively modest. The presence of Chinese technicians and Chinese equipment may have some intangible effect in enhancing Chinese prestige, although, in the long run, the effectiveness of the Chinese model of economic development will have to speak for itself.

[29] Yuan-li Wu *et al., op. cit.*, II, p. 29 *et seq.*, and Oleg Hoeffding, "Sino-Soviet Economic Relations, 1959–1962," *Communist China and the Soviet Bloc, The Annals, loc. cit.*, p. 102.

The Balance of International Payments and Economic Development

The preceding discussion has stressed the principal items in Communist China's international receipts and payments. As mentioned before, trade with the free world yielded in most years a net in-payment. This was needed to finance other expenditures in Western countries and to service the Soviet debt. In more recent years, a surplus in trade with the Soviet Union, accomplished at the cost of a substantial reduction of imports, had succeeded in practically eliminating the indebtedness to the Soviet Union. However, not all food imports have so far been fully paid. Other purposes requiring large expenditures include Communist China's foreign-assistance program, as well as diplomatic, propaganda, and subversive activities abroad. On the other hand, remittances from Chinese living abroad continue to constitute a major source of in-payments.

For the eleven-year period in 1950–60, one estimate of Communist China's balance of payments may be shown below:

In-payments		Out-payments	
(In millions of yuan)			
Soviet credits	5,294	Trade deficit	4,323
Overseas Chinese remittances	859	Interest on loans	2,882
Narcotics traffic	1,295	Foreign aid by China	3,543
Foreign expenditures in China	129	Expenses paid to foreign advisers and technicians	1,059
Use of foreign reserves	942	Communist China's governmental expenditures abroad	259
Deficit owed abroad	3,547		
Total	12,066		12,066

However, because of the uncertainties caused by changes in debt service, present data are not sufficient for us to project the structure of the current balance of payments. Additional study will also be needed to arrive at better approximations of other items.[30]

[30] A recent study by Wu Chun-hsi (unpublished manuscript) has, for instance, placed the current value of overseas remittances at about $40 million a year, substantially larger than the figure shown above.

Yet there is little doubt that the predominant form of in-payments will continue to be exports and that, consequently, the capacity of export will determine the volume of imports. It would not be unreasonable, therefore, to expect the volume of imported machinery and other industrial goods to be rather limited, barring the availability of large external credit, especially if import of food or means to produce food must be maintained. The only effective substitute for external credit is, in the circumstances, not so much domestic savings as technological innovations to be attained through increased research or, in the terminology of the economist, sustained improvements in the production function. The planned economy of Communist China has been able to restrain personal consumption, but it still has to achieve real self-reliance in technological knowledge, the detonation of a nuclear device by Communist China in October, 1964, notwithstanding.

CHAPTER X

An Evaluation of the Communist Chinese Economy

In conclusion, we turn to the question of evaluation. How good, after all, is the economic model of Communist China? An attempt will be made to answer this question from several points of view.

As a model of economic planning in resource allocation, the Chinese economy is subject to a number of strictures. As we have seen in Chapters 2 and 3, an optimal allocation of resources is impossible under the Chinese system of planning as long as the optimum is defined in terms of the population's own preferences, which the price system is not permitted to reflect. This is of course a common criticism of all economic planning systems operated without a freely functioning price system. In addition, it has been shown in Chapter 3 that even if the optimum is defined in terms of the planners' scale of preferences and priorities, an optimal allocation of resources would still be impossible under the economic accounting system and the profit and cost concepts employed in Communist China. The principal difficulty lies in the ideological disinclination to account for interest charges in the use of capital, thus leading to the curious phenomenon of not being able to allocate investment efficiently, although the economy is faced with severe restrictions on the capacity to save. However, this again is not a unique problem confronting Communist China. Other Soviet-type economies have similar difficulties. Apparently, some Chinese planners have become fully aware of this problem, although its logical correction would necessitate the embracing of "revisionism."

As a model of economic development, whether Communist

China offers an example of a successful "bootstrap" operation is a matter of concern to many of the less-developed countries. If economic growth is measured in terms of the gross national product or its per-capita value, and if we grant that the composition of the GNP in any particular period may not be optimal in the sense mentioned above, then the answer really depends upon whether the malallocation of resources during such a period or such periods can be compensated for by a higher rate of growth over a greater length of time. In the case of Communist China, however, economic growth has not been accompanied by stability. If stability is not obtained so that the average rate of growth would vary with the length of the period examined, and if the downswing in any cycle is a severe one, the compensatory effect of rapid growth would be largely illusory. In fact, the rate of growth of the GNP in Communist China would be 6 per cent a year if we take the 1952–60 period, whereas it would be only 3.7 per cent if we take the 1952–62 period. On a per-capita basis, the annual growth rate of the GNP would be 3.6 per cent for 1952–60, but only 1.5 per cent for 1952–62.

If by "economic development" we mean the growth of personal consumption or of per-capita personal consumption, the annual growth rates would be

	Total (Per cent)	Per Capita (Per cent)
1952–60	.25	−2.5
1952–62	1.4	−0.75

The major obstacles to a steady rate of expansion are (1) the desire on the part of Communist China's political leaders, and perhaps of some of the planners, to increase the total output too rapidly, (2) their determination to achieve excessive autarky, (3) their inability, for ideological and political reasons, to obtain a steady and reliable inflow of foreign capital, (4) their failure to devise an adequate system of incentives independent of material benefits or to divorce productivity from labor incentive, and (5) lack of flexibility on the part of the economic system to make up shortfalls in any one sector by substitution from other sectors. While none of these circumstances is really unalterable, any modification of the first four conditions would necessitate a radical reorientation of Communist China's ideological or political position. The last condition, on the other hand, could be altered through success in scientific and technological developments. This, however, cannot be depended upon and would in any case take time.

Is it possible for the Communist Chinese leaders really to abandon the desire for rapid economic development even though as a short-run concession or tactical retreat they may be sufficiently realistic to slow down the pace somewhat, as they have done since 1961? Is it conceivable for them to abandon the goal of autarky without seriously compromising their attitude toward Communist China's military and defense requirements? Is it possible to patch up their quarrels with the Soviet Union sufficiently so that a constant and reliable flow of foreign capital and technology from the Soviet Union would be resumed? Alternatively, is it possible for long-term credit to be forthcoming from Western countries that are willing to step into the breach? It would be most improbable that any of these things could happen for a long enough time to be meaningful unless the Chinese Communists are prepared to undergo some radical change in their fundamental outlook.

As a model of income distribution, Communist China may have achieved a greater degree of income equality than pre-Communist China. Yet there is no evidence that greater equality in the distribution of economic or political power has been attained. One may in this connection raise the basic question why income inequality is undesirable. One objection to such inequality is that where it exists, the low end of the distribution may represent too low an income level. Another objection is that the distribution of economic and/or political power tends to be uneven. A third objection is the lack of security of employment and livelihood. Still another objection, in the opinion of some, concerns the inequity or social injustice. If we examine all these aspects, we find that the lowest level of personal income in Communist China, a level shared by many, has been kept at the subsistence point or below, that greater income inequality has given way to greater inequality in the distribution of power between Communist Party members and non-members, and that greater security in employment—by no means absolute—has given way to greater personal insecurity. Whether these exchanges have yielded a net increase in the well-being of the population cannot be determined. It must be evaluated by the individual observer on the basis of his personal beliefs and system of values.

As a model of a "command economy" which can get specific things done, the Communist Chinese economy enjoys the same advantage as a well-organized war economy or as the Soviet economy. A new bridge across the Yangtze River, a steel mill in Inner Mongolia, a railway extending westward toward Central Asia, these are all examples of tangible accomplishments which have bedazzled many an observer who is not aware of the cost of these undertakings and does not inquire into the alternatives that have been forgone. Of course, if these costs do not have to be considered once the constructions have been completed, one might claim that future generations would benefit from the cost paid by the present generation. Whether this would justify the present cost depends upon (1) who the decision-makers are, and (2) why they should make the decisions. What is the justification for the leaders of the Communist Party of China to decide on the number of years for which they should plan and the nature and degree of the burden the people must bear? Whence have they derived their mandate? Obviously, no answer to this question can be given on purely economic grounds. We must instead appeal to the political and moral philosophy which is part of one's personal beliefs and value system in a pluralistic society, but which, in Communist China, is imposed from above.

Yet it is important to point out that in spite of the advantage of the Chinese model as a command economy, the efficiency of its performance and planning has not been above reproach. Furthermore, to the extent that it has been efficient, the accomplishments have been possible only as a result of the strict discipline and organization of the Communist Party. One might even go so far as to say that Communist China's economic successes, such as they are, owe much to the political astuteness of her leadership and the dedication of the Communist Party's rank and file. The political astuteness of the Party leaders is of course relative. To point to their outstanding success is to indict their opponents, both domestic and external, for their monumental failures. However, one must hasten to note that even Mao Tse-tung's astuteness cannot be taken for granted, and the failure of the commune and of the Great Leap Forward has been unmistakably his. Not the least inference to be drawn from the above is the practical conclusion that for an underdeveloped country without China's type of political organization, leadership, and following, to adopt the Communist Chinese model of operation bootstrap would be an invitation to failure. And to try to set up this type of totalitarian organization and leadership would be suicidal for a free society.

Nor will even such a totalitarian society necessarily endure. As

Mao Tse-tung is reported to have said,[1] the continuation of the Communist revolution is in the hands of the future generation, and no one can tell what future generations will choose for themselves, however hard the present generation of planners may attempt to mold them.

[1] See report of Edgar Snow's interview of Mao Tse-tung in *The New Republic,* February 27, 1965.

Appendixes

APPENDIX I

A CHRONOLOGICAL CHART OF GOVERNMENT STRUCTURE

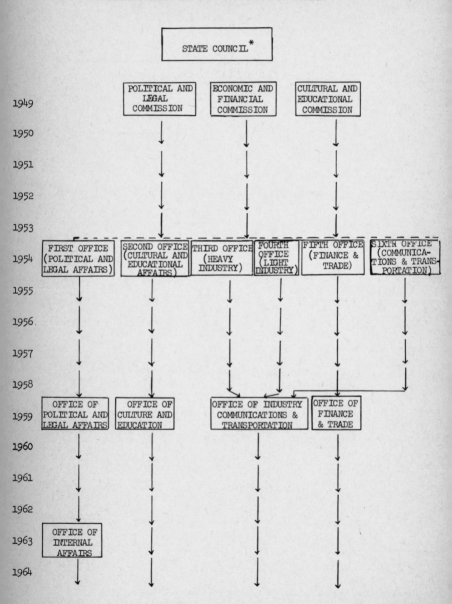

* UNTIL 1954 THE GOVERNMENT ADMINISTRATIVE COUNCIL.

A CHRONOLOGICAL CHART OF GOVERNMENT STRUCTURE
(CONTINUED)

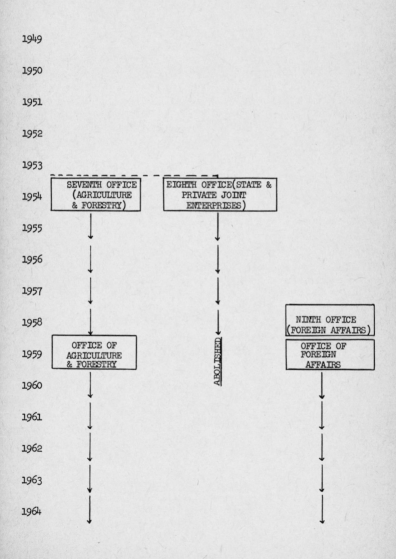

APPENDIX II

ORGANIZATION OF THE STATE COUNCIL, 1964

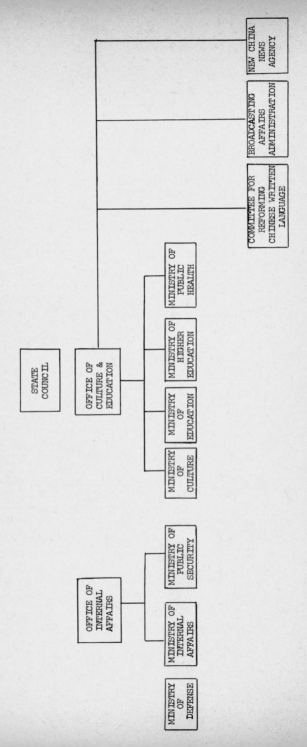

APPENDIX II

ORGANIZATION OF THE STATE COUNCIL, 1964
(CONTINUED)

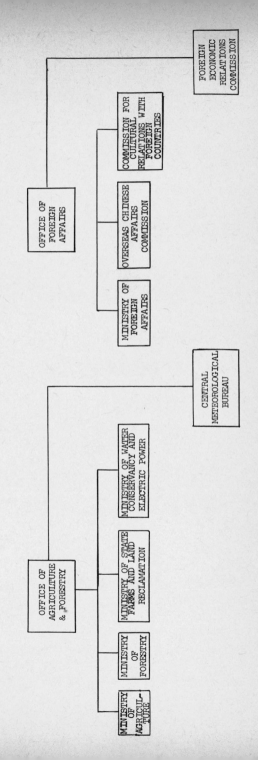

APPENDIX II

ORGANIZATION OF THE STATE COUNCIL, 1964
(CONTINUED)

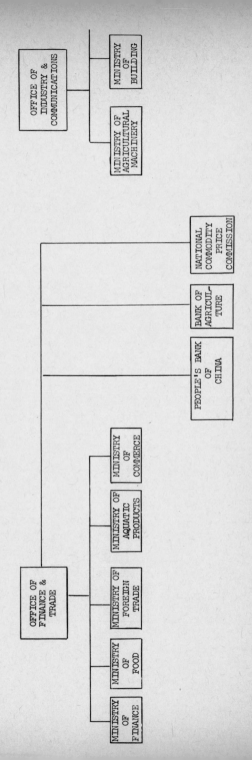

APPENDIX II

ORGANIZATION OF THE STATE COUNCIL, 1964
(CONTINUED)

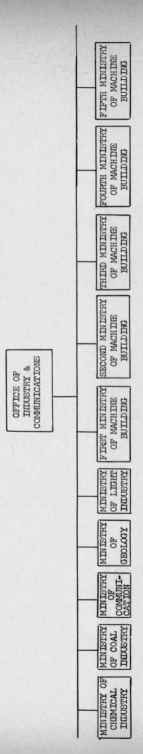

APPENDIX II

ORGANIZATION OF THE STATE COUNCIL, 1964
(CONTINUED)

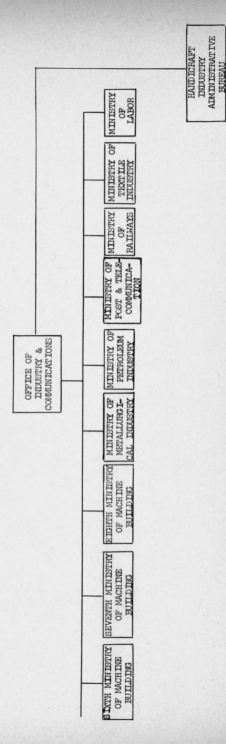

APPENDIX II

ORGANIZATION OF THE STATE COUNCIL, 1964
(CONTINUED)

AGENCIES UNDER THE DIRECT JURISDICTION OF THE STATE COUNCIL

A. COMMISSIONS

STATE ECONOMIC COMMISSION	STATE PLANNING COMMISSION	SCIENTIFIC AND TECHNOLOGICAL COMMISSION	PHYSICAL CULTURE AND SPORTS COMMISSION	NATIONALITIES AFFAIRS COMMISSION

B. BUREAUS AND ADMINISTRATIONS

STATE STATISTICS BUREAU	STATE SURVEY & CARTOGRAPHY BUREAU	RELIGIOUS AFFAIRS BUREAU	STATE ARCHIVES BUREAU	CHINA TOURIST BUREAU

APPENDIX II

ORGANIZATION OF THE STATE COUNCIL, 1964
(CONTINUED)

AGENCIES UNDER THE DIRECT JURISDICTION OF THE STATE COUNCIL

B. BUREAUS AND ADMINISTRATIONS
(CONTINUED)

| GOVERNMENT OFFICE ADMINISTRATIVE BUREAU | FOREIGN EXPERTS BUREAU | CENTRAL ADMINISTRATIVE BUREAU OF INDUSTRY AND COMMERCE | PREMIER'S OFFICE | BUREAU OF MATERIAL SUPPLY | STATE BUILDINGS ADMINISTRATION | CIVIL AVIATION GENERAL ADMINISTRATION | COUNCILORS' OFFICE | STATE OCEAN TRANSPORT BUREAU |

Index

Index

Academy of Sciences, 36, 121
Administrative Bureau of Industry and Commerce, 38
Africa, trade with, 173
Afro-Asian relations, 38
Agricultural sector, 130–56; collective ownership, 77, 80, 135; crop yields, 148–51; farm income, 133–35; food production, 22, 36, 143–51; government controls, 131; gross-value output, 108–9n; investment in, 96; labor force, 86, 130, 132, 150–51; land, 143–44, 147–48; mechanization program, 154–55; "mutual-aid teams," 77, 135; per-capita output, 132; prices of products, 94; production and distribution, 22, 36, 133–35, 143–47, 151–53; relative importance, 130–33; right to private plots, 78, 92; socialization of, 76–77; statistical reporting, 136–45; yield and acreage estimates, 137–43; technological improvements, 153–56; values-added, 105; wages, system of low, 79–80; *see also* Cooperatives, State farms
Argentina, 175n; trade with, 196–99
Asia, trade with, 173, 180–85
Association for Asian Studies, 137
Australia, trade with, 196–99

Balance of payments, 104, 132; economic development and, 200–201
Banking system, 34; state control of, 66–67
Barr, Robert J., 171n
Belgium, trade with, 196–99
Birth control, 92
Buck, John Lossing, 133n, 144, 148

Bureau of Standards, 36
Burma, trade with, 171, 180, 196–99

Canada, 175n; trade with, 196–99
Capital: accumulation, 19–21, 49, 51–54, 63, 78–79, 89–90; accumulation-income ratio, 51–54, 89n; constant, 57; expropriation of, 10; fixed, 64; Marxian concepts, 57; turnover of fixed, 59; variable, 57; working, 50, 59
Capital construction, 22, 34, 36, 50, 93; investment in, 28, 97
Central China, 116
Central planning, 26–27
Ceylon, trade with, 171, 180, 196–99
Chandrasekhar, S., 92n
Chang Chu-Chung, 52–53, 89n
Chang, K. N., 4n
Chao Kang, 111, 112n, 189n, 190n
Chekiang Province, 117
Chemicals, 12, 36; fertilizers, 54, 123, 154, 155
Cheng Chu-yüan, 150n
Chiang Kai-shek, 10n
Chin Li, 64n
Chou En-lai, 123n, 159, 169
Coal, 36, 70, 101; production, 122
Collective bargaining, 12
Collectivization, 12–13, 53, 77, 135
"Command economy," 13, 204–6
Commerce, Ministry of, 38
Commodities, 49; controlled, 24, 36, 68–71; selecting commodity-output targets, 54–55
Common Program, 11–12, 16
Commune system, 13, 54, 68, 77–78; consumption, 102; crop yield, 149; Khrushchev on, 102n; failure of, 151, 205; farm income, 149–50;

Commune system (*Cont.*)
incentives, 152–53; labor force, 151; mismanagement, 151; number of, 151–53; organization, 78, 152; problems of costing, 70, 151; "production brigade," 135, 151, 152; reorganization of, 151–53

Communications, investment in, 96

Communist Party of China (CPC): Central Committee, 10; Economic Program of the 1954 Constitution (1954–57), 12–13; Eighth National Congress, 51, 159; executive departments, 32–38; historical background, 9–11; importance to world economy, 195–99; leadership, 15, 205–6; national goals, 3–17; nature of, 3; planning organs, 32; political directives, 47; political opposition, 15–16; rise of, 4, 11; tactical shifts, 9; training of staff and activists, 24

Constitution (1954), 12, 16, 21

Construction industries, 36, 123

Consumer-goods industries, 12; government agencies responsible for, 34

Consumption, level of, 78–79, 90–91, 160, 163; controlling, 19; curtailment of, 78, 91, 164; estimates of gross domestic product, investment and (1952–62), 91; minimum subsistence level, 90; population growth and, 91–92

Control figures, 47–48, 54, 65; adjustments, 47–48; economic indicators, 65; selection of, 48

Cooperatives, 11, 67, 77, 135–37, 149–50; crop yields, 148–49; distribution process, 73; profit rate, 58; replaced by communes, 13

Costs, 60; problems of costing, 70; profit rate and, 57–59

Cotton, imports, 174–75

Counterrevolutionaries, 21

Credit, availability of, 104–5

Crimes, economic, 71, 75, 78

Cuba, trade with, 172, 183, 185

Cyclical fluctuations, 166–68; conditions underlying fluctuations, 166–68

Dawson, Owen L., 133n, 144, 148

Decentralization program (1959), 71

Decision-making, economic, 27–46, 205; evolution of the apparatus, 27–46; imports and exports, 171; state apparatus, 25–26

Deficit financing, 94

"Democratic dictatorship," 9

Denmark, trade with, 196–99

Depreciation, 58, 64

Depressions, 13, 158

Distribution system, 13, 38, 67–68, 73; description of process, 73; free market, 68, 78, 96; government control, 67, 96; national economic plan, 24

Dualism, economic, 104, 115–16

Eckstein, Alexander, 88n

Economic accounting system, 58, 61–65, 69–70; continuing emphasis on, 120; indicators used, 65; inefficiency of, 70, 121

Economic growth: assumption of "normal conditions," 160–61; Chinese-U.S. differences, 6–8; cyclical fluctuations, 157–69; downward adjustment, 164–65; factor underlying long-term, 168–69; favorable shocks or windfalls, 165, 166; new economic policy, 168–69; over-all economic record (1949–64), 87–106; rates of, 104, 203; deviations between actual and planned, 161–65; planned versus feasible, 159–61; shortfalls, 165, 203; target-setting process, 160

Education, 34; national economic plan and, 24

Electric power, 12, 36, 106, 163, 166; Ministry of, 38

Electrical equipment, manufacture of, 12

Employment, 157–58

Emulation campaigns, 83, 121

Energy resources, 122

Equipment, industrial: import of, 103–4, 155; supply of, 34, 155

Exchange rate, 85n, 170, 189

Exports and imports, 130, 132, 154–55, 161; *see also* Foreign trade

Fan Jo-i, 58–61, 97, 105
Federal Republic of Germany, trade with, 196–99
Ferrous metallurgy, 12
Finance, Ministry of, 34, 70, 188
Financial and Economic Commission, 27
Financial institutions, 12, 34, 66–67
Fiscal and monetary policies, 4, 11
"Five-anti" campaign, 71, 75
Five-Year Plans, 85; First Five-Year Plan, 13, 14, 16, 55, 62, 64, 78, 81, 82, 85, 118–20, 159; Second Five-Year Plan, 55, 159; Third Five-Year Plan, 169
Foods, 38, 118, 133; curtailment of consumption, 144; import policy, 103–4; production, 22, 36, 143–51; see also Grains
Foreign aid, 15–16, 52, 55, 94, 104–5; see also Soviet Union, economic aid to China
Foreign Economic Relations Bureau, 38
Foreign exchange, 21
Foreign trade, 170–201; balance of international payments, 200–201; Coordinating Committee (COCOM) countries, 173, 177–80, 183–85; cost comparisons, 170; decision-making, 171; direction of, 175–85; dumping of exports, 180; economic-warfare measures, 180; exchange rate, 170, 189; foreign policy reasons, 172; general principles of policy, 170–73; importance, to world economy, 195–99; imports, 174–75; index of exports and imports, 191; Ministry of, 34; multilateral trade deals, 171; national economic plan, 24; with other Asian countries, 180–84; for political purposes, 173; price comparisons, 170; purpose of, 182; with Soviet bloc, 172, 173, 175; with Soviet Union, 176–77; potentials of reorientation, 190–95; scale and significance, 185–90; trade agreements, 185; trade balances, 172; underdeveloped nations, 173; with Western countries, 173, 177–80, 183–84, 190–97

Forestry, 96
France, trade with, 196–98
Free markets, 68, 78, 96
Fukien Province, 117

Geology, Ministry of, 29
Gould, Sidney H., 36n
Government revenue, distribution of, by sources, 93–95
Grains: imports of, 16, 144, 171, 174, 175n, 191, 194; output statistics, 143–45, 155
"Great Leap" period (1958–59), 16–17, 54, 81, 83, 158, 166, 167; effect on industrial output, 129; failure of, 27, 82, 102–3, 205; investment policy, 97–98; level of consumption, 102
"Great Slide," 158
Greater Administrative Regions, 26, 27
Gross domestic product: allocation by end-use, 87–106; estimates of, 157–58; estimates of investment and consumption and (1952–62), 91; originating in agriculture, 131–33
Gross national product (GNP), 87–88, 130; during "Great Slide," 158; rate of growth, 203

Handicraft industries, 38, 99, 109–10, 115
Health, Ministry of, 34
Heavy industries, 14, 58, 60, 114
Ho Chien-chang, 58n
Hoffman, Charles, 82n, 83n
Hollister, William, 88, 89
Hong Kong, trade with, 173, 177, 182, 185, 194–99
Hsü Heng-mo, 81
Hsü Kang, 79
Hsü Ti-hsin, 89
Hsüeh Mu-ch'iao, 29
"Hundred Flowers" campaign, 16
Hung, Fred C., 111, 112n
Hydro and thermal power plants, 38, 122; see also Electric power

Imports, composition of, 174–75; see also Foreign trade

Incentives for labor, 81–84, 152–53, 203; negative, 84; nonmaterial, 83

Income: choosing investment-income ratio, 51–54; per-capita annual "consumption," 85; planning, 72–86; reduction of property, 74–78; pre-emption of national income for accumulation, 78–79

Income distribution, 9, 19, 72–86; commodity supplies, 77–78; in the commune, 77–78; differentials between farmers and industrial workers, 84–86, 149–50; effect of nationalization, 74; evaluation of, 204; farm, 84–86, 133–35, 149–50; fluctuations in, 157–58; labor productivity and wage rate, 80–81; pre-emption of national income for accumulation, 78–79; principles in, 72–79; reduction of property income, 74–78; system of low wages, 79–84

Indonesia, trade with, 173, 180, 182, 185, 196–99

Industrial equipment, 34; import of, 103–4, 155

Industrial sector, 107–29; dual economy, 115–16; emphasis on production goods, 119–20; few modern industries, 166; First Five-Year Plan, 118–20; gross-value output, 108–9; handicraft production, 119; historical background, 113–18; income of workers, 84–86; industrial centers, 116–17; investment, 96–97; retrenchment of, 123; location of industry, 116–17, 119; optimal course, 120–23; output statistics, 108–13, 123–29; overestimate of production (1960), 131; performance in, 107–29; planning errors, 121–23; pre-Communist period, 4, 113–18; productivity of investment, 105–6; rate of development, 120; reorientation of policy, 123–24; small-industry drive, 98–102; under Communist regime, 118–20; values-added, 97, 105

Industrialization, 3–5, 13, 51–52; accelerated program, 13; historical background, 3–5

Inflation, 4, 66n, 82, 95

Interest charges, 57, 63, 202

Inventory policy, 121, 162, 166

Investment-consumption ratio, 49

Investment funds, source of, 78

Investment-income ratio, 51–54

Investment plans, effect of actual and planned rates of growth on, 161–65

Investments, 8; allocation by sectors, 96–97; capital construction and, 22–23; changes in policy after First Five-Year Plan, 97–98; estimates of gross domestic product, consumption and (1952–62), 91; financing, 93–96; foreign-capital inflow, 93; level of consumption and, 90–91; productivity of, in modern sector, 105–6; rate (1960–62), 103; ratio of, 89–90; retrenchment during economic crisis, 102–3; small-industry drive, 98–102; Soviet loans, 93

Iron-and-steel industry, 105, 121; output, 123; small-industry drive, 98, 102

Irrigation works, 100–101, 153–54

Italy, trade with, 196–99

Japan, 4; trade with, 180, 182, 196–99

Jasny, Naum, 145

Kapitsa, M., 187

Khrushchev, Nikita, 102n

Korean War, 172

Kung, H. H., 10n

Kuo, Leslie T. C., 154n

Kuo Mo-jo, 36n, 121

Kuomintang, 4, 10n

Labor, 21, 64; control over, 66; forced labor camps, 21, 34, 64, 84, 104; number of, 79; incentives, 81–84; mass labor projects, 78–79; Ministry of, 34; national economic plan, 23, 69; surplus of farm, 86, 130, 132, 150–51; transfer of workers, 103; unpaid workers, 70; wages and productivity of, 65, 80–81; supply and training, 34

Labor unions, role of, 84

Land: area of cultivated, 143–44;

Land (*Cont.*)
competing uses of, 147–48; reclamation, 36; redistribution, 10; reform, 11, 76, 134–35; rent, 57; utilization, 134, 144, 148
Larsen, Marion R., 175n
Latin America, trade with, 173
Li, C. M., 27n
Li Cheng-kan, 36n
Li Hsien-nien, 188–89
Li T'ien-min, 79n
Liao Lu-yen, 149
Light industries, 38, 114
Lin Li, 7n
Liu Chi-chuen, 36n
Liu Ta-chung, 8, 88, 89, 109n, 115, 118n, 119n, 133n

Ma Wen-jui, 83n
Machine industry, 12, 36, 38, 54, 111, 114, 123
Mah Feng-hua, 93, 133n, 189n, 190n
Malaya, trade with, 171, 173, 177, 182, 185, 194–99
Manchuria, 4, 64, 186; industry, 116–17; Soviet despoliation, 114–15; wage scale, 82–83
Mao Tse-tung, 9–11, 53, 85, 146, 167, 205–6
Marshall mission, 10
Meier, Gerald M., 116n
Meteorological installations, 29, 96
Mexico, trade with, 185
Military equipment, 38
Mining, 12, 116
Modern sector, investment in, 105–6
Monetary and fiscal policies, 19, 24

"National capitalists," 10, 12
National goals, 3–17; Chinese-U.S. differences, 6–8; compared to goals of a pluralisitc society, 5n, 6–8; conflict between private and, 8–9; economic aspects, 5, 13–17; historical development, 3–5; industrialization, 3–4; long-term, 15; maintaining Communist Party in power, 7, 9; modifications of economic policy, 14–17; nature of, 3; near-term goals, 14–17; near-term objectives and operational plans, 9–13; pluralistic society, 6–8; po-

National goals (*Cont.*)
litical considerations, 3, 5–6; private goals versus, 8–9; and economic plan, 18–22; selection of, 3–17; self-sufficiency, 4–5; short-term, 15–17; Soviet goals compared with, 3, 7; transition to socialism, 74
Nationalist Government of China, 4–5, 10, 180
National income: concepts, 87–89; pre-emption of, for accumulation, 78–79; rate of growth, 89
National-product index, 87–88
National Resources Commission, 5
Natural resources, 29
Net domestic product, 87–88
Net material product, 87–88
Netherlands, trade with, 196–99
Nieh Jung-chen, 36n
Niu Chung-huang, 89n
"Normal conditions," 160–61
North China, 116
Nove, Alec, 11n
Nuclear program, 36n, 201

Ou Pao-san, 8n

Pauley, Edwin W., 114n
People's Bank of China, 34, 66–67, 70n
Petroleum, 36, 54, 119, 174
Planning Bureau, Financial and Economic Commission, 27
Po I-po, 51–52, 89n
Political campaigns and drives, 17, 21, 83, 121
Population growth, 91–92
Port Arthur, 186
Power industries, 123; *see also* Electric power
President's Commission on National Goals (U.S.), 6, 8
Prices and pricing, 56–57, 60–63; commodity price, 60; costs and, 56–57; discrepancies between controlled and free-market prices, 96; effect of demand and supply, 60–61; financing investment and stability of, 95–96; indices, 95; problems, 105; producer-prices, 63; "transfer prices," 60, 62

Private property, nationalization of, 9–10, 21, 66, 74–78; "five-anti" campaign, 71, 75; reduction of property income and, 74–78; state ownership of trade groups, 75

Producer goods, allocation and supply of, 23–24, 34, 38

Product mix, 113, 123, 161

Products, standards for, 103, 111, 123

Profit rate, cost concept and, 57–59

Profits: Marxian position, 62–63; non-inclusiveness of production costs, 62–63; planned profits, 62; problem of computing, 64

Propaganda, 172

Property income, reduction of, 74–78

Quality improvement, 103, 111, 123

Railways, 36, 108, 186

Rationing, 78, 95–96

Regional planning, 24, 26–27, 71

Research and development, 121, 203–4

Resource allocation, 47–71; commodity mix, 49; divergence between theory and practice, 68–71; "deviations," 71; economic accounting system, 63–65; errors in, 105–6; evaluation of, 202; financial and direct controls, 65–68; government enterprises, 63–65; inclusiveness of cost concept and profit rate, 57–59; investment-consumption ratio, 49; investment-income ratio, 51–54; national goals and, 8, 19; optimal, conditions for, 55–63; principles for general guidance, 50; problems of, 71; selecting targets, 54–55; two basic sets of decisions, 48–50

Retail outlets, 67–68

Rewards and punishments, 74, 75, 121

"Rich peasant" economy, 12, 76, 135, 149

Rostow, W. W., 4n

Savings, 8, 49; forced, 78, 94

Scientific and Technological Commission, 32, 36, 121

Scientific Planning Commission, 36

Self-sufficiency, 3, 12, 20, 160; national goal, 4–5

Shabad, Theodore, 102n

Shen, T. H., 148

Sino-Japanese War, 4, 117

Sino-Soviet dispute, 93, 104, 190

Small-industry drive, 98–102, 119, 151, 167; failure of, 100–102; investment in, 98; opportunity cost, 100–102

Snow, Edgar, 146n, 206n

Soong brothers, 10n

South China, 116

Soviet bloc countries, 177n; economic aid from, 104

Soviet Union, 159; accumulation-income ratio, 52–53; despoliation of Manchuria, 114–15; economic aid to China, 55, 93, 104, 185–90; economic growth, 6–7, 14; emulation campaigns, 83; national goals, 7; New Economic Policy (NEP), 11; output, 83, 108–9; statistical reporting, 29, 108–9; trade with, 176–77, 199; decline in, 190; withdrawal of technical experts, 123, 160, 167, 188

Spulber, Nicolas, 22n, 23n, 50n, 52n

Standard of living, 79

State Administrative Council, 27

State Economic Commission, 32, 34, 51, 67; formulation of the plan, 47–48

State farms, 36, 77, 154; see also Agriculture, Cooperatives

State Planning Commission, 32

State Statistical Bureau, 28–29, 47, 89n, 137, 144

State trading companies, 11

Statistical Bureau, see State Statistical Bureau

Statistical reporting: accuracy of data, 69, 110, 136–37, 166; decentralized, 69; food-grain production, 136–45; gross industrial output, 109–10; information-gathering agencies, 27–32; Soviet system, 29

Steel, see Iron-and-steel industry

Supply and demand, 49

Supreme National Defense Council, 5

Szechwan Province, 117

T'ang Kuo-chün, 80n

Taxes and taxation, 12, 34, 86, 93–94; agricultural, 133, 147

Technological improvements, 20, 23; agriculture, 153–56

Teng Hsiao-ying, 22n

Teng K'ang-ning, 69

T'eng Tai-yüan, 108

Textile industry, 12, 54, 115, 118

Tractors, 154

Trade, Ministry of, 34, 38

Transportation, 36, 101, 116; investment in, 96, 108; national economic plan, 22

Ts'ao Chü-ju, 70n

Ts'ui Ch'i, 65

Tung Fu-jeng, 49n

Underdeveloped countries, 163; Chinese Communist aid, 199; trade with, 180, 185

United Arab Republic, trade with, 196–99

United Kingdom, 160; trade with, 196–99

United Nations, 173

United States: economic growth, 7–8; national goals, 6–8

Wage bill, 49, 69, 79, 81

Wage system, 79–84; government regulation, 74; differentials between farmers and industrial workers, 84–86; incentives for labor and, 74, 81–84; low-wage principle, 79–80

Wall Street Journal, The, 63n, 136n

Wang Cheng, 154

Wang Foh-sheng, 116, 124

Wang Hsiao-t'ang, 71n

Wang Kuang-sheng, 137, 142

Wang Kuei-wu, 26n

Wang Ssu-hua, 29

Water conservation, 36, 38, 96

West Germany, see Federal Republic of Germany

Workers' Daily, 63n, 69

World War II, 9–10

Wu Ch'eng-min, 117

Wu Yuan-li, 4n, 12n, 27n, 66, 75n, 77n, 79n, 84n, 85n, 88n, 91, 92n, 93n, 95n, 97n, 100n, 104n, 108n, 111n, 112n, 115n, 118n, 119n, 122, 124n, 132n, 133n, 150n, 158n, 171n, 174n, 175n, 189n, 199n

Yang P'o, 73n

Yeh Kung-chia, 8, 88, 109n, 118n, 119n, 133n

Yuan, value of, 85n, 170, 189